How to Be Childless

How to Be Childless

*A History and Philosophy of Life
Without Children*

RACHEL CHRASTIL

OXFORD
UNIVERSITY PRESS

Oxford University Press is a department of the University of Oxford. It furthers
the University's objective of excellence in research, scholarship, and education
by publishing worldwide. Oxford is a registered trade mark of Oxford University
Press in the UK and certain other countries.

Published in the United States of America by Oxford University Press
198 Madison Avenue, New York, NY 10016, United States of America.

Library of Congress Cataloging-in-Publication Data
Names: Chrastil, Rachel, author.
Title: How to be childless : a history and philosophy of life without children / Rachel Chrastil.
Description: New York : Oxford University Press, [2020] |
Includes bibliographical references and index.
Identifiers: LCCN 2019015698 | ISBN 9780190918620 (hardback) |
ISBN 9780190918637 (updf) | ISBN 9780190918644 (epub) |
ISBN 9780190066765 (online)
Subjects: LCSH: Childlessness—Psychological aspects. | Childlessness—Social aspects. | Infertility.
Classification: LCC HQ734 .C5554 2019 | DDC 306.87—dc23
LC record available at https://lccn.loc.gov/2019015698

for Beeto
and
for John

Contents

Acknowledgments

This project has benefited from many, many conversations with colleagues and friends. Thank you to all who have read and discussed the project, including Suparna Chatterjee, Hwisang Cho, Roger Chrastil, Liz Chrastil, Bella DePaulo, Catherine Dunlop, Carolyn Eichner, Rebekah Eklund, Jean Friedman, Walker Gollar, Gabe Gottlieb, Steve Harp, Jennifer McFarlane Harris, David Mengel, Julie O'Hara, Paul O'Hara, Niamh O'Leary, Lisa Ottum, Kristen Renzi, Kathleen Smythe, Vanessa Sorensen, Amy Teitelman, Karim Tiro, Jim Uhrig, Miti von Weissenberg, Tyrone Williams, Jodi Wyett, and the anonymous readers for Oxford.

I've also gotten advice and support from Margaret Andersen, Naomi Andrews, Michael Bess, Jennifer Boittin, Steve Harp, Anne Kwaschik, Karen Offen, Richard Polt, Sarah Sussman, Karim Tiro, and Rachel Weil, along with audiences at Stanford, the University of Tennessee, the Western Society for French History, the Society for French Historical Studies, the Colloquium of the Deutsch-Französisches Historikerkomitee, and the Berkshire Conference on the History of Women, Genders and Sexualities. At multiple key stages, David Mengel, Dean of the College of Arts and Sciences at Xavier University, has ensured that I have had the time to develop this project. John Merriman has given, as always, his unwavering support. Early work on this project was funded by a Xavier University Faculty Development Leave and by a fellowship to research at the Gustave Gimon Collection on French Political Economy at the Stanford University Libraries.

I owe special thanks to my editor at Oxford, Abby Gross, for believing in the project, and to Susan Ferber for bringing me to OUP. Early portions of the book were originally published in "Paths to Zero: Childlessness in France and Germany in a Historical Perspective," in *La 'condition féminine': Féminismes et mouvements de femmes aux XIXe–XXe siècles*, ed. Françoise Berger and Anne Kwaschik (Göttingen, Germany: Franz Steiner, 2016): 227–237. In addition, portions appeared in two blog pieces, "Mary Astell: A Life with No Children in the 1600s" (https://internationalchildfreeday.com/mary-astell/) and "No Kids in Pre-Revolutionary France: Louise Le Mace" (https://internationalchildfreeday.com/louise-lemace/); both are used by permission of International Childfree Day founder Laura Carroll (https://internationalchildfreeday.com, https://lauracarroll.com).

I particularly want to acknowledge my debts to Jacob Melish, who has been everywhere to talk through everything; Amy Whipple, the maven of exquisitely crafted sentences; Randy Browne, the sharp-shooting editor of structure; and especially Michelle Brady, who always knew what I was trying to do long before I did. Thank you to my mom, Mary Chrastil; my dad, Roger Chrastil; and my siblings, Mike and Liz, for everything.

I have dedicated this book to Beeto Lyle and to John Fairfield, with whom I have not had children, but with whom I have had, and continue to have, long and essential conversations about that and everything else. They know the rest.

Introduction

How to Talk about Childlessness

In the twenty-first century, millions of women around the world will reach the age of fifty without having given birth. Some will experience infertility, others will choose childlessness early in life, and many will spend years debating whether or not to have a child.

Childless women may think that they are alone in this experience, but, in fact, they can draw on a long history of childlessness that extends for centuries. With the exception of the baby boom, widespread childlessness has been a long-standing reality in northwestern European towns and cities from around 1500 onward.

What are the pathways that lead to childlessness? How does childlessness shape our adult lives, beyond work—from our households and the people who live in them to our debates over national security and global population? Do childless women regret not having children? What challenges do the childless face as they grow old? What relationship do the childless have with future generations? Childless women of the past can help us to consider how childlessness comes to be and how it can be part of a good life.

Whether you are wondering about whether you want to have children or have made that decision long ago, whether you are childless or childful, I hope you'll find in this book insights, comfort, and answers to questions about childlessness. We might think that we're living in a unique situation with little to guide us. In reality, we can draw on the vast human experience with childlessness for inspiration, warnings, and guidance.

How Not to Talk about Childlessness

We so often talk past each other—friends, sisters, daughters, and mothers—when it comes to childlessness and reproduction. On a visit home shortly after I'd embarked on this project, my mother asked me the question I'd been dreading.

"So tell me what you're working on this summer."

She sat across from me at her kitchen table, hands folded, expectantly. I did not think she'd want to hear the answer.

"Um, that project on childlessness."

Now, my mother has always supported my work and career. But let's face it: no undertaking could have been more antithetical to producing grandchildren. She replied, "You know, when I think about having children. . . . It's not that I grew up playing with dolls or thinking I would have children. But when I had them, it was the best thing that's ever happened to me." She stopped. We didn't make eye contact.

"Well, I am writing about what it's like not having them."

"It's not just the tangible aspects of children. It's the intangibles."

I took a shallow breath and hazarded, "I'm interested in the intangibles of not having children."

My mother changed the subject. I gratefully accepted it. Conversation over.

I can't blame my mother for not understanding why I don't have children. After all, I had never tried to tell her.

As a white, middle-class, middle-American girl growing up in the 1980s, I assumed that I would grow up to have children. Childlessness did not appear to be an option. My parents were baby boomers, and their experiences overshadowed my understanding of how life had always been. All the adults I knew had children, and I didn't think I'd be any different. In fact, I didn't think about it much at all.

I started down the path to childlessness without even realizing it. It began in the winter of seventh grade, when—with a twinge of pain in my belly and a rush of hormones through my blood—I became capable of pregnancy and childbirth. But instead of being hurried off into marriage, as would have happened in other times and places, the very next morning I climbed onto the bus to go to school, just as I had always done—to locker combinations, to science class, to vocabulary quizzes and algebra, to the Presidential Physical Fitness Test, to lunchroom gossip, to learning how to handle all of these things with no family members in sight. My parents and my government had plans for me other than immediate reproduction: they wanted me to become a stable and independent person, perhaps even an individual capable of crafting a life for herself. I don't suppose that they thought that I'd stay childless forever, though; I certainly didn't imagine on that day that I was embarking on a path toward childlessness. I assumed that I'd one day have a family of my own.

As it turned out, I stayed in school and unfertilized for the next fifteen years. I came of age in the 1990s, after medical contraception, after free love, after AIDS. And, as it turned out, well after voluntary childlessness was already the experience of millions of American women. In the late 1970s, rates of childlessness in the United States had begun to rise. By 1999, the year I graduated from college, nearly one in six women had reached age forty-five without having borne a biological child.[1] The same was true in most wealthy countries, from Britain to Australia.

As I slowly became aware of these childless women, I assumed that they were overturning all manner of natural and historical precedent. They seemed thoroughly modern: educated, Pill-popping careerists who either callously put ambition over nurturing or were so thoughtless as to forget to have children until it was too late. Even as I joined their ranks, childless women seemed novel and contrarian.

I had my own motivations for remaining childless, including both a career path and a disinterest in raising children (let's face it: even as a kid, I'd never played with dolls; I'd played "going to college"). I also had the good fortune of experiencing two (consecutive) long and loving relationships with men who, for their own reasons, also did not want for us to have children.

In my twenties, I positioned childlessness against parenthood, as two states in conflict. I began to find intolerable any whiff of an insinuation that I might change my mind. I talked about the superiority of childlessness all the time with my partner and friends, justifying and rejustifying the choice, but for some reason—perhaps that special twenty-something bravado regarding one's decisions, perhaps an unwillingness to point out that my life was going to be different from theirs—I rarely talked about having children with my own parents.

As I became a professional historian and entered my thirties, the notion that childlessness is a new phenomenon began to sound suspiciously naive. Over and over again, I'd found that ideas that seemed fresh to twenty-first century ears, like disruptive technology or globalization, had turned out to be at least as old as civilization itself. What about childlessness? I knew that exceptional women, like Queen Elizabeth of England, had preserved their virginity for reasons of state. Nuns opted for a holy family rather than an earthly one. Were there others, too? I wondered why some women in the past did not have children and whether their stories had anything in common with my own. Two questions particularly intrigued me: What have been the pathways to childlessness, and how can childlessness be part of a good life?

I soon learned that in earlier centuries, lifelong childlessness often extended to about twenty percent of women in areas of northwestern Europe, especially among urban women, whether they lived in a Renaissance town or an industrial city. The twentieth-century baby boom was an exceptional moment, a hiatus, when ninety percent or more of all women bore children. I realized that childlessness is a distinct category of human experience with a history of its own. I also started to put these women in conversation with the findings of researchers who ask about childless women in the twenty-first century, who study regret, old age, global population trends, and the very meaning of human flourishing. I found that childless people in the past had secrets to reveal.

By this time, I was going through that crucial set of years when the door was starting to close on giving birth. While I'd never doubted my path, I knew that I was passing slowly through a point of no return. At the same time, as I began to find out more about the history and present of childlessness and to talk about the project with just the slightest gap of distance between myself and my study, I found my own attitudes softening. There is something about framing a difficult issue as a topic of study that can, ironically, allow for a new openness to arise. Simply by posing childlessness as an area of research, colleagues that I barely knew shared the most intimate struggles and the most exquisite insecurities. Childlessness became a site of exploration rather than certainty. I began to see childlessness and parenting in counterpoise, a balance of each other, rather than in conflict. As the project evolved, my questions and tone turned from defensive to open. This book, then, encompasses my own journey from assuming I'd have children, to snarky defensiveness when I decided not to, to seeing childlessness and parenting both as part of the unfolding human condition.

Why We Don't Know Much about How to Be Childless

Conversations about childlessness can be fraught with difficulty because through them we are making ethical claims about personal issues as well as ideas about family, work, and the purpose of life. It can be hard to get beyond our differences. Mutual suspicions of selfishness get tied up with mundane family guilt. Some people have a hard time even hearing the word *childless*. They hear "infertility" instead of "voluntary childlessness." They hear "unmarried women" rather than "women without children." In the past, they heard "nun" or "witch" or "prostitute."

It's still difficult to assign the appropriate term: "childfree" can be too aggressive; "childless," too much a lack. "Nulliparous" is technically accurate but frankly unappealing. I've defaulted to "childless," since that is the defining characteristic of the people I'm interested in, but with the caveat that I don't view the absence of children as a deficit to be overcome.

Childless individuals might be forgiven for feeling that they are following an uncharted course. After all, their own existence results from an unbroken chain of childbearing that extends back to the dawn of sexual reproduction.[2] Having children is part of their family stories, and for many it is the primary way of understanding their history and their place in the world. Furthermore, our culture's sustained focus on mothering overpowers conversation about alternatives. Archetypes of the family from the nineteenth century—with the breadwinner father, the homemaker mother, and a brood of children—remain pervasive in the twenty-first century.[3] We can get a sense of the long-term imbalance from the corpus of books scanned by Google and made visible in the Google Books Ngram Viewer, a revealing set of data.[4] For the past two hundred years, as Figure I.1 shows, *mother* has appeared approximately one hundred times more frequently than *childless* or *old maid*.

All of these phrases are overshadowed by *children*. As Figure I.2 illustrates, *children* has appeared twice as frequently as *mother* over the last fifty years.

Similar results occur in French- and German-language publications. In all three languages, books concerning mothers have held an increasingly large share since the end of the baby boom, even as childlessness has returned to prominence.

Figure I.1 The word *mother* has appeared in print more frequently than the words *childless, old maid,* or *child free.* Google Books Ngram Viewer, http://books.google.com/ngrams.

Where else might we turn? A search in a scholarly database of historical works also reveals a disproportionate focus on children (24,911 results) and mothers (5,648), rather than on childlessness (96).[5] Historians rarely write directly about childless women; they either focus on the family (understood to include children), or they write about singlewomen instead—often written as one word, especially when discussing early modern Europe (roughly 1500–1800). For the most part, childlessness has escaped the notice of historians of the 1800s and 1900s, because it lingers, pervasively but silently, in the shadows of major historical events and trends: childlessness didn't cause World War I, it wasn't the obvious solution to industrialization, it didn't serve the cause of national expansion and integration, it wasn't

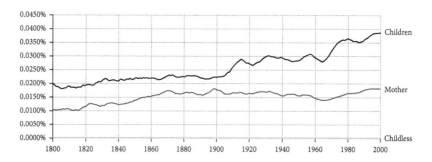

Figure I.2 The word *children* has appeared in print more frequently than the words *mother* or *childless.* Google Books Ngram Viewer, http://books.google.com/ngrams.

the way to claim citizenship, and it flew in the face of the dominant cultural belief that women were natural full-time mothers who find themselves through the care of others.

Contemporary global population studies such as the United Nations World Population Prospects focus on overall fertility rate or average family size rather than the distributions of family size—that is, how many families have zero children, one child, two children, and so on. But if we only look at fertility rate, childlessness easily escapes notice.

Commentators who do pay attention to childlessness tend to present it as a new trend, propelled by contraceptives, 1970s Second Wave feminism, and women's higher education and drive for high-powered careers.[6] Childlessness appears as a lifestyle choice and a lucrative, liberating one at that. Much of the discussion concerns the work–life balance, navigating education and career, and *leaning in*.[7]

Questions about choice and work–life balance are important, but they are not the only ones. In fact, once we start to examine childlessness, the list of possible topics is almost limitless. In this book, I'm focusing on the pathways that fertile individuals have taken to childlessness over the last five hundred years, and how childless lives can help us to better understand human flourishing—from our households, to our old age, to the legacies we leave.

Artificial reproductive technology, infertility, forced sterilization, reproductive justice, pronatalism, and eugenics play only a small role in this book; these are important topics, but they direct our attention toward reproduction rather than toward childlessness.[8] Likewise, sexual orientation and singleness play a role, but they are not the primary focus of this book. And while there is no denying that individuals often form close bonds with children they did not physically birth, I'm less interested here in adoption, othermothers, or the fruitful relationship that childless people might have with their stepchildren, with nieces and nephews, with the children of friends, or as caregivers for children in schools, hospitals, or daycare.

Childlessness is a feature of all cultures, with different expectations riding on it at different times and places. I've chosen to focus on the history of western Europe and the United States, a history with a rich set of sources that capture the voices of women: a few drops in northwestern Europe since the 1500s, a trickle since the mid-1800s, and, since the late 1900s, a flood.

When I envision a childless person, I think about the domestic servants of Elizabethan England and the activists of the 1970s. I think about the social reformers of the 1890s striving to improve the lot of urban workers and the flappers of the 1920s making sense out of world turned upside down. The pathways they took will look, in some ways, remarkably similar to our own. They provide us with companionship as we navigate childlessness and liberate us from thinking that we're alone.

Who Is Childless?

Let's establish some ground rules. In general, I define someone as childless if they never had a biological child and have never been deeply involved in raising a child, whether through legal adoption or otherwise. Many studies that compare childless people with parents explicitly include adoptive parents with parents of biological children. This combination is used when studying questions related to life satisfaction, aging, or household composition. Stepparents are not usually included. However, adoption as a legal, regular matter dates back only to the late nineteenth century; in earlier centuries, it is difficult if not impossible to trace whether a given person had a parental relationship with a nonbiological child. As much as possible, I honor the self-identification of women, especially when I am dealing with their personal writing. In historic demographic studies that draw on marriage and baptismal records, however, these nuances are not available.

It is harder to define childlessness when women have experienced the pain of miscarriage, abortion, or stillbirth. It's difficult to know what to make of Suzanne Voilquin (1810–1876), a Parisian seamstress turned journalist turned feminist turned midwife, who traveled extensively in Egypt, Russia, and the United States. She suffered three miscarriages before finally giving birth to a daughter who died at age two weeks. Voilquin despaired, "O! holy maternity, my dear ideal!! why did you always flee?"[9] She was a mother, and yet the brevity of the experience led her to write that motherhood eluded her. So, I will occasionally tell the stories of women like Suzanne Voilquin, to the extent that they can illuminate aspects of a life without children. At the same time, I recognize that her experience of involuntary childlessness is not the same as someone who has chosen to remain childless and that other women in her position would identify themselves as mothers.

Of course, many parents do not live with their children due to divorce, separation, or abandonment, or simply because their children have grown and moved out. Some parents outlive their children. In some cases, children do not have contact with their parents at all. Some researchers have distinguished among these situations, but in all cases, for obvious reasons, they consider these estranged parents to be parents, not childless. Childless lives from the past can offer insight to these parents, too.

Women, Men, Humans

Childlessness affects all genders, but it is often perceived to be a women's issue. After all, there is something specific happening to women who pass from childhood to puberty and fertility to infertility. Time is scarce. Bodies matter. We all have bodies whose physicality and appearance shape our experience of the world, and so we should not imagine that we are simply brains acting independently of our embodiment; that has been the mistake applied to free men in the Western world when they are conceived as minds who are seeking rights and developing selfhood without any physical presence or limitations.

Demographers interested in fertility rates tend to focus on women for more prosaic reasons: it's easier for a woman to know whether or not she's had a child than it is for a man. In addition, the fact that women experience the end of fertility at menopause allows researchers to bracket women's fertile years in a way that would be difficult for men. Some historical demographers exclude women who died before age fifty from their studies, since they cannot be said with certainty to have completed their reproductive years.

Of course, the focus on the reproductive female also results from, and can perpetuate, the assumption that motherhood plays a more fundamental role in a woman's life than fatherhood does in a man's. And this assumption is often used to justify women's lower status and to preclude their full participation in citizenship. Women have often not been allowed to let go of their bodies, to be rights-bearing individuals, to hold the status of full selfhood independent of a male head of household, to be considered as separate from the messiness of menstruation and reproduction and breastfeeding, to be other than the powerful and feared giver and taker of life.[10] To rectify or draw attention to this imbalance, some historians examine women of all ages, including those who died before age fifty and those who lived well beyond menopause. They ask questions about the lives and experiences of singlewomen, not just about their marital status and reproduction. They avoid the time-worn mistake of seeing women's bodies as all-determining. In other words, while bodies matter, they don't define us completely.

And so I don't mind thinking about childlessness as having a particular resonance for women, at least on certain questions. This book honors the biological possibilities and limitations of fertility that are the special circumstance of women, without making reproductive capacity the only marker of their lives and experiences.

Still, many of the questions that I have about childlessness affect men as well as women. Some of these issues, such as work opportunities, household membership, or inheritance strategies, play out differently for men than for women, as cultures past and present create gendered legal constraints and social expectations. Other issues, such as aging, differ between men and women for biological reasons: women tend to outlive men, so their experience of aging differs, too. Fortunately, historians and social scientists have recently begun to include single and childless men in their studies.[11] Finally, for some issues, such as the characteristics of human flourishing or the elusive pull of future generations, we have access to answers in which the stamp of gender is less profound, at least, in certain times and places. And so at times the gender of the childless person will be less salient.

Voluntary versus Involuntary

Everyone is born childless, but few plan to stay that way forever. Yet many end up childless anyway. One of the central aims of this book is to uncover the many *pathways to childlessness*. Is childlessness driven by economic hardship? Or individualism? By culture? Or careers? What is the relationship between marriage and reproduction, between singlehood and childlessness?

How should we understand Joséphine Bruyère?[12] Bruyère was born in France in 1917 to a soldier father. She grew to become a schoolteacher and a poet, a translator of Petrarch and literary critic with a publication record spanning decades. At age thirty-eight, she earned second place in a competitive national exam. Bruyère did not seek marriage; when a colleague wished for her a husband, she responded, "Oh! for the moment I'd rather have a 2CV!"[13] A new car figured higher in her estimation than a companion.

When Bruyère met and married Louis at age thirty-nine, the union did not replace so much as it sustained the rich life that she had already built. The couple hoped to have children. But during a trip to the Antilles—as a civil servant born in the Caribbean, Louis had the right to a roundtrip visit every five years—a fibroid caused her body to hemorrhage.[14] She had known about the fibroid before her marriage and discussed it with Louis, having been told by her doctor that it was benign and would not prevent her from having a child. Now, surgery revealed smaller fibroids clinging to her internal organs. To her deep disappointment, she required a hysterectomy. The couple considered adoption, but Louis's parents made it clear that an adopted child would never be accepted into the family. They gave up on the idea. Instead, Joséphine profited from the time of her convalescence to turn her notes from the Antilles into a prizewinning collection of poems.[15]

In Joséphine Bruyère's memoir, we see the complexity of the pathways to childlessness. Could she have become pregnant earlier in life? Did she choose childlessness because she postponed marriage to pursue education and a career? Should she have stood up to her in-laws? Did her infertility represent a limitation or a new possibility? Who has the right to decide?

Perhaps the most difficult dimension of childlessness to define is that of "voluntary" and "involuntary." In fact, you might say that the inquiry into this distinction lies at the heart of this project: the pathways of childlessness can be so varied and complex, and the motivations, so multifaceted. It's tempting to create a sharp distinction between those who are childless by choice (#childfree) and those who are childless by circumstance. The difference is clear between those who gleefully decided against children at an early age and those who desperately wanted children but could not overcome infertility. Yet childlessness is not a one-time choice but an outcome of a dynamic process that unfolds over a person's lifetime. Between those who could not become pregnant despite their long and earnest efforts and those who articulated a preference to remain childless early in life lies a vast swath of women whose reasons for childlessness are subject to interpretation.

It can be difficult to find direct evidence. Until recently, few women wrote about these most intimate of questions. Personal writing by childless individuals prior to 1900 are rare and fragmentary. Even when they exist, they are subject to question: brief snippets of diaries recorded at the end of a trying day, exculpatory memoirs written decades after crucial decisions, poems capturing one facet of experience, census forms filled out in front of a government worker. Even as they illuminate, these records raise questions about the reliability of our narrators, about memory and trust, about the passage of time. They are idiosyncratic, insightful, and beyond category.

The difficult doesn't go away when it comes to women who are still alive and available for us to interview. Ask childless women to list the reasons why they don't have children, and you'll hear similar themes: It wasn't the right time, I didn't find the right partner, I had to finish my education and get a job. Then ask them whether they are childless by choice or by circumstance, and you will find that there is a wide divergence of interpretation. One person's barrier is another person's postponement.[16]

Researchers at the National Center for Health Statistics have defined the voluntarily childless as those who state that they do not expect to have children and are either fecund or surgically sterile for contraceptive reasons.[17] According to these criteria, about six percent of American women aged fifteen to forty-four were voluntarily childless (3.735 million American women) in the years 2006 to 2010. This is an increase since 1982, when only 4.9 percent of women were voluntarily childless, but a slight decrease from the 6.6 percent reported in 1995.[18]

Yet eighteen percent of American women end up without children, which suggests that many women who expected to eventually have children never do. And fewer and fewer of these women have biomedical barriers to pregnancy and childbirth, due to improvements in overall health, less sterility from sexually transmitted diseases, and better treatment for infertility.[19] What is going on?

One study provides some insight. Psychologists Sherryl Jeffries and Candace Konnert categorized women aged forty-five to eighty-three using seemingly straightforward criteria.[20] Women were considered voluntarily childless if they gave the following reasons for not having children:

1. She and her partner never wanted children;
2. At one time they wanted children by changed their minds; or
3. It was "never the right time" or the decision was postponed until it was "too late."

Women were considered involuntarily childless if they provided one of the following reasons:

1. It was physically impossible for her or her partner to have children;
2. She had difficulty conceiving or carrying a pregnancy to term;

3. She had not used contraceptives and did not get pregnant;
4. She tried (or wanted) to adopt but was unable to do so; or
5. She stated that her circumstances made it impossible to have children.

None of the women in the study gave reasons that would have placed her in both categories; in the minds of the researchers, each woman was clearly either "voluntarily" or "involuntarily" childless. But when the women were asked to give their own self-identification, their own categories often differed from the ones produced by the study criteria. More than one out of three of the women that the researchers had considered to be "involuntarily" childless referred to themselves as voluntarily childless.

What had happened? At some point in their lives, despite being unable to conceive or adopt or find the right circumstances to have a child, these women had re-evaluated their lives. They faced a decision of whether or not to continue trying to have children, to pursue fertility treatment or adoption, and they chose to embrace a life without children rather than focus on what they did not have. They redefined themselves as childless by choice.

One of these women stated,

> Definitely in my 30s and my 20s [I wanted to have children], because everyone else did, that was the norm then. . . . I was single until 41. . . . By the time I married there really was no choice . . . but by that time I had changed my mind. I changed my mind because my family and friends who were having children were having quite a problem with them and I thought that's one thing I don't have to face. I really changed my mind around the age of 45.[21]

In other words, she changed her mind just as her natural fertility had likely conclusively come to an end. In addition, eight out of the ten never-married women under consideration self-identified as voluntarily childless (rather than childless by circumstance, or involuntarily).[22] We need to understand this dynamic of changing narratives to make sense out of the pathways to childlessness.

In addition, we might fruitfully make distinctions among the voluntarily childless. As early as the 1970s, sociologist Jean Veevers distinguished between two groups of voluntarily childless. The first group rejected children all together. They tended to have decided early against having children, before they married. That means that the two spouses had a high degree of consensus and commitment regarding their decision not to procreate. These childless individuals and couples were more likely to avow a dislike of children, or at least of a child-centered lifestyle, and accepted that they differed from individuals who became parents.

The second group, by contrast, came to childlessness over a longer process, often after marriage or late into their thirties.[23] They might have said that they expected to have a child, but at the same time they made choices that indefinitely postponed childbearing. "I am not childless by choice," writes Canadian journalist Mary Jane Copps, "although many of my choices have contributed to my being childless."[24] Some of these postponers found that when they decided to pursue motherhood, they had waited too long. Or, they finally decided to forgo children rather than disrupt the lives they had built.

More recently, Kyung-Hee Lee and Anisa M. Zvonkovic propose an even more complex model that concerns couples rather than individuals. Among childless but fertile couples in which both partners play a role in decision-making, they discern three types: mutual early articulator couples, mutual postponer couples, and nonmutual couples. This model discerns three phrases: *agreement, acceptance*, and *closing of the door*.[25] Lee and Zvonkovic suggest that even when significant barriers are removed—biomedical limitations and the difficulty of finding a partner—there remain multiple gradations of "voluntary" childlessness.

Like other debates over reproduction, childlessness is often couched in terms of freedom: free choice, right to choose, a decision point, an issue of privacy. But, in reality, women operate under all kinds of constraints that are not of their choosing, and they narrate and interpret these constraints in a multitude of ways. Childless women of the past show that individual choices about procreation do not exist in a vacuum. Their opportunities and values were part of a community, an economy, and a set of cultural expectations.

And so rather than seek out a percentage of women who were "choosing childlessness" in earlier centuries, it's more useful for us to understand the possibilities and constraints available to them, including the jobs they could hold, how they understood their personal development, and the marginalization they faced if they contravened their neighbors' expectations. I have no interest in either vilifying parents or in fetishizing the freedom of life without children; rather, I want to examine how and why folks have gone without children over the last five hundred years.[26]

What's at stake for us is not just our ability to make a choice about our reproductive lives, although this ability is crucial. At issue as well is our confidence to think and judge for ourselves, with fuller knowledge of the range of possibilities and pathways available to us in the present. *How* we make decisions matters—not just the outcome of the decision. The intentions we have and the care with which we contemplate the options matters, even though we don't have complete control over whether or not we will, in fact, conceive and take a child to term.

Personal, Political, and Philosophical

Pathways to childlessness is the first major theme of this book. The second theme is *how to be childless*, which is a personal, political, and philosophical issue.

Reproduction is a personal matter, the fruit of our intimacy, shaped by and shaping our bodies. Whether or not we have children, our status as a (non)parent exerts a powerful influence on nearly every aspect of our everyday lives, from our household goods to the food we prepare to the people we meet.

Because reproduction entails our roles as members of society and the contributions we're expected to make, it is also deeply political. Childlessness, as a part of the basso continuo of demography that hums under us, informs macro issues from political economy to climate change. This isn't identity politics for childless folks; I'm not claiming to uncover the oppression of the voluntarily childless. Instead (and this is a subtle difference), I am trying to draw attention to the uninterrogated supremacy of family and reproduction in our political lives, that is, in the moments when we try to get things done collectively. After all, we define ourselves not just as atomized individuals, but in relation to others, through talking with and watching others and by engaging in traditions and setting up a household, making dinner, celebrating holidays, voting, and working together. The diversity of human experience includes the always-present fact that some humans do not reproduce, and this fact should inform how we operate collectively.

Furthermore, because reproduction involves birth, death, and our connection to the human past and future, reproduction raises timeless philosophical questions about the meaning and purpose of life. Childlessness is an issue concerning not only the meaning of freedom and choice but also the most fundamental questions about the human condition, about how our lives take shape and what troubles us in the darkest corners of the night. Childlessness invites a meditation on morality and permanence, on the tension between egoism and selflessness, and on our place in the chain of existence.

After all, self-conscious childlessness, like religion and philosophy and all manner of culture, marks us as human, with all the richness that entails. While life in all of its forms encompasses those who reproduce and those who do not, only humans can think about it and act accordingly. Ever since humans acquired the capacity to make decisions and plan for the future—alongside the physical capacities and resources to enact that decision—humans have been able to limit procreation and even to prevent it all together.

Childlessness brings to the surface different facets of these personal, political, and philosophical issues. It draws our attention to tensions often left unspoken. In this book, we will consider how childless lives can help us all to explore the meaning of a good life and the development of our collective capacity for human flourishing. I'm interested in claiming the language of values and the good life for lives that fall outside of traditional norms. It is an ethical issue about how we interact with each other. I am committed to the project of creating space for childlessness—not just acceptance or toleration or in the sense of promoting freedom of reproductive choice (though all of these are part of the project) but also space for the encounter between the childful and the childfree. I'd like to turn the childless person from the avatar of a finite, meaningless life into a fully fleshed flourishing human.

Raising these difficult conversations can lead to silence or blame or general snarkiness. It's a rough ride as we try to navigate the waters of childlessness, buffeted back and forth by waves of anger and insight. We can do better than that. Philosopher Michael Sandel argues, "To achieve a just society we have to reason together about the meaning of the good life, and to create a public culture hospitable to the disagreements that will inevitably rise."[27] This book aims to contribute to debates over the meaning of childlessness and the good life in a way that is civil and evenhanded.

I wrote this book for childless adults seeking perspective about their lives. It's for the eighty thousand women in the United States with an advanced degree who reach age forty-five each year without having had children, women with experience and authority.[28] It is also for parents, including those whose grown children are considering a life without children.

This book is also for those who are conflicted about whether or not to have children, though I won't try to convince them to remain childless. It is possible, after all, that we might come to reasonable, different conclusions about whether or not to have children.[29] This isn't a self-help book offering concrete steps to personal fulfillment. It does not seek to define personalities or prescribe action. It doesn't promise happiness or better relationships.

Instead, this book is the answer I wish I had given my mother. What am I working on? A conversation about childlessness that goes beyond the stale debate over career versus kids and that transcends fertility technologies; a humanistic approach to help us tell our stories and empower us to navigate our lives; and a historical perspective to debunk myths, provide a longer view, and expand the range of our possibilities.

1

Delay

London, 2011. After grappling with finding herself childless during her mid-forties, Jody Day founded Gateway Women, a blog and support network for women coming to terms with not becoming a mother. "The room called childlessness has many doors," she writes, "not just the ones marked 'didn't want' or 'couldn't have.'" In her September 2013 piece "50 Ways Not to Be a Mother," Day lists reasons that twenty-first-century women find themselves without children:

31. Our partner or ourselves being ill during our most fertile years . . .
32. Caring for a sick, elderly, disabled or vulnerable family member during our fertile years . . .
34. Losing a key relationship because of family disapproval on religious, cultural, class, financial or other grounds, and then not meeting another partner in time to start a family . . .
38. Needing to save enough money to buy a home and pay of college debts before we could afford to start a family, only for it to be too late.[1]

Day's list captures the space between choice and constraint: the problem of delaying childbirth, for whatever reason, to the point where having children is no longer an option. These reasons may appear at first to reflect fresh challenges facing the modern woman. In reality, however, Day's "50 Ways" echoes the pathways to childlessness that women have experienced since at least the time of Queen Elizabeth. They share in common the problem of *postponement*.

Postponement

We might be tempted to place the origins of postponement in the 1960s, after the Pill. We might imagine that earlier women uniformly pursued childrearing as a primary goal. Natural instinct and lack of options drove them to continue the species. Under the thumb of priests and patriarchs, we might think, women in the past surely could not have exercised enough control over their minds and bodies to avoid childbearing.[2]

Indeed, in most agricultural societies worldwide, including those of medieval Europe, women typically married upon reaching puberty.[3] They often joined the household of their husband's parents and lived by the rules of their mothers-in-law. Almost every woman married, and all but those who were physical incapable had children.

By the 1500s, however, if not before, women in the towns and villages of northwestern Europe began to marry later, in their mid-twenties, rather than in their teens.[4] Marriage occurred not when women were capable of becoming mothers, but when they were ready to set up their own households. Instead of joining an established household in which they played a minor role, they sought to set up independent households of their own. And so as young adults they worked to save for a dowry to purchase the linens and household tools—the pots, the pans, the sheets—that would last their entire marriage. They labored as domestic servants, apprentices in the art of household management. For example, in 1610, Dorothy Ireland, a London servant, married her fiancé, a stable hand, when she was thirty-six and he was forty. For eight years they had been together; only after they saved enough to start their own business did they decide to marry.[5]

To be sure, male dominance continued to exert a real force on women's lives—in their negotiations with the men who they lived and worked with and whenever they reported a crime or made confession. Yet early modern European women among the Christian majority often slipped out of direct parental control.[6] And sometimes they married men of their own choosing.

Since this marriage system relied on the relative prosperity and independence of young people, it left wide open the possibility that many people would never marry, and never have children, at all. In England, in Denmark and Sweden, and in northern France and the Netherlands, the temporary single life crept without ceremony into a permanent state. In the larger towns especially, where female domestic servants abounded, many women remained single for their entire lives.[7] The precise percentage varied from place to place and over time; in seventeenth- and eighteenth-century French cities, 15 to 22 percent of the adult population—millions of people in each generation—were lifelong single.[8] A conservative estimate for the total of lifelong singlewomen for late seventeenth-century England is 15 percent.[9] It is true that some women lived in clandestine relationships—with priests in Catholic countries, with men separated from their legal wives, or just because they didn't see the necessity of marriage. Yet marriage itself was not the bastion of strength we might assume. Up to 10 percent of the married women in early modern England were abandoned by their husbands at some point.[10] Many never married or did not live long in a marital couple.

Meanwhile, until the mid-eighteenth century, illegitimacy remained low, as pregnant couples married under pressure from family, village elders, and the local priest.[11] The social prohibition against having children outside of marriage was a crippling constraint. In other words, as we seek childless individuals, it is a safe bet that most unmarried people did not have children.

Of course, marriage did not guarantee children. The later the marriage, the less likely pregnancy became. Dorothy Ireland's postponement of marriage for eight years tripled her chances of infertility. In England, for the years 1600 to 1800, infertility occurred in 3.3 percent of couples in which women married at age twenty to twenty-four, 8.4 percent for those aged twenty-five to twenty-nine, and 14.8 percent for those aged thirty to thirty-four. For women who married in their late thirties, like Dorothy Ireland, the rate of infertility reached 25 percent or higher.[12] These numbers correspond more or less with current estimates for natural age-related infertility.[13]

In the American colonies, free women married at a younger age and more universally than their English counterparts: about 90 percent. One in twelve married women was infertile. And so, even in this higher-fertility society, around 15 percent of free women never raised a child. In other words, those who married seem to have tried to have children, but not everyone was successful.[14]

Slowly, however, couples began to limit their number of children, that is, to delay or space out their children. In seventeenth-century France, some couples—mostly urban and with middling status or higher—began to talk about family size not only as God's will, but also as a goal to try to achieve.[15] Louis XIV's Edict on Marriage (1666), which aimed to promote procreation, also reflected the belief that people could exert influence on the size of their families.[16]

In these early centuries of widespread childlessness, then, we can already discern a pattern of *postponement*. Childlessness for many was not a destination but a detour, a way station that turned out to be a home. By putting off marriage and child-rearing for a decade or longer, women could achieve other goals: a job, some savings, and the respect of their neighbors.

To survive, these early modern women learned to take risks, make plans, and act responsibly.[17] In the end, some women never married, and others waited so long that they turned out to be infertile by the time of marriage. Waiting for babies became an acceptable, deliberate strategy that has continued to the present day. But it wasn't easy.

A Precarious Gamble

1758: Marie Caton left her family house in Varacieux, France, a farming village then as it is now, and set off toward Lyons, fifty-one miles away.[18] She was looking for work. In her village, the lucky ones found a job on a neighboring farm to milk and make hay, to cook and carry water, to tend sheep and vegetables, to be a farmer's wife-in-training. In such a position she'd also have an inside chance at marrying a local—a son or a nephew or another farm worker, or a villager from down the way. But with a growing population, opportunities to earn wages in the countryside were few.

So Marie Caton walked away, in the footsteps of many others, toward the city. Upon arrival, she faced competition from the girls from town, who could work for their own families, in a tavern, in a vegetable stall, or alongside their mothers as a washerwoman, a seamstress, or a spinner. Perhaps through connections with a family member or a friend, Caton managed to find a job with a satin manufacturer. Later, she spent a few years as a maid-servant for a parish priest and then cobbled together two jobs as a servant for two silk manufacturers. There she likely learned how to make silk: unwind the delicate thread of a silk worm from its cocoon, drop the cocoon into near-boiling water, wait for the sticky binding to dissolve, and pluck it out—one, two, three, four threads, spun together between thumb and finger. The task, easily learned in the smell and the damp, grew tedious fast, and it took only a single careless plunge to scald one's fingers.

Throughout these labors, Marie Caton kept a notebook, in which she recorded (or had recorded for her) eight years of wages and, more rarely, expenditures. Shoes, an item of clothing—these were purchases reluctantly made, for they lengthened the number of months she had to work to save the money she needed for the real prize: a marriage. Marie Caton was pursuing a dowry, a financial accumulation that she could invest in household goods such as a bed, a chair, a table, and cupboard, perhaps some cooking pots and some chickens. Like countless others, Caton recognized the central importance of this dowry for her future and its security. She labored for a few coins and managed to save fifteen to eighteen livres per year—one-ten-thousandth the amount of Marie Antoinette's annual dress allowance—for a total accumulation of about one hundred livres.[19]

But it was a precarious gamble, with no guarantee of success. Typhus, typhoid, smallpox, and pneumonia crept in through the water, the humidity, and the small, shared spaces. With no more of a bed than a cupboard or the kitchen floor, women like Marie Caton were vulnerable to abuse and disease. They were fired during economic slumps. For Caton, the calculation did not work out. Her diligent saving was derailed by illness, probably tuberculosis, that lead her in 1766 to the Hôtel-Dieu—the hospital—where she died leaving only a change of clothes, a pair of shoes, a buckle, and a hope-laden notebook.

Caton's story cautions us that we should resist any temptation to romanticize the situation of singlewomen. The very freedom that allowed women to make plans and strategize also led to the frightening risks of poverty, dependency, and cruel mockery. Some lived with physical or mental disabilities that made them less likely to marry. Others worried about the toll that large families would take on their bodies. At the end of the 1600s, Elin Stout of Lancaster remained single due to ill health. Her brother William Stout recorded, "My sister had the offers of marriage with several country yeomen, men of good repute and substance; but being always subject to the advice of her mother, was advised, considering her infirmities and ill state of health, to remain single, knowing the care and exercises that always attended a married life, and the hazard of happiness in it."[20] Her health did not preclude Elin, however, from caring for her brother's household and children.

Others, like Marie Caton, never accrued enough money to marry. Securing a dowry entailed years of labor to save for linens and utensils expected to last a lifetime. Even with a steady job, a favorable marriage was not inevitable. A young woman whose father had already died lost his economic support in securing a dowry and his wherewithal in negotiating a marriage; as many as 47 percent of women lost their fathers by age twenty.[21] The poorest women never acquired enough savings to set up a household or attract a partner. Economic hardship was also a consequence, not just a cause, of childlessness. For these generations, childlessness in marriage could spell disaster. A household without children lived at the margins, struggling to make the harvest, manage the shop, or earn a few more coins.

Single and Surviving

Yet, even for women of Shakespeare's time, it is presumptuous to assume that all unmarried women bemoaned their fate—to surmise that all women wanted to marry and raise children, but only the unfortunate did not. Some singlewomen could support themselves, and therefore they could imagine a life without children, even if it was not what they had planned.

In recent years, historians have uncovered an astonishing record of early modern women's work and capacity to support themselves and each other. Women worked as domestic servants; they lent money, sold hot food, traded in stolen goods, sewed, and made lace. In the city, they laundered dirty linens. They worked in hospitals and orphanages as cooks or assistants. In plague times, they turned the sick in their sheets and sewed the dead into burial cloths. They worked at public baths, assisting visitors as they dressed and bathed, shaving them or beating them with switches for better circulation. Some worked in brothels.[22] They built alliances both within and across households to make it work.

Although women's work was often illegal or excluded from guilds, the black market for such labor abounded. Furthermore, many trades were not regulated by guilds: "making brooms, brushes, soap, sauerkraut, or candles during the winter months, gathering firewood or herbs in the spring and nuts, berries, fruit, or mushrooms in the summer, and harvesting grain or picking grapes in the fall."[23] Female textile workers—bent over their stitches in small workshops or in rented rooms—drove economic growth and innovation.

In some regions, singlewomen, like widows, enjoyed the legal status of *feme sole*, and therefore (unlike married women) they were legally allowed to enter into contracts, take on debt, or sell property.[24] Municipal authorities nevertheless often restricted singlewomen from these actions, especially in the 1500s and 1600s. In Augsburg, the weaver's guild protested to the city council that singlewomen undercut their business by spinning thread on their own; the weavers wanted the women to work and live with them at a third of the wages. It wasn't enough to denounce the women for economic dealings—no, they complained of the women's complete freedom to choose their working hours, their lack of oversight when out walking with journeymen, and their bad example to girls arriving from the countryside. The city council listened: in 1597 they passed ordinances to banish women who worked on their own or who made demands on their employers.[25]

The situation changed by the late 1600s. In England, women won more latitude to open businesses with less municipal harassment. By the 1660s, the French government, too, recognized the importance of women's work and taxed them accordingly.[26] Women not only earned wages but also could support themselves with this labor. One study of London women between 1695 to 1725 suggests that "77.8 percent of singlewomen and 71 percent of widows were wholly maintained by their own paid employment, while another 4 percent of singlewomen and 8 percent of widows were partially self-supporting."[27] They may still have lived with others, and this independence remained precarious and more so as they aged, but more women were able to survive outside of marriage than we might have otherwise believed.

These studies suggest, therefore, that some women may not have remained single and childless only because they were too poor to marry. Mary Rowte and Elizabeth Shergold, both of whom lived in early modern England, did not prioritize marriage and childbearing. Instead, they worked alongside their mothers in successful businesses, training to take over the family enterprise after their mothers died. Rowte set up shop as an iron-monger selling hardware and iron tools at age thirty-five, and Shergold ran a number of businesses starting at age forty, after the death of her widowed mother. With their own economic security in hand, Rowte and Shergold might have married, and bearing a child was not yet conclusively out of the question, but they did not. Marriage would have entailed a loss of independence, as they would have been subject to laws turning their property over to their husbands. Instead, they each enjoyed decades of running their own businesses—Rowte until her early seventies and Shergold until age eighty-two.[28]

These "exceptions" in the historical record are becoming so common that we need to start seeing them as part of the structure of the economy and of the story of women's lives. Women, including childless women, formed a crucial, productive part of the economy, and some of them could make decisions about how their lives would unfold. When demographers corelate fertility rates with economic downturns, the implicit corollary is often that women's natural, universal desires to have children were thwarted by the economy, instead of assuming that women exercised choices, albeit within a set of constraints. And yet we do women of the past a disservice if we assume that they were simply unable to contemplate a life without children. As tempting as it may be to assume that all women before the Pill either actively or unthinkingly sought to have children, this is an oversimplification. When one in five women don't have children, is it really the case that all of them—*all* of them?—regretted their situations? It's a mistake to assume that people blindly followed tradition. After all, this was the era in which millions of Europeans engaged in religious warfare to establish what they believed in their hearts to be the true Church. If the Reformation entailed the consolidation of the patriarchal family, it also led to widespread nonconformism and indifference and skepticism about religion, sometimes hidden and sometimes open, but always and everywhere complained of by clergymen. Time and again, ordinary people put their personal judgment first.[29] Indeed, the religious, legal, familial, and cultural pressures designed during this time to ensure that women would reproduce and do so within acceptable parameters testify to the fear that women might somehow opt out.

Unmarried Sisters

Meanwhile, the nobility and the well-to-do afforded their sons and daughters little choice in the timing and partner in their marriages. These families continued to marry off their teenage daughters to hand-picked suitors. In cities across early modern Europe, whether London, Paris, or Florence, two marriage tracks ran side by side, one for the rich and one for the poor.[30] In seventeenth-century Geneva, women from the middle classes married before they were twenty, while the women who washed their linens did not marry until almost age twenty-seven. Royal families in particular married their daughters at a young age and expected them to produce multiple heirs. Kings and queens could make use of every child in politically and diplomatically advantageous marriages.[31]

Nevertheless, in many wealthy families, early marriage the elder children led to postponement or lifelong singleness for the younger. In 1729, almost one in every six women born to a British ducal family could expect to remain single; in Scotland during that same century, as many as one in three aristocratic daughters did not marry.[32] One study of the elite in the French city of Montauban found that fully 37 percent of those who died and left a will between 1800 and 1824 were single—23 percent of men and 52 percent of women.[33] The strategies of elite and moneyed families entailed celibacy for younger children.

It was a difficult balance: with so much doubt over the survival of children, families needed to reproduce plenty of sons to carry on the name and daughters to provide favorable matches. But if too many survived, the families ran the risk of not being able to provide adequately for all.[34] Parents did not want to dilute their wealth and property across multiple marriage settlements.

The monastery and the merchant's ship provided safe vessels for surplus men, conferring honor to those who were not first-born and (hopefully) rescuing them from vice. Some women entered a convent, but more often they attended to their extended families. The common stereotype of the spinster assumes they were an unwanted burden on family, and, indeed, for many, dependency was intolerable misery. In 1716, a young woman, unnamed in the diary in which the event was recorded, hanged herself: "The reason of it seems to have been a too sensible resentment of her unhappy circumstances which reduced her to the necessity of receiving her subsistence from her uncle. She seems to have been a great while melancholy . . . but last Sunday she several times expressed her thoughts about self murder, that she thought it was reasonable where a person was neither serviceable to the world nor herself." Despite her family's care to watch out for her, "she slipped away and hanged herself with her garters."[35]

Yet unmarried sisters often proved indispensable to household labor and management as well as a source of affection and companionship.[36] By 1654, Frances Blundell, aged only twenty-three, had already become essential to her brother William's household. In this family brimming over with children—fourteen born, of which ten survived infancy—Frances was valued as a sister, an aunt, and a companion. William knew this well. When a sister-in-law tried to snag Frances for her own household, William intervened: "But give me leave to lament humbly the damage you have done to my Family," he wrote to his mother-in-law. "You have taken from my sister Winifred a husband [a reference to another unmarried sister in William's household], from [my daughter] Milly a Tutoress, a companion from my wife, and from myself a most excellent player of shuttlecock."[37]

Far from a burden, Frances was sought after for her skills and companionship. She was a stakeholder in the estate, as well, though as a dependent rather than a legal proprietor. She allowed her brother to use several hundred pounds of her inheritance to repurchase the family estate (the Catholic, Loyalist family had lost property during the English Civil War of the 1640s) and received a twenty-five pound annual allowance in return.

Yet the relationship between Frances and her brother, nieces, and nephews extended far beyond a simple calculation of reciprocal support. She accompanied her nieces and nephews in their travels, which included six years in Ireland to help her married niece set up household. Later, with both sister Winifred and William's wife Anne deceased, William and Frances lived out their lives in a brother–sister household.[38] Over the course of decades, the Blundells built alliances within and across households; each individual held unequal amounts of power, to be sure, but they all held some standing in the collective effort to support the family fortune.

Similarly, Marie and Marianne Lamothe, the only daughters in a family of seven children in eighteenth-century Bordeaux, ran the family household and supported their unmarried brothers. Their letters suggest that, for these sisters, such a situation was fulfilling and satisfying.[39] Marie thought of her elder brothers as surrogate husbands and the younger ones as surrogate children. Marie wrote to brother Victor in 1760, "I think of you and Alexandre as my two children, I love you with the love of a mother . . . my title of godmother, along with my sentiments gives me, I think, much leeway."[40] The Lamothes, like many unmarried women, were variable pieces in a constantly shifting household whose members came and went and who carefully negotiated their power and influence.

Attitudes toward Singlewomen

Early modern people were aware of increasing numbers of unmarried and childless women among them. While most commentators suggested that childlessness was a sign of deviance or societal impairment, a few voices questioned the wisdom of the direct path to marriage and children.

The emergence of the term "spinster" in the late 1500s as a neutral descriptor of unmarried women—young or old, both those who might later marry and those who never married—indicated a growing prominence of the social category "unmarried person." Before this time, in the European Middle Ages, portrayals of unmarried women—both religious and secular—had focused on the young maiden, the pure virgin who would eventually find either marriage or a religious vocation.[41] The life-long single woman had had no place. Another common term, "singlewoman," also dated from the Middle Ages, when it could refer to prostitutes and widows as well as to unmarried women.

By the 1500s, however, "singlewomen" came to indicate only never-married women. Lifelong unmarried women now became a recognized social group, appearing in legal documents, wills, and civil records.[42] The word "childless" came into more frequent usage; on rare occasions, early modern writers used the word "orb" as an adjective to describe a childless person, as when Giles Fleming (d. 1665) wrote of "Edward the Confessor, who dyed Orb or Childless."[43]

Although singlewomen were becoming more common, they were not always welcome. The single and the childless were often mocked, and pamphleteers assumed that remaining unmarried was a sign of dysfunction. In England, the Reformation meant that women lost a sanctioned option. No longer legally allowed to become nuns, marriage was considered to be a goal shared by all—even though late marriage made it difficult for everyone to marry. To many in England, celibacy meant Catholicism, a dangerous connection. Singleness became a sign of damnation, enshrined in this proverb, first captured in English in *The Book of Fortune* (c. 1560):

> A mickle truth it is I tell
> Hereafter thou'st lead Apes in Hell:
> For she that will not [marry] when she may,
> When she will she shall have nay.[44]

We can debate the meaning behind the apes: perhaps they represented the husbands or children that the women did not have in life, or old bachelors, or the only lovers these unnatural women could find. In any case, the image became an undisputed part of the culture, appearing in Shakespeare's *The Taming of the Shrew* and *Much Ado about Nothing*. Queen Elizabeth's virgin status did not elevate the position of ordinary singlewomen.

In the 1600s, childlessness was common, but it still seemed abnormal. Singlewomen walking alone at night were subject to harassment from the local watch committee. Their living arrangements were also a concern for parish and town governance. Robert Burton in 1621 wrote, "Surely nothing is more unprofitable than that they die old maids, because they refuse to be used to that end for which they were only made."[45] Singlewomen could be suspected of witchcraft and hanged for the offense.[46] A witness in a 1625 Venetian witch trial was asked, "Are there any witches in your neighborhood?" "No," replied the witness. "They are all married women."[47]

In English pamphlets and satires appearing in the 1640s to 1690s, wits and wags came up with schemes to address the alarming rise of never-married women in their midst. These anonymous pamphlets took on the voice of women—upstanding daughters of citizens, servants, virgins—though it is unlikely that they were in fact written by young singlewomen.[48] In 1642, at the outset of the English Civil War, the first petition appeared: *The Virgin's Complaint for the Losse of their Sweet-hearts, by these Present Wars, and their owne Long Solitude, and Keeping their Virginities against their Wills: Presented in the Names and Behalfes of all the Damsels both of Country and City, January 29, by Sundry Virgins of the City of London.* The 205,000 maids claimed by this satirical pamphlet called on the end to war so that men might return home to marry. Unlike individual maidens portrayed in medieval literature, these women claimed men for marriage as a group collectively wronged.[49] Other pamphlets claimed that widows and prostitutes prevented men from marrying singlewomen. In all of these cases, the unmarried women themselves were portrayed as victims left out of the game.[50]

In the late 1600s, childless women were the objects of particular scorn.[51] John Dunton's *The Challenge . . . Or, the Female War* (1697) attacked singlewomen as "envious, malicious, loquacious, ugly, deceitful, odoriferous, and vain 'Lump[s] of *Diseases*' with 'terrible Fangs' who resemble 'She-Canibbals,' 'Man-Catchers,' and 'Flesh-Crows.'"[52]

But not every commenter disapproved of childlessness. Bernard Mandeville's *The Virgin Unmask'd* (1709) argued, through the character Lucinda, "If you wish to come to a fair Trial, you must take your Married Women of the same Age with the maids, and if you do, you will not find One in Five Hundred, but what has repented a Thousand Times, that ever she submitted to the Yoak: Whilst all the Old Maids, as soon as that troublesome [sexual] Itch is over, rejoice at having kept their Liberty, and agree unanimously in the Comforts of a Single Life."[53] Moreover, "is it not a Thousand pitys, to see a Young Brisk Woman, well made, and fine Limb'd? as soon as she is Poyson'd by Man, reach, Puke, and be Sick, ten or twelve times in a Day, for a Month or Six Weeks; and after that, Swell for Seven or Eight Months together; till, like a Frog, she is nothing else but Belly."[54]

In the 1700s, "spinster" ceased to be a neutral term and instead became associated with bitter, unattractive, and either prudish or hypersexualized women.[55] By the end of the 1700s, the old maid morphed into an object of pity and ridicule, a piece of useful furniture over in the corner of the household, beheld in a temper much less virulent than a century before.[56]

By this time, women were marrying younger—at age twenty-three rather than twenty-six; the peak of nonmarriage had passed, and the population expanded at a rapid clip, allowing England to engage more intensively in production and in empire-building.[57]

At the same time, a new trope of childless womanhood began to appear: the wealthy irresponsible socialite. Adam Smith observed in *The Wealth of Nations* (1776), "A half-starved Highland woman frequently bears more than twenty children, while a pampered fine lady is often incapable of bearing any, and is generally exhausted by two or three. Barrenness, so frequent among women of fashion, is very rare among those of inferior station. Luxury in the fair sex, while it inflames perhaps the passion for enjoyment, seems always to weaken, and frequently to destroy altogether, the powers of generation."[58] Not for the last time, childless women were seen as having too much fun for their own good.

Meanwhile, free Americans in the early republic celebrated their freedom to reproduce. Childlessness and positive portrayals of celibacy, such as William Wirt's "On Celibacy," published in the *Richmond Enquirer* in 1804, enjoyed little currency.[59] Instead, Benjamin Franklin's salute to population increase through early marriage, published in *Observations Concerning the Increase of Mankind and the Peopling of Countries* (1755), remained popular in the early republic.

Thomas Jefferson aligned population increase with democracy and expansion. In a letter dated just one month after taking possession of the Louisiana Purchase in 1804, Jefferson reasoned that in America, "the immense extent of uncultivated and fertile lands enables every one who will labor to marry young, and raise a family of any size."[60] This position took on geopolitical importance as Jefferson aligned the United States with France during the Napoleonic era. Free trade, freedom of circulation, and freedom to procreate within marriage and to populate new land acquisitions: these were Jefferson's promises.[61] For enslaved women, however, pronatalism was cruelly enforced; those who did not bear children were subject to punishment or sold off.[62]

Unyoked Is Best!

It's more difficult to find female voices written by women, but we can find signs that some early modern women questioned the assumption that everyone should marry and have children. Anna Bijns (1493–1575) survived the tumult of the Reformation in Antwerp through her sharp wit and barbed pen. "Sour rather than sweet" was her motto, and this unmarried—indeed, misogamic—schoolmistress attacked Lutherans with gusto. She was the most widely read woman of her time in Dutch; some considered her to be among the most famous women of the sixteenth century. In her lifetime, Bijns published three collections of poems, mostly anti-Reformation and works of prayer and piety. She also wrote voluminous refrains in other modes, from the amorous to the wise. Throughout, Bijns expressed the need for self-reliance, freedom from domination, and independence. It's not clear why Anna Bijns never married. The daughter of a master tailor with property, she was not impoverished or in ill health. But her sister's marriage was unhappy, and this may have influenced Anna's disposition. While the following poem does not refer explicitly to child-rearing, it expresses clear antipathy to the circumstances in which children would be born:

> How good to be a woman, how much better to be a man!
> Maidens and wenches, remember the lesson you're about to hear.
> Don't hurtle yourself into marriage far too soon.
> The saying goes: "Where's your spouse? Where's your honor?"
> But one who earns her board and clothes
> Shouldn't scurry to suffer a man's rod.
> So much for my advice, because I suspect—
> Nay, see it sadly proven day by day—
> 'T happens all the time!
> However rich in goods a girl might be,
> Her marriage ring will shackle her for life.
> If however she stays single
> With purity and spotlessness foremost,
> Then she is lord as well as lady. Fantastic, not?
> Though wedlock I do not decry:
> Unyoked is best! Happy the woman without a man.
>
> Fine girls turning into loathly hags—
> 'Tis true! Poor sluts! Poor tramps! Cruel marriage!
> Which makes me deaf to wedding bells.
> Huh! First they marry the guy, luckless dears,
> Thinking their love just too hot to cool.
> Well, they're sorry and sad within a single year.

Wedlock's burden is far too heavy.
They know best whom it harnessed.
So often is a wife distressed, afraid.
When after troubles hither and thither he goes
In search of dice and liquor, night and day,
She'll curse herself for that initial "yes."
So beware ere you begin.
Just listen, don't get yourself into it.
Unyoked is best! Happy the woman without a man.[63]

Katherine Phillips (1632–1664) expressed a similar view. Phillips wrote the poem after her own marriage, at age fifteen or sixteen, which led to two children. She used much of her poetic work to decry women's lack of choices. Her description of mothering duties suggests that women could and did contemplate the possibility of not becoming a parent:

A married state affords but little ease;
The best of husbands are so hard to please.
This in wives' careful faces you may spell,
Though they dissemble their misfortunes well.
A virgin state is crowned with much content,
It's always happy as it's innocent.
No blustering husbands to create your fears,
No pangs of childbirth to extort your tears,
No children's cries for to offend your ears,
Few worldly crosses to distract your prayers.
Thus are you freed from all the cares that do
Attend on matrimony and a husband too.
Therefore, madam, be advised by me:
Turn, turn apostate to love's levity.
Suppress wild nature if she dare rebel,
There's no such thing as leading apes in hell.[64]

Some felt compelled to circulate their criticisms of marriage in the form of pamphlets. *The Maid's Vindication: or, The Fifteen Comforts of Living a Single Life* (1707) called marriage a prison from which women could only be freed through death or adultery. Why would women rush into marriage, when their hopes will be so easily dismantled by a tyrannical, inept, or unambitious husband? Similarly, *Matrimony; or, Good Advice to the Ladies to Keep Single* (1739) warns the young against a hasty marriage. Abusive husbands who belittle their wives were not much of a prize. Such pamphlets encouraged women to think carefully before committing themselves in marriage.[65]

Nowhere do we more strongly see evidence of a woman choosing a single life than in the poetry and prose of Mary Masters (*c.* 1694–1771). While she did not condemn marriage for all—indeed, her poetry celebrated the weddings of her friends—Masters clearly preferred spinsterhood for herself:

> And really, my dear,
> I'll be very sincere,
> And make you an honest reply;
> For since life began
> I never knew the man
> For whom I could languish and die.[66]

Masters may or may not have expressly chosen to remain single; she wrote of financial troubles that dissuaded potential suitors. But once her single-ness became a given, Masters made clear her embrace of the single life.

It's not known whether Dorothy Ireland and her stable-hand husband had children. It is likely that they did. But there is a good chance—about one in four—that this older married couple never had a child. After all, they had not merged their lives together with children as their primary goal. They had sought stability first.

The new marriage trend in a small region on the tip of the Eurasian continent has great bearing on patterns of marriage and childbearing today. Just as we now know that early modern women profoundly shaped the economy, as both producers and consumers, we need not wait until the 1970s to see how female workers shaped family characteristics, including childlessness. The pattern of postponement continues to dominate.

In the early modern period, one did not choose childlessness so much as decline (or fail to acquire) the entire package of marriage and childbearing. Husband and child came almost in the same breath. Early modern women poets and pamphleteers assumed that marriage and procreation were one and the same. With marriage and childbearing so closely entwined, it was difficult to separate the one from the other. Childlessness was part of a marriage system that could not accommodate everyone, a system whose economic flexibility depended on the fact that some would lose out. The women of the early modern period referred more commonly to their skepticism about the possibility of a happy marriage than they did about children.

Could one choose to be childlessness? Postponement meant that childlessness unfolded over the course of decades within a network of responsibilities and obligations. While the rise and fall of wages affected overall fertility rates—better jobs led to more babies—the fact of one particular woman's childlessness may have turned on any one of myriad factors, such as a favorable employer, a fluke injury, or a sustaining and influential friendship.

For early modern women, childlessness shifts shapes, appearing at one moment as the sorry lot of the losers in the marriage market and at another as a secret treasure shared with winks and laughs in a tavern by servants on their day off. The very adaptability of the marriage market allowed some individuals to exert their will on their lives. Women in the past could reason about their reproduction: in fact, voluntary childlessness could be a rational and evolutionarily compatible response to socio-economic stress. For others, childlessness was a loss that was worth the trade-off of avoiding a potentially tyrannical husband.

Early modern women could not make the same choices that twenty-first century women would make. They faced different sets of constraints and a narrower range of possibilities. The very notion of individual choice may be anachronistic in times and places where women discerned God's will in their marital fortunes.[67]

Yet early modern women opened up a space for something other than economic determinism in our understanding of childlessness, a space for something other than bemoaning childlessness as a sad and tragic fate. Like all of us, these early modern women were strategizers interacting more or less effectively within the constraints of the world around them. They discerned among possibilities, even if they did not link this discernment to freedom or choice.[68] The Gateway Women of the twenty-first century continue a long tradition of navigating postponement.

2

Whispers

On the wall in my grandmother's house hung a photograph of her own grandmother's family. It's a formal picture circa 1906 of a Nebraska farm family, of German immigrants and their children (Figure 2.1). Wilhilmine and John Puls are seated, surrounded by seven daughters and four sons, plus an infant clutching a teddy bear on her father's knee. The girls wear high-collared dresses and the boys, un-ironic bow ties and hair parted down the middle, each one a distinct variation of the others. The photographer's backdrop, wrinkled in the top left corner and not quite big enough to contain the family, evokes the piety of a Lutheran church. My great-grandmother Marie stands to the left of her father's shoulder. She is about nine years old, still in short skirts, the fringes of her blond hair in ringlets. About a decade later, she will marry and establish a farm. Like every one of her sisters, she'll have children of her own—five of them. In the thirties, she'll lose the farm to the dustbowl and a son to polio. Another son will drive ambulances on D-Day. Her eldest daughter, my grandmother, will marry a musician and move to the city.

As a child, I thought that this family was typical of the time: My great-great-grandmother Wilhilmine, the mother in the photograph, had twelve children by 1906 and one more on the way.

As it turns out, however, for women like Wilhilmine who were born in the 1860s, childlessness within marriage became a possibility, at least in some regions.[1] And for American women of Marie's generation—born between 1885 and 1915—at least one in five never had children. Similar rates of childlessness, the highest ever recorded, occurred across western Europe, Canada and Australia.[2]

We don't hear much about these women for a simple reason: they didn't become anyone's mother, let alone anyone's great-great-grandmother. They fade out of our family history. And yet, childless women did exist. Many of these women postponed marriage and childbearing for the same reasons as they had for centuries: to set up a household or save for marriage.

Figure 2.1 The Puls family circa 1906. Photographer unknown. Photograph courtesy of Roger Chrastil.

Some never married and never had children. In addition, more women—especially urban women—began to limit their childbearing within marriage, even if they wed during their fertile years. Childlessness within marriage now became a secret reality.

Childless within Marriage

London, 1890. Beatrice Potter had a problem: Sidney Webb wanted to marry her. This was not how things were supposed to turn out. To her mind, she should not have been available in the first place. At the age of thirty-two, the handsome, accomplished daughter of a wealthy businessman should have found a husband years before. She ought to have married in her twenties, like each one of her eight sisters.

But Beatrice had spent her youth reading and writing and investigating poverty. She had donned the simple dress and cap of working women and labored among them to study their plight. She had endured a long and painful love for radical politician Joseph Chamberlain that ended in disappointment. After her mother died, Beatrice had served as hostess in her father's house. And when her father fell ill, Beatrice had taken care of him. She had long reconciled herself to spinsterhood.

Sidney Webb would not hear of it. When they first met, he fell in love instantly. They shared socialist political views and a faith that research could combat social evils. Beatrice admired Sidney's diligence and intellect but found him personally unimpressive. The small, bulbous son of a Cockney hairdresser would not do in her social circles. She feared losing her independence and the time she needed for writing. And in any case, she was done with love. "Marriage is to me another word for suicide," she proclaimed in her diary. "Personal passion has burnt itself out."[3]

Yet Sidney's determination that their forces combined could do good for the cause—that one plus one equals not two, but eleven—finally persuaded Beatrice to marry. "I am not 'in love,'" she recorded, but "our marriage will be based on fellowship, a common faith and a common work."[4] Marriage would not cause her to give up her writing, but rather sustain and improve its usefulness. At the time of her engagement, she did not express a hope that her union with Sidney Webb would lead to children: "We have honestly only *one* desire—the commonweal."[5] They deliberately chose not to procreate.

By the time of Beatrice and Sidney's wedding in 1891, increasing numbers of British couples were going childless. In fact, from the mid-nineteenth century on, childless women were more likely to be married than unmarried. As early as 1857, *The Times* of London had suggested that some French couples were "deliberately marrying with the intention of having only one or two children, or none at all."[6] As so often happened, the French stood in for fears of what was actually happening in Britain. For those English and Welsh couples who married at ages twenty-five to twenty-nine between 1891 and 1896, 11.6 percent were childlessness, compared to 9.8 percent for their parents' generation and 8.4 percent for the early modern period.

The increase in childlessness is even more striking for those like the Webbs who married in their early thirties: 23.4 percent in the late 1890s, up from 15.8 percent in the 1860s and well above early modern infertility for that age (14.8 percent).[7] Similar patterns have been found in Germany and the United States.[8]

For white American women born in the early 1860s, about the age of Beatrice Webb and my great-great-grandmother, childlessness *within marriage* surpassed 13 percent in California, Nevada, and New England, reaching a maximum of 19.3 percent for women in New Hampshire. Table 2.1 provides the percentages of childless married women by state.[9]

Declining Fertility

The increasing importance of childlessness within marriage occurred as overall fertility plummeted.[10] It started in France, where fertility declined from 5 to 3.5 children per woman between 1790 and 1855, followed by a second drop from 3.5 to 2 children between 1880 and 1940.[11] France's rivals later experienced the same changes. In Britain, the average family size declined from 5.8 children for couples who married in the 1870s to 3.4 for those who married in the first decade of the 1900s. Other countries soon reached 3.5 children per woman: Germany and the United States (1914), Italy (1930), and Japan (1950).[12] In the United States, white women in 1800 had seven children; by 1900, they had three or four.[13]

Most historians agree that the decline in fertility occurred independently in different areas, but they don't fully understand why.[14] According to the theory of the demographic transition, as child mortality decreased, parents began to raise fewer children. A version of this theory holds that parents in wealthier, industrializing countries shifted their priorities from quantity of children to quality. Still others have emphasized that female education, too, triggers lower fertility, including in poorer countries.[15] Education makes it more possible for women to make long-term decisions and have a say in how their households are run. Educated women are more able to strategize about the number of children they bear, either alongside or in spite of their husbands. In another debate, some demographers view the decline in the number of children as a form of altruistic investment in a small family, whereas others see it as emblematic of the rise of individualism.[16]

Demographers also debate whether the decline in fertility occurred because women spaced out their pregnancies, or, at a certain age prior to menopause, stopped having children all together. Evidence from eighteenth-century France suggests that many women began to bear their last child

Table 2.1 Percentage Childless for All White Women and for Ever-Married White Women by State: Cohort Born 1861–1865

State	% Childless of All Women	% Childless of All Ever-Married Women
Oklahoma	5.7	4.1
Utah	8.1	3.2
Idaho	8.2	5.3
Arkansas	8.4	4.3
Texas	8.6	4.6
South Dakota	8.7	5.1
North Dakota	9.1	5.9
Kansas	11.8	6.9
Nebraska	12.0	6.8
New Mexico	12.2	8.2
Wyoming	12.2	8.1
Washington	12.9	8.9
Montana	12.9	8.6
Minnesota	13.0	7.0
Tennessee	13.0	6.2
Wisconsin	14.0	6.3
Mississippi	14.0	7.1
South Carolina	14.2	5.2
Georgia	14.2	5.8
Alabama	14.3	5.9
Oregon	14.3	9.6
Florida	14.3	8.4
Missouri	14.5	7.0
Iowa	14.6	6.9
North Carolina	15.5	6.1
Michigan	15.7	9.8
Arizona	15.8	12.0
Colorado	16.2	10.7
West Virginia	16.6	8.1
Kentucky	16.7	7.4
Indiana	16.9	9.9
Louisiana	17.2	6.9
Illinois	17.4	9.3
Delaware	17.5	6.3

(continued)

Table 2.1 Continued

State	% Childless of All Women	% Childless of All Ever-Married Women
Virginia	18.7	7.4
Pennsylvania	19.8	9.0
Nevada	19.9	15.7
Ohio	20.2	10.4
New Jersey	21.1	11.7
Vermont	21.7	13.4
California	21.8	13.0
Maryland	22.5	10.5
New York	24.3	12.7
Maine	24.8	14.9
Connecticut	26.0	14.3
Rhode Island	28.3	14.4
Massachusetts	30.0	16.3
New Hampshire	32.1	19.3

S. Philip Morgan, "Late Nineteenth- and Early Twentieth-Century Childlessness," *American Journal of Sociology* 97, no. 3 (November 1991): 785, Table 1, citing the US Bureau of the Census (1943, Table 32).

around age thirty-five, instead of age forty or later—and this, even though they were starting to marry even later than before, at age twenty-six.[17] The difference could be startling; a change from five children per woman to four may sound small, but it represents a 20 percent decline.

Whatever the cause, the average fertility rate masks the wide range of outcomes for women in the midst of the fertility decline. Beatrice Potter and her eight sisters, who married between 1867 and 1891, produced a total of 43 children, an average of 4.78—perfectly in line with the British national average of the time. This number might lead us to assume that childlessness remained rare. But two sisters, Catherine and Beatrice, never had children, despite long marriages. Mary had only one, a son born when she was twenty-one. The other six sisters raised between five and ten children. In this wide range of family size, too, the Potters fit British trends. Childlessness became more frequent during the transition to smaller family size. It was not only that more families ended at three, four, or five children but also that more families stopped at one or even zero children.[18]

Victorian Birth Control

What explains the rise in childlessness? As before, some women found the independence of remaining single more attractive than marriage. They took advantage of job opportunities in the cities: in industry, shops, and businesses.[19] In Britain, the Population Census of 1851 reported more than one million unmarried women above the age of twenty-five.[20] Rates of singleness in the United States increased from 7.3 percent for those born in the 1830s and peaked at 11 percent for those born in the 1870s.[21] The ideology of republican motherhood created more space for single women in the United States. For some, the demands of Victorian motherhood seemed so all-encompassing, so conclusive, that they believed that having children would prevent them from working to achieve pressing social reforms.[22] Others simply wanted time to teach, to write, to create art. Louisa May Alcott, like other "busy, useful, independent spinsters," chose to remain single, "for liberty is a better husband than love to many of us."[23] In fact, if we include these unmarried women, almost one in three women in New Hampshire born in the early 1860s never had children.

But the persistence of single women doesn't fully explain the trend that we have already uncovered: the women who married and yet ended up with fewer children than in the past, or none at all. We might wonder how couples could have avoided having children without access to the Pill or other medical contraceptives. Despite a three-million-word diary, extensive letters, and autobiographies, Beatrice Webb remained silent about her sexual life with Sidney. Few women talked openly about sexuality and menstruation; even the most private and detailed diaries included only elliptical references. For decades, Mary Pierce Poor, an upper-middle-class American who married in 1841, tracked her periods with a + and sexual intercourse with her husband with an x. Surely one purpose was to trace pregnancy: Poor had seven children, sometimes with long intervals between them. But these codes were never explained, and the layers of their meaning were never openly dissected, not even in the privacy of this diary.[24] Nineteenth-century literature, too, almost never referred to contraception. "Readers may wonder yet have to remain ignorant about how Dreiser's Sister Carrie avoided pregnancy," writes historian Janet Farrell Brodie. "Even the boldest French novelists skirted the subject, and readers never learn how Madame Bovary or Zola's courtesan, Nana, controlled their fertility."[25] Only a handful of novels, including Leo Tolstoy's *Anna Karenina*, broach the subject, and even then with the use of ellipses to signal the impropriety of the conversation.

Yet despite this silence, contraceptive practices were hardly new.[26] Even in early marriage societies, women limited fertility through prolonged breastfeeding, contraceptive herbs, withdrawal, and taboos on the timing of sexual relations; such practices, applied to a greater or lesser extent at different times and places, meant that the average number of children per woman who married at age twenty to twenty-four ranged from 6.61 to 9.15.[27] Women without the resources to raise their children neglected them so they would die or abandoned them at foundling hospitals.

In the nineteenth century, knowledge of birth control practices and the wherewithal to use them increased, but unevenly across time and place. For those who were fertile, it took new habits, planning, and luck to pull off the family of zero or one child. To take charge of one's sexuality—to track the dates, procure the devices, and negotiate with one's husband—did not always come easily.[28] Yet in times and places where matrons used birth control to slow down or end reproduction, some of their newly married sisters did, too. Supply of birth control advice and devices and demand from women who wanted to limit the number of births mutually reinforced each other. New instruments and practices were devised, some of which were effective and safe, and others that were not. Well before Beatrice Webb's marriage, couples also inserted soapy douches and stretched on dried gut condoms. By the 1880s diaphragms, vaginal sponges, and pessaries were also widely available, if only somewhat reliable.[29] Advice manuals conflicted over the timing of the monthly "safe" period. Some advised waiting for intercourse until the eighth day after the onset of menstruation, precisely the wrong time if a couple sought to avoid pregnancy. Doctors were unlikely to counsel birth control, but they may have indicated that fragile women might take care in becoming pregnant. Furthermore, some manuals for young wives published in the 1890s implied that women had the right to avoid sex with husbands they found repulsive.[30]

Abortion, the birth control of last resort, was common. In France at the end of the century, where abortion was illegal, there were 100,000 to 500,000 abortions annually, compared with 900,000 live births. In the United States in the early twentieth century, estimates range between 250,000 and 1 million illegal abortions per year.[31]

Yet many never spoke openly about techniques to limit conception. At times, secrecy was legally enforced. In the United States, the Comstock laws of the 1870s suppressed the circulation and possession of contraceptive devices.[32]

While the use of birth control remained controversial, the birth control movement slowly opened up conversation—however horrified and hushed—about sexuality and the control of reproduction, sometimes in public debates. In 1877, free-thinkers and socialists Charles Bradlaugh and Annie Besant defended at the Queen's Bench Court in London their right to distribute a pamphlet—Charles Knowlton's *Fruits of Philosophy*—advocating contraception with the aim of alleviating the misery of overpopulation in Dickensian London.[33] In 1887, four years before her marriage, Beatrice Potter joined a crowd gathered around a man at Speakers' Corner in Hyde Park. He'd run his voice raw on a "delicate" subject: "the rival methods of checking population."[34]

For those willing to discuss birth control openly, it inspired thoughtful, complex deliberation. Debates over the use and implications of birth control cut across politics in ways that might surprise us. Neo-Malthusian liberals, who sought freedom from government intervention and the uplift of the worthy, believed that restricting family size through various forms of birth control was the only way out of poverty. Fewer births would help women become better mothers. Neo-Malthusian anarchists Paul Robin and Marie Huot argued against procreation as an act of resistance; why should women produce more cannon fodder for the armies of the state?[35] (Neo-Malthusians are not to be confused with T. R. Malthus himself, who did not advocate for birth control other than abstinence. More on him in Chapter 8.)

The far left, including many socialists, deplored contraception as a tool of oppression. It is not overpopulation that causes poverty, they argued, but the capitalist system that enriches a few at the expense of the many.

Fabian socialists, however, including the Webbs, promoted contraceptives to create a more efficient, reformed society.[36] The state ought to play an active role, they argued, to prevent "our most inferior stocks"—Sidney Webb's reference to Irish, Jews, and Poles—from outnumbering the "right" sort of people.[37] Eugenicists, who promoted one of the ugliest ideas conceived in the modern era, supported the conversation about contraception.[38]

Yet many feminists of the era opposed birth control if it only gave men more power and pleasure and deprived women of the affection and prestige that raising children conferred. French socialist-feminist Léonice Rouzade espoused the position that "motherhood is women's principal social function and deserves to be subsidized by the State."[39] By 1900, Blanche Edwards-Pilliet, a female doctor and republican feminist argued—much like Rouzade—that the state ought to fully subsidize motherhood.[40]

Advocates of contraception slowly legitimized concerns about the pain and high mortality associated with pregnancy and childbirth. The French neo-Malthusian League of Human Regeneration published a "manifesto for women" in 1903 exhorting women to limit fertility when it threatened their health or well-being: "This depends entirely on you, you are mistresses of your destiny . . . you must not be ignorant of the fact . . . that science has emancipated you from the dreadful fatality of being mothers against your will."[41]

Only a few radicals, such as John M. Robertson in England and Nelly Roussel in France, openly made the argument for contraception most familiar in the twenty-first century: the right for a woman to control their bodies and their family size. Although such claims aroused vehement disapprobation from the mainstream press, Roussel—whose unique combination of feminism and neo-Malthusianism led her to advocate the liberation of female sexuality—delivered dozens of lectures annually to crowded rooms throughout France. Her most popular lecture, "La liberté de maternité" (which, historian Elinor Accampo notes, might be translated as "freedom *in*, *for*, or *from* motherhood") advocated the use of contraception to give women control over their pregnancies.[42]

Why?

If more couples knew how to control pregnancy, why did some of them decide to prevent it all together? It is one thing for techniques and technologies to control birth to become more available, and it is quite another for them to be used. Which married women were more likely to remain childless? The answer cannot be simply a matter of preference; couples did not exist in a vacuum, but moved in a broader web of relationships bound by sentiment, economics, politics, and social norms that shaped their family size.[43]

Surely, some remained childless for the same reasons that they had in previous centuries: they postponed having children to gain firmer economic ground and, in the end, did not have children at all. The economic depression that started in 1873 may have encouraged later marriage, which rendered some women childless. By the late nineteenth century, the rising cost of raising, educating, and securing a place for children might have led some couples to postpone reproduction until they felt more financially secure.

Still, economic hardship can answer only part of the question. By the late 1800s, even as the cost of raising children expanded, wealthier American couples were less likely to have children than poorer ones.[44] In the long term, economic well-being is negatively correlated with fertility: as the standard of living improves and the economy grows, fertility falls.[45] Furthermore, as a very few voices began to articulate their reasons for childlessness, these reasons extended beyond finances to include other values. In 1911, *Good Housekeeping* published a letter from a twenty-eight-year-old woman who wrote "without any shame or hesitation. . . . I have been married seven years and have deliberately avoided having children. I have seen many women look horrified at such an admission. . . . Then these same women go on to tell of their difficulties in making ends meet."[46] In addition, her marriage had been "a pure love match," and she had no interest sacrificing this relationship for the sake of children. For her, the reasons for childlessness included both marital happiness and financial constraints.

Another woman, who told her story in the 1907 *Independent,* gave the economic motive a sharp political edge. Although she wanted to have a child of her own, she feared the prospect of raising a child in poverty. She already needed to work to support herself, her husband, and another relative; bearing a child would cut into her ability to work and therefore the family income, while adding to its expenses. Her despair extended into a critique of capitalism itself. She would not bear a child "destined from birth for wage slavery and exploitation or worse. . . . Are the bodies of women to be regarded merely as baby machines, to supply the losses which civilization creates by its awful mismanagement? . . . The master class can't force me to furnish food for its factories."[47]

Childlessness within marriage was more common in urban, secular areas. Cities in turn-of-the-century Germany with over 100,000 souls had significantly higher rates of childlessness than those with fewer than 2,000.[48] In London, in spa towns, in ports and textile towns, women who married later than age twenty-five were at least ten percentage points more likely to be childless than might be expected according to natural fertility rate.[49] Couples in the Netherlands who were more religiously liberal or who lived in urban areas were less likely to have children. So, too, were those who lived in areas that voted for progressive parties and in towns with a higher standard of living as measured by the density of shops.[50] In Scotland, social groups with unusually high numbers of small or zero-child families included professionals such as doctors and lawyers as well as hawkers and performers who were particularly mobile, small greengrocers and shopkeepers, whose wives were likely to be involved in the work, or domestic servants.[51]

Some professional women may have preferred to be able to work outside the home, and some women who performed unpaid civic or intellectual work, like Beatrice Webb, preferred this life to childrearing.[52]After all, women who held jobs such as a teacher were routinely fired when they became pregnant.[53] In the northeastern United States, women who worked in the mills may have continued to do so after marriage.[54] Men, too, may have preferred their chances in life if they remained childless. The golden handcuffs of middle-class status led some struggling young aspirants to renounce marriage or to marry only with the restriction of offspring.[55]

National Insecurity

Not surprisingly, then, childless couples in the late nineteenth century immediately gained suspicion. Pronatalist activists, researchers, and policymakers spoke openly of issues that remained whispered among women. In the late nineteenth century, concern about childlessness and low fertility became an issue of national security. Childless men were deemed weak and self-absorbed—those money-obsessed social climbers perched in some damp and sooty Edinburgh accounting house, brushing their suits and upgrading their pocket watches, mindful to preserve the crease in their pants legs, oblivious to their national duties. Women fared even worse. Whereas early modern conversations about "old maids" had referred primarily (but not exclusively) to personal relationships in the domestic sphere, discussions of married childless women at the turn of the twentieth century thrust them into the national spotlight. T. R. Malthus had advocated limiting the population to alleviate misery, but these later generations believed that having more children—and more of the "right" children—would support the nation and the interest of the "white" race.

As early as the 1860s, childless women in the United States were portrayed as obsessed with youth and health and uninterested in domestic duties. Critics were certain that some women chose childlessness and that these wayward young wives were destroying the fabric of American life. Foster Barham Zincke, who wrote of his travels through the United States in 1867–1868, found that "childlessness allows comfort, society, amusement; husband and wife agree to have but one child or none. Another reason which often has much weight with husbands is the short duration of female beauty; the young wife does not care to dilapidate herself prematurely."[56] In the end, he argued, the couple divorces out of mutual alienation.

The situation became so common that in 1899 the president of the American Association of Obstetrics and Gynecology could write in an open letter to his colleagues, "I am sure we have all often been perplexed by the shameless confession of a handsome and what is apparently correct young married woman that she prevents conception; even more, that she entered the marriage bed with the distinct understanding that she desires no off-spring and does so because of the inconvenience it would give her. It has been my sad experience to note this antipathy to be more frequent in the young woman than in the young man."[57]

In France, too, childlessness had become an issue of national concern. France's devastating loss to Prussia and its allies in 1870 led to the annex-ation of the populous regions of Alsace and part of Lorraine. The war laid bare France's demographic deficit in comparison to the newly founded German Empire. Consensus soon emerged across the political spectrum that depopulation and degeneracy lay at the root of France's problems.[58] The anticlerical republican state and the Catholic Church did not agree on much, but they both decried the loss of population and France's demo-graphic might. As in the United States, many feared that the "right" people were not reproducing.

In 1896, the government released census data showing that France's population had grown by only a quarter million over the previous decade, whereas Germany's had increased by eight million.[59] Pronatalists pounced. Childlessness was believed to be part of the problem. Theories abounded on how to fix the problem (and few questioned that it was a problem). Jacques Bertillon believed that men had fewer children because they were reluctant to break up their property and so proposed new inheritance laws. Others recognized that this issue was one that involved women, too. Henri Thulié attributed the decline to infant mortality, something that reformers had been working to address for decades.[60] Still others viewed childlessness as a moral issue and so emphasized educational reform.[61] A few believed that population decline had resulted from women's low status in society. The pronatalist platform called for tax penalties against single persons and married couple without children. It also sought to criminalize sharing information about birth control.[62]

French fears of childlessness and depopulation arose just prior to their claims to control vast territories in Africa and Asia. By the 1890s, the French empire encompassed some sixty million colonial subjects, as compared to approximately forty million French in the metropole.[63] But these subjects alone would not in themselves make up for the decline of the French population; pronatalists viewed the French reliance on colonial soldiers as harkening the decline of French greatness, much as ancient Rome's use of colonial subjects heralded the fall of the Roman Empire.[64] Instead, pronatalists focused on the salutary effects of life in the colonies, away from the poverty and disease of urban life. The colonies provided space, so they thought, for wayward and overcivilized French men and women to recover their lapsed fecundity and redeem their modern ways—the unmasculine man and the professional woman would recover their true selves by reproducing in the fecund and rural colonies, where they would fulfill their true natures as virile men and fertile women, healthy and moral.[65]

The Twentieth Century

Despite these exhortations for women to have more children, rates of childlessness continued to increase into the twentieth century and reached unprecedented heights for women born in 1900. One in five American women born at the turn of the last century remained childless throughout their lives, and similar rates occurred in Germany (26 percent for women born in 1900), France (25 percent), Canada (22 percent), Italy (18 percent), the Netherlands (23 percent), and Australia (31 percent).[66] Childlessness continued to become more common within marriage. Sixteen percent of all British couples who married in 1925 were childless. [67] By 1940, a study of 382 long-term childless couples in Indianapolis could estimate that just over 40 percent had chosen to remain childless.[68]

Childlessness remained a piece of lowering birth rates. Fertility fell below the number of children needed to maintain the population—the replacement level—for a number of years in the 1920s and 1930s across many parts of Europe as well as in Canada and the United States. The low point fell in the mid-1930s. Germany's cohort completed fertility slipped below replacement level at the outset of the twentieth century, when the cohort born in 1885 reached adulthood and started to bear their 3.36 children, below the replacement level of the time of 3.44 children (the replacement level was higher than today due to higher mortality rates among the young). For the 1900 cohort, which reached childbearing age in the late 1910s through the 1930s, completed fertility was 2.1 children in both France and Germany. In cities, particularly, birth rates plummeted; in Berlin between 1880 and 1900, the number of births fell by 32 percent.[69]

The generation of 1900 came of age in the turbulent early twentieth century. The Great War, the influenza pandemic, the Great Depression, and World War II disrupted normal family planning. Over 40 percent of women born in Berlin between 1885 and 1904 ended up childless, and surely the trauma of the twentieth century shaped this outcome.[70] In fact, some demographers attribute the low fertility rates and high rates of childlessness primarily to the events of the twentieth century.[71] It is indeed the case that short-term fluctuations in economic well-being were strongly correlated with fertility: when the economy declines, people have fewer babies.[72] Despite the decimation of potential marriage partners in the Great War, 90 percent of women born in 1900 eventually married, including in their forties, but marriages may have ended all too quickly due to the war and the pandemic, and the Great Depression led many to postpone childbearing until it was too late.[73]

But these events, as disruptive and traumatic as they were, do not fully explain the high rates of childlessness. Childlessness had been on the rise since the mid-nineteenth century, especially among married couples; it was not an unusual blip in a particularly tragic era. And it doesn't make sense to say that childlessness occurred in the 1920s due to the losses in the Great War, but that the baby boom started after the even more destructive war against fascism. Something else was going on.

During the 1920s and 1930s, leading demographers did not simply ascribe low fertility to the aftereffects of the Great War or to the Great Depression of the 1930s. Instead, they believed that low fertility occurred due to long-term changes. Women, they believed, were no longer going to church; they were less God-fearing and more interested in themselves, their clothes, and their electric appliances. They were using contraception and enjoying sex and eroticism within marriage. They were voting and driving and becoming more free. By the 1920s, images of couples enjoying a loving, fun marriage entered mainstream culture in movies and novels. At the same time, critics churned out pamphlets, magazine articles, films, radio programs, and novels showing nonmothers as dried up, frustrated, sad, and lonely.[74] British single women, including teachers (who were barred from marriage) who were entrusted with the education of young people, were seen as sexually frustrated or as lesbians who, ironically, exerted too much influence on young girls.[75] In other words, demographers did not see low fertility as a short-term issue related to acute problems in the early twentieth century, but rather to long-term developments in the modern condition. These long-term changes seemed to them a revolution with an uncertain outcome. They feared that the population might never stabilize at a new equilibrium.[76] They anticipated that the "perfect contraceptive" could be invented at any time and that it would support this new unstable regime. They saw motivations for this change not as the altruistic devotion to fewer children, but as individualistic and dangerous.[77]

Often these arguments took on racist tones, as when Italian Corrado Gini argued in 1930 that "the white races" of Europe had entered a period of decline, or when Frederich Burgdörfer, who became the director of the demographic department in the *Statistiche Reichsamt* in Nazi Germany, promoted policies to prevent the extinction of the "white" or "Teutonic race."[78] In the United States, childlessness, fewer children, and later marriages among the "native element of the population"—that is, those descended from English settlers—elicited the standard ugliness of the xenophobic crowd. They believed that childlessness among the English was leaving America to be taken over by Italian, Russian, and Jewish immigrant families. The proportion of childless American-born wives increased from 14 percent in 1910 to 21 percent in 1940, but, to the alarm of eugenicists, these percentages were lower for immigrant women (11 and 13 percent, respectively).[79]

The threat to the family, and therefore the nation, reputedly stemmed from a crisis in values among the "descendants of the colonizers of the United States," who "preferred material luxuries to spiritual realities, lustful conceits to correct theories of life, and self gratifications of inordinate ambitions to unselfish acceptance of the duties of parenthood."[80] They were perfectly aware of the "movement of childlessness among American women," especially in New England, Pennsylvania, and New York.[81] Arthur Calhoun wrote in 1919 that "many families run out in the third generation."[82] (To his mind, generations only counted if they started on American soil.) He cited women's "selfish shrinking from [the] burden restraint, anxiety, [and] expense" of children: "Tho New England girls married they rarely became mothers."[83] In 1936, eugenicist Paul Popenoe asked adults why people they knew did not have children.[84] They put "self-centered" at the top of the list, followed by wife's career, economic pressure, health, dislike of all children, eugenics, and marital discord. Popenoe took these answers at face value: "The great bulk of the voluntary childless marriages are motivated by individualism, competitive consumption economically and an infantile self-indulgent frequently neurotic attitude toward life."[85]

Concern about racial purity contributed to forced sterilization campaigns in the United States and elsewhere; to the enforcement of mothering norms for women of the "right" background through culture, laws and violence; and, in fascist and authoritarian regimes, to the murder of those who were deemed enemies of the race.

But demographers did not need to subscribe to racist and traditionalist ideologies to notice the prevalence of subreplacement fertility or to interpret it as part of a long-term trend. These interwar demographers recognized that people were choosing something other than the traditional family. They knew that the personal was political: that family size would shape national standing and the ability to wage war, grow the economy, and exert power over colonial territories. They saw that family size was related to class, to civil society, to citizenship within a representative democracy, and to the notion of the public sphere and who was allowed to participate in it.[86]

While pronatalists interpreted childlessness as a neurotic, selfish, and antiwhite source of anxiety, others saw childless women as trying to do their best in a complex world. It was possible, both then and now, to notice that some women took the path of childlessness neither because of dire need arising from the circumstances of war nor from a selfish impulse to seek pleasure, but because they had other worthy goals in mind. Indeed, even to make the argument that women could and did marry after the Great War reproduces the notion that marriage is the ideal state and that unmarried women are marginal figures.[87] Alternatively, it could also be, historian Katharine Holden points out, that the lack of men after the Great War changed women's views and aspirations and encouraged some women to seek alternatives. In 1916, Leta S. Hollingworth published in the *American Journal of Sociology* her arguments against the notion of a maternal instinct. Hollingworth, a childless, married psychologist, argued that maternal instincts were nothing but the work of "those in control of society" who "invent and employ devices for impelling women to maintain the birth rate sufficient to insure enough increase in the population to offset the wastage of war and disease."[88] Hollingworth found "no verifiable evidence to show that a maternal instinct exists in women of such all-consuming strength and fervor as to impel them voluntarily to seek the pain, danger, and exacting labor involved in maintaining a high birth rate."[89] Hollingworth's argument fit the behaviors of many women of the generations before and after, whatever they might have been able to say out loud.[90]

During and after the baby boom, demographers developed a different interpretation of the interwar period, one that provided a reassuringly straightforward ending: lowered fertility in the late nineteenth and early twentieth century was heading toward a new equilibrium of low fertility and low mortality, one that would quell the fears of either dying out or unsustainable population growth.[91] Populations shifted from relatively high mortality and fertility to a new equilibrium with relatively low mortality and fertility.[92] And so, demographers in the late twentieth century interpreted the subreplacement fertility of the interwar period as an exception caused by the Great War and Great Depression rather than as part of profound and long-lasting demographic instability. The story of childlessness during that time was masked.

Despite external pressures to procreate, couples in the nineteenth and early twentieth centuries like Beatrice and Sidney Webb began to postpone childbearing from the beginning of marriage, despite the risk that such postponement might turn into permanent childlessness. Some of them, it seems, started to realize, individually or in whispered conversations, that they might continue this way indefinitely. With infertility a real possibility, who was to probe if a couple never procreated? "And, if they did," writes demographer Michael Anderson, "a sad shrug of the shoulders might well have been enough to put off further inquiry."[93] The events of the twentieth century exacerbated trends that had been developing since the late nineteenth century.

What was new about these generations? Not the large numbers of unmarried people, not the conscious limitation of fertility, and not the methods, many of which had been part of European families for centuries. Rather, the change came in the acceptance, however reluctant, of the possibility of childlessness even within marriage. A new act of imagination allowed couples to dissociate sexual activity from procreation, to practice the art of making a choice, even if they never openly put it into words. Bearing children no longer came as part of a package that contained marriage and an independent household. As in the past, age at marriage strongly influenced whether or not a married couple had children. Now, marrying at an older age brought not just greater risk of infertility but also, for some, more knowledge about deliberate fertility limitation and a greater willingness to use it. Demographers in the 1920s and 1930s believed they were witnessing a revolution whose outcome could not be predicted, in which subreplacement fertility was a structural piece of the puzzle.

But then, there was a brief interlude called the baby boom.

3

Interlude

The Baby Boom

For many of us who came of age in the late twentieth century, the baby boom seemed to set the standard for how life had always been: middle-class women had married their high school sweethearts, given birth to two or three children, and stayed home to raise them. They wore rubber gloves and aprons during the day and nip-waisted emerald dresses at night. The family provided the cornerstone of national security and a haven from the evils of the outside world.

As children, these women had experienced the Great Depression, World War II, and quite possibly dislocation and food shortages. But by the time they came of age in the 1950s, they enjoyed economic prosperity, improved prenatal care and relative political stability.[1] In the United States, raising a family became synonymous with adulthood and independence. Personal fulfillment through domesticity became fundamentally linked to national security.[2] Government support in the form of the GI Bill, tax credits, and mortgage lending also encouraged family formation in suburbia.[3] Family became a refuge from the horrors of World War II and fears of the Cold War, from the great swirling acceleration in the human capacity to destroy itself. Children played a necessary role in this domestic drama. Conventional wisdom dictated that everyone have their Suzy and Johnny, or at least everyone but the most deviant outsiders and unfortunate souls.

In France, the baby boom was fueled by government aid. As the dark years of World War II gave way to postwar reconstruction, General Charles de Gaulle imagined a brighter future for France starting with the birth of "twelve million beautiful babies."[4] In the years that followed, the French government developed a system of policies and institutions unrivaled in Europe with the primary aim of raising the national birthrate, including family allowances, publicly funded nurseries, and centers of population study.[5] Beautiful babies—healthy and French—soon followed. French postwar family policy both supported the breadwinner–homemaker model that paid women allowances to stay home to raise children and also provided access to preschools that allowed women to work for wages outside the home.[6] Compared with other industrialized countries, France's rates of fertility remained high and rates of childlessness stayed low from the baby boom years through the 1970s and right down to the twenty-first century.

In both countries, the baby boom included both an increase in the number of children born per woman and an increase in the percentage of women having children. Many women had children all at the same time.[7] In the United States, family size rose between the 1930s and 1950s from 2.4 to 3.2 children.[8] And from the late 1940s though the mid-1960s, a higher proportion of women married than ever before—about 95 percent—and they did so at a younger age.[9] In France, the average age for a mother at birth (including second or third or higher births) was only 26.1 years, two full years younger than the age of their own mothers.[10]

In this "golden age of marriage," women born around 1935 had the lowest levels of childlessness on record in Europe and America: in the United States and in France only 10 percent of women and in Germany, 7.1 percent.[11] The very notion of a baby boom only makes sense in contrast with an extended previous period of lower fertility and higher rates of childlessness.

In one respect, however, the baby boom provided continuity: these parents nurtured the belief that they could and should plan their families. Although it's easy to criticize the baby boom parents for leading cookie-cutter lives, we might not give them enough credit for the care it took for American women to bear only 3.2 children in the era before the Pill.[12] On average, French baby boom mothers stopped having children at age twenty-nine, a decade or more before their fertility came to an end.[13]

How did this happen? While marriage and children remained the goals and the defining characteristics of most women's lives, young women in the 1950s began to consider themselves in a new light. In the 1950s, people became more habituated to seeing others as having a psychological development, as having a self and seeking personal satisfaction. This shift occurred as the ideas of Sigmund Freud became popularized and the Alfred Kinsey report legitimized female sexual desire and as Simone de Beauvoir encouraged women to see themselves as a self, not just as objects defined by the men in their lives.[14] In 1955, Françoise Giroud, one of the founders of *Elle*, celebrated the kind of woman who understood the freedom they could have, "that of choosing one's life," whether in a career or in the home.[15]

These conversations included discussion about the number and timing of pregnancies. As early as 1949, American sociologist Pascal K. Whelpton noted, "For more and more couples the question of whether to have none, one, two, three, or some other number of children, depends on motivations rather than age at marriage or age at starting childbearing."[16] In the 1950s, *Constellation*, a French women's magazine that aimed at rural and working-class audiences, began to discuss variations in fertility during the menstrual cycle and even noted that this knowledge could help women avoid pregnancy.[17] For the first time, then, the ultimate number of children a woman bore was not governed by her age at the time of marriage.

The baby boom was an anomaly, an interlude that lasted about twenty years. Then, childlessness returned, more controversial and openly debated than ever before.

4

Shouts

In 1976, advice columnist Ann Landers asked her readers, "If you had your life to do over again, would you have children?" Some ten thousand people responded, and 70 percent said no! It wasn't scientific in the least—a representative poll taken in 1974 showed that only 10 percent of parents wished they had not had children—but who needs data when you can tap into emotion?[1] A woman in Fargo, North Dakota, reported that she and her husband had waited eight years before having children and then quickly had three. "We both agree our happiest years were before we had the kids," she wrote. "They have brought us a lot of heartache and very little pleasure. If we had it to do over again, we'd have remained childless."[2] A mother of twins in Tampa complained, "I was an attractive, fulfilled career woman before I had these kids. Now I'm an overly exhausted, nervous wreck who misses her job and sees very little of her husband. He's got a 'friend,' I'm sure, and I don't blame him. . . . I'm too tired for sex, conversation or anything else."[3] Both of these women lamented the damage that raising children did to their marriages and to their own fulfillment.

Another woman, signed "Sad Story" from New York, decried the kinds of people that her five children turned out to be: difficult, rebellious, mentally ill, the followers of religious cults. "Not one of our children has given us pleasure," she complained. "God knows we did our best, but we were failures as parents, and they are failures as people."[4] One letter writer wisely advised potential parents to examine their motivations: "Should you have children? It depends on what you want them for. Do you want a child who will be everything you weren't? Someone whose achievements you can brag about? Do you want company in your old age? Forget it. Have children only if you can give them unselfish love and expect nothing in return. Only then will you have a fighting chance of turning out emotionally healthy individuals who will appreciate and respect you and themselves."[5]

In the 1970s, after the baby boom hiatus, childlessness returned to prominence. A twenty-five-year-old American woman reading Ann Landers's column stood a one in six chance (17 percent) of never having a child. Her counterparts in West Germany and Switzerland were even more likely to remain childless: 18 percent and 21 percent, respectively, would reach age forty-five without ever having a child. As Table 4.1 shows, childlessness became a powerful alternative in many countries for women who were born in the early 1950s and came of age in the 1970s.

All of the respondents to Ann Landers's query shared a common assumption: having children was something you could choose to do, for good reasons and for bad. In previous centuries, the notion of choice had remained shadowy and largely unexpressed. Childlessness had signaled, almost universally, either a disappointed life, shaped by forces beyond one's control, or a sign of selfishness. By the 1970s, however, the complex reasons that women ended up without children were openly reframed as the willful exercise of choice.

The puzzle remains: Why did childlessness become common again in the 1970s? The expansion of choice in both reality and perception helps to explain the rising rates of childlessness. But "choice" as an explanatory mechanism is unsatisfactory on its own; it doesn't explain why childlessness was more common in Germany than in France or why these choices were so hotly debated. As we'll see, it's crucial to understand the context in which choices were made. Once again, the historical perspective helps us to understand the pathways to childlessness.

The Pill

It's tempting to ascribe the return of childlessness to the Pill. The Pill! a medical technology that operated with such predictability and ease that it not only prevented conception but also, so it seemed, changed the reproductive preferences of millions of women. The Pill leaped out of its intended marital scope within a few short years and changed premarital sexuality, gender relations, and politics forever.[6] The early baby boomers, born in the late 1940s, came of age during the "sexual revolution" with access to the Pill from the very beginning of their reproductive years. They openly challenged many of the behaviors and attitudes of their mothers. Without the Pill, how could so many women have avoided pregnancy? How else could so many women today remain childless?

Not so fast. Many of the features of the 1970s had been common in northwestern Europe for centuries, including postponement as an accepted

Table 4.1 Percentage Childless
at Aged Forty-Five for All Women
by Country: Cohort Born 1950 to 1954

Country	% childless
Northern Europe	
Denmark	11
Finland	15
Norway	11
Sweden	14
Western Europe	
Austria	14
Belgium	14
England and Wales	14
France	13
Germany (former West Germany)	18
Ireland	13
Netherlands	15
Switzerland	21
Southern Europe	
Greece	9
Italy	12
Portugal	10
Spain	10
Eastern Europe	
Bulgaria	4
Czechoslovakia (former)	8
Germany (former East Germany)	7
Hungary	9
Poland	unknown
Romania	8
Balkan countries	
Bosnia and Herzegovina	14
Croatia	9
Macedonia	8
Serbia and Montenegro	3
Slovenia	4

(*continued*)

Table 4.1 Continued

Country	% childless
Yugoslavia (F.R.)	4
Yugoslavia (former)	8
Non-European Countries	
Australia	13
Canada	14
United States	17

Pearl A. Dykstra, "Childless Old Age," in *International Handbook of Population Aging,* ed. P. Uhlenberg (Berlin: Springer, 2009), 673–674, Table 30.1.

stage of family formation, systematic childlessness, and a wide range of family sizes. The Pill alone can't explain why women born in 1900 were more likely to be childless than they are today. After all, the Pill is only one of a long list of inventions and practices that have allowed people to limit childbearing: abstinence, condoms, withdrawal.

Furthermore, the Pill alone can't account for the variety of rates of childlessness in different countries. We can see this variety most clearly in the generation that grew up with the Pill. In the former West Germany, for the cohort born in the early 1960s, one out of every four women reached age forty-five without bearing children. In France, it's only one out of every nine.[7] Yet French women use contraceptives more than others do. In 2000, nearly 63 percent of French women aged twenty to forty-four were using either the Pill or the IUD. Ninety-five percent of French women born in the mid-1960s used medical contraceptives at some point in their lives before age fifty.[8]

In fact, there is not a direct line between the use of the Pill and the return of childlessness. Within the context of countries with lower fertility, childlessness and low fertility are no longer strongly correlated. In Western countries in the twenty-first century, there is little variation in family size, but a wide range of childless rates. In 2014, the range of fertility averages among European countries was only 0.82 children, between 1.26 in Bosnia and Herzegovina and 2.08 in France, but rates of childlessness for women born in 1965 (who were forty-nine in 2014) ranged between 5 percent and 27 percent.[9] It's true that these aren't exactly the same women, but the overall pattern is nevertheless revealing. We'd see a different pattern if it were a simple matter of pent-up demand for childlessness, actualized by the invention of the Pill—or if the Pill itself caused the desire for childlessness. Context matters.

Take Germany for example. Figure 4.1 shows that women born in West Germany any time after 1940 have been more likely to be childless than those in communist East Germany—more than twice as likely for cohorts born after 1950. For women born in the late 1960s, childlessness rose to nearly 30 percent. Only Switzerland had similarly high rates. By contrast, in East Germany, childlessness among those born c. 1945 to 1960 declined to about 7 percent. For those who completed their fertility in the uncertain years after reunification (1990), childlessness in the former East Germany rose to 14.4 percent, but this number remains far below that of their western counterparts.[10]

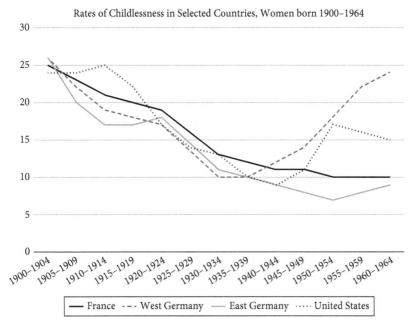

Figure 4.1 Rates of childlessness in selected countries, women born 1900 to 1964. *Sources:* Pearl A. Dykstra, "Childless Old Age," in *International Handbook of Population Aging,* ed. P. Uhlenberg (Berlin: Springer, 2009), 673–674, Table 30.1, and Laurent Toulemon, Ariane Pailhé, and Clémentine Rossier, "France: High and Stable Fertility," *Demographic Research* 19, (July 2008), art. 16, 518, Figure 10.

Attitudes toward children differ, too. In 2004, 16.6 percent of females in the former West Germany said their desired fertility was "no children," as compared to 5.8 percent of females in eastern Germany.[11]

Despite their divergent patterns of childlessness, western and eastern Germany now have virtually the same, ultra-low fertility rate: 1.44 in the west, 1.47 in the east.[12] In the former East Germany, one-child families are common, but few women do not have children. In the former West Germany, many women do not have children and are not married. But these women are balanced out by the many women who have three or more children.[13]

It's far too simple, then, to argue that the Pill allowed women to exercise choice about their fertility. It may describe *how* childlessness happened for millions of women, but it doesn't explain *why* it happened.

Self-Actualization

The Pill is better understood as a tool that allowed women to exercise choice about reproduction and to see options that they might not otherwise have seen. To better understand why they made one choice or another, we can turn to two major positions. The first is an argument about self-actualization, and the second is an argument about economics. Both arguments hinge on the notion of choice, but they do so in different ways. While neither argument is completely convincing, they both illuminate the issue of how and why childlessness returned in the 1970s.

Let's start with self-actualization as formulated by demographers Dirk van de Kaa and Ron Lesthaeghe in 1986 as part of a theory they call the Second Demographic Transition. Van de Kaa and Lesthaeghe argue that since the 1960s, more people have been willing and able to pursue their own self-actualization, and this has led to more variety in family size and structures—including widespread childlessness.

In formulating the Second Demographic Transition theory, Van de Kaa and Lesthaeghe borrowed from American psychologist Abraham Maslow's famous hierarchy of needs. In 1943, as the most destructive war in history stripped men, women, and children of their lives and affronted their human dignity, Maslow wondered about a different world, one in which people have enough food to eat and do not fear for their safety. He theorized that once these basic needs are met, we humans are not satisfied: we then need love. We seek affection and a secure social place with friends, family, a sexual partner, children. Having found love, we still chafe for more. We seek the esteem of others, respect for our accomplishments and abilities, a sense of confidence that we can contribute to the world. Even then, Maslow reasoned, we still are not content. Having secured food, safety, love, and esteem, Maslow argued, we seek *self-actualization*, "to become more and more what one is, to become everything that one is capable of becoming."[14] This drive to become our best self takes many forms; he continued: "In one individual it may take the form of the desire to be an ideal mother, in another it may be expressed athletically, and in still another it may be expressed in painting pictures or inventions."[15]

In 1943, Maslow lamented that self-actualization remained rare.[16] For too many people, the basic needs of food and safety were not met. But after the war ended, across the industrialized West, decades of postwar economic prosperity changed expectations. The rise in affluence paralleled a growing attentiveness to the psychological self. The conversations about choice and the self that had started in the 1950s intensified in the 1960s. In the early 1960s, a subtle shift occurred in the relationship between the self and family life; rather than fit the self into prescribed family roles, women were supposed to discover self-actualization through family life.[17] Women began to be viewed not only as wives and mothers, but also as women who found fulfillment as wives or mothers.[18] In the late 1960s, it was a crucial step, then, for women to seek self-actualization outside of the family all together.

These greater expectations and this more salient sense of self, argue van de Kaa and Lesthaeghe, profoundly reshaped the family. By the late 1960s, the driving principle behind the contemporary family became the "right to self-realization granted to each individual," which can be manifested in a wide variety of family structures.[19] Prospective parents now ask themselves, "'Will our lives be enriched by having a child, or an additional child now?' The couple will weigh a great many aspects, including the direct and opportunity costs, but their guiding light will be whether it would be self-fulfilling."[20]

Together, the advent of the Pill and the rising importance of self-actualization can explain much about the return of childlessness. They both heralded the emphasis in the 1970s on personal choice. In *The Journal of Nervous and Mental Disorders*, in 1970, Edward Pohlman embraced freedom of choice so that adults "might choose whichever life style—parenthood or childlessness—suits them best."[21] He explained that childlessness, including voluntary childlessness, ought not to be viewed as a sign of disorder. Contrary to received wisdom, Pohlman wrote, "Parenthood has many disadvantages, many husbands and wives might be better off without children, many couples cannot provide very favorable environments for children, and population pressures would be eased by an increase in the proportion childless."[22]

The concept of choice, tightly linked with the desire to become the person who you want to be, had been developing in both theory and practice over the previous centuries. Choice-making, by the 1960s firmly attached to ideas about democracy and liberty, became ordinary and celebrated as a goal across the political spectrum. In fact, the concept of self-actualization helps us to understand that the difference between East Germany and West Germany in terms of childlessness might be related to the relative lack of individual choice under communist rule. In the east, raising children may have provided a measure of autonomy that could not be found in other areas of life.

In the west, it was a small but fateful step that "choice" emerged as a rallying cry for reproductive freedom. The language of choice appeared everywhere, from the Supreme Court's *Roe vs. Wade* decision, to the rhetoric of the National Organization for Non-Parents (NON), to a 1974 episode of the television program *All in the Family*, which reached forty million viewers, in which Gloria argued, "Ma, I believe a woman is meant to be a person first, and then maybe a mother. I don't need to give birth to a baby to make me feel useful!"[23]

Eventually, the question "Should we have children?" became a topic of open conversation. Women gained more knowledge about their fertility, a greater ability to deliberate about means and ends, and greater self-confidence to judge and make decisions regarding the terms of sexual encounters.[24] Once women could plan their pregnancies with more precision, it became possible for more of them to pursue formal education and employment and easier to openly discuss the fact that not all females are destined for motherhood.[25]

Slowly, childlessness became more openly discussed and accepted. Singleness and childlessness, which in earlier societies were deemed to be social conditions worthy of shunning, shame, pity, and economic dependency, now often became associated with greater liberty.[26] The Pill, coupled with the liberating notion of self-actualization, appeared to make this all possible. Women could now exercise choice.

And yet, the liberating culture of choice can't fully explain the differences in rates of childlessness. After all, self-actualization cut both ways. It could justify postponing or foregoing childbirth, and it could justify raising children. In a 1973 article published in the *American Journal of Psychiatry*, Henry Greenbaum, a follower of Erik Erikson, argued, "Adults, both men and women, have a need to rear children in order to enhance their own self-realization and to achieve fulfillment of some of their emotional, mental, and social aspirations."[27] Lestheage has found that those who become parents rely on reasons of self-fulfillment just as readily as those who did not.[28] Looking back over the decades since the 1970s, philosopher Elisabeth Badinter puts it this way: "The individualism and hedonism that are hallmarks of our culture have become the primary motivations for having children, but also sometimes the reason not to."[29]

So, the notion of self-actualization and the theory of the Second Demographic Transition might account for the variety of family structures, including the prominence of childlessness. Yet self-actualization doesn't fully help us to understand how and why some people make the decision to remain childless.

Rational Economic Actors

A second argument to explain the return of childlessness developed in the middle of the twentieth century, at about the same time as the argument about self-actualization gained currency: the theory of the rational economic actor maximizing household economy. This theory was most famously formulated by economist Gary Becker of the University of Chicago in his collection of papers *The Economic Approach to Human Behavior* (1976). Becker, who won the Nobel Prize in 1992, claimed that people act in ways to maximize their welfare, whatever the situation, from choosing a new car, to selecting socks in the morning, to marrying and having children. According to Becker, individuals make rational choices by weighing the costs and benefits. Becker assumed that people seek to maximize their outcomes, that the underlying values that shape their preferences are stable (values like health, prestige, etc.), and that everything can be traded on a market.[30]

In an essay first published in 1960, Becker extended his analysis to include the raising of children. In particular, he claimed that there is a relationship between the quantity of children and their "quality"—that is, the amount of resources voluntarily spent on a child to increase that child's utility to the parent. By the mid-twentieth century, given low child mortality rates, couples preferred to invest in a few children rather than have more children. Contrary to Malthus, an increase in income would not lead to an increase in population. In economic terms, "the quantity elasticity should be small compared to the quality elasticity."[31]

In terms of childlessness, the logic of the economic approach works like this: as more women gained access to professional employment and higher education, the opportunity costs of raising children increased, leading to higher rates of childlessness. The choice was less about becoming the person they wanted to be and more about direct and indirect costs. Or rather, from this perspective, self-actualization was just one weight in the balance of opportunity costs, one that could be traded against other weights, such as state subsidies, a bigger paycheck, or accessible child care.

Although Becker did not claim that he had worked out the entire complicated incentive structure for parenthood, he argued that such a structure does exist: "The economic approach provides a valuable unified framework for understanding *all* human behavior, although I recognize, of course, that much behavior is not yet understood, and that non-economic variables and the techniques and findings from other fields contribute significantly to the understanding of human behavior."[32] Becker's ideas became wildly influential by the late twentieth century, as market mechanisms have become a normalized—but also highly contested—way to address social problems.[33] Indeed, a true believer will expand the concept to include not only direct and opportunity costs, but also any of the other values that we hold dear. According to this line of thought, all of the freedoms, values, and identities that we seek can be conceptualized as commodities and therefore traded on a more or less efficient market, using more or less effective incentives.

Over the years, researchers have made an effort to better understand how to measure the value of children and the benefits that they might confer on parents to better understand how opportunity costs function with regard to human reproduction. Lois Wladis Hofmann and Martin L. Hofmann first developed the "value of children" model in 1973. This model acknowledges that different people will have different attitudes toward children under a variety of circumstances. Children can add value to parents in many ways, through the new social status or sense of self that they confer to parents, the fun they add to daily life, the feeling of achievement and creativity, the sense of moral correctness, or the competitive advantage that children might bring.[34]

In Bernhard Nauck's much later formulation, children add utility in four dimensions: labor contributions to the household's production or income, insurance against life's difficulties, enhancement of the parents' status by creating new connections or changing the ones that already exist, and emotional value through bonds of affection and other positive emotions.[35] The economic approach can, in this view, encompass and account for differing amounts that parents might invest in their children.

The economic approach also helps to explain the disparity between East and West Germany. In West Germany, family policy is generally seen as a failure due to its limited choices for women; it encourages women to stay home with children but doesn't provide enough options for those who work. In reunified Germany, the state's family policies, writes Elisabeth Badinter, "provide considerable financial help, but they essentially encourage mothers to remain at home, promoting the role of the father-provider and obliging women to choose between family and work from the moment the first child is born."[36] One could say that the incentive structure is inefficient. Women never make up for postponed children. Many remain childless. Policies designed to incentivize motherhood often backfire in this way, argues Badinter: "Those countries with the lowest birthrates—Japan, Italy, Germany—also seem to offer women the least choices."[37]

In East Germany, by contrast, the government provided greater economic and structural support for parents in the form of child allowances, maternity leave, birth assistance, and preferential housing allocations for parents. The state encouraged and expected women to work outside of the home, so it provided support for working mothers. Starting in the early 1970s, women were allowed to take maternity leave after childbirth and then return to their jobs. In 1986, a policy allowed women to stay home for up to a year while keeping 70 to 90 percent of her salary. When they returned to work, they had the benefit of shorter working hours and low-cost public child care.[38] The social security provided in East Germany—training, employment, and basic goods—also meant that people were more willing to undertake the irreversible decision to have a child.[39] With these supports in place, few women in East Germany forewent childbearing, though they had very few children in total. In this view, the communist East reveals starkly that, however important culture and history may be, immediate economic circumstances profoundly shape fertility.

Outrage

Like the Second Demographic Transition theory, the economic approach tried to impose order on the emotional chaos surrounding reproduction by elevating the belief that we are rational actors exercising choice. But neither theory could capture or explain the disillusionment expressed in the Ann Landers survey or the mutual antipathy and moral outrage that arose in the 1970s between parents and the voluntarily childless.

Again, context is key. The two choice-oriented theories failed to take seriously the fact that individuals operate within constraints not of their own making, within contingent realities that shape their attitudes from a young age and often fall along gendered lines.[40]

Becker wrote his essay on children at a time when gender roles were assumed to be unproblematic, in which identity and value were ascribed rather than problematized.[41] But the focus on economics does not always recognize a household power dynamic that might place certain burdens on only some citizens; for instance, it might be assumed that women would be solely responsibility for caring for children, without there being a rational conversation weighing the pluses and minuses of this arrangement. The economic approach can lack awareness of gender inequities and assumes that preferences are pretty much stable across and within populations.[42]

In reality, however, gender roles were about to undergo a radical challenge. Take West Germany for example. We've already encountered two choice-related reasons for its high rates of childlessness: greater personal freedom but fewer economic incentives for having children than in East Germany. But those explanations don't fully capture the story of sexual liberation in the West after the highly restricted and punitive sexual mores of the 1950s. Compared with the United States, West Germany in the 1950s opened proportionally fewer family planning clinics, sold fewer diaphragms or spermicidal jellies, and published less medical literature on birth control.[43] Many German states retained the 1941 Himmler ban on contraception (except for condoms, which protected from venereal disease), and doctors who had trained during the Third Reich had not received education in birth control.[44] Forms of sexuality outside of vaginal penetration—petting, masturbation, oral and anal sex—were all widely deemed unacceptable in the backlash against the open embrace of premarital and extramarital heterosexuality in both Weimar and Nazi Germany.[45] Yet between 80 and 90 percent of young people engaged in premarital sex, a much higher percentage than in the United States.[46] Many women, married or not, took recourse in illegal abortions. During the 1950s, in any given year, it is estimated that between 5 and 10 percent of all German women had an abortion: they visited a midwife or paid off a doctor for the insertion of soapy water or knitting needles.[47]

In the late 1960s, the spread of the Pill in West Germany occurred at the same time as an increased conflict about sexuality through debates over sexualized advertisement and through the women's movement. The transition to a more open conversation about alternative families occurred within conflicts and anxiety about male performance and sexually free females.[48] These conditions more fully explain why fertility rates plummeted and childlessness became common in the late 1960s and 1970s.

Or take the situation of women's work in the United States of the 1970s. For Linda Gordon, whose *Woman's Body, Woman's Right* was published in 1976, the "motherhood mystique" contributed to the continual relegation of women to menial, domestic jobs and even had the side effect of preventing women from engaging in the "genuine pleasures of motherhood." When so many women had few opportunities for meaningful paid work, she argued, they found domestic work more rewarding, even though it was not for pay. Child care may have been difficult, but in comparison with most low-paying, menial work, it was a more creative and engaging form of labor, one that required skill and afforded some amount of discretion and control in how time is spent.[49] "Women learn to like themselves in mothering roles," she wrote, "which allow them experiences of love and power not easily found in other situations."[50] For Gordon, childbearing could never be a free choice so long as children were saddled with "being useful to adults"—by giving adults an arena for validation and creativity.[51]

When questions about one's sexuality, work, and bodies were so publicly and rapidly challenged, choosing childlessness could not be taken to be a rational choice only. In fact, the very act of framing reproduction as a rational choice may have heightened the sense of anxiety and outrage even more, raising mutual antipathy between the voluntary childless and parents. By the 1960s, the interest in the psychology of the self had led those who were not interested in marriage to reframe the issue as one of normality: Am I normal?[52] The increasing effectiveness of artificial reproductive technology made parenthood seem like a choice, an achievement—and, therefore, to borrow the words of Katharine Dow, "a site of ethical deliberation."[53] Anxiety characterized the criticisms that many voluntarily childless raised as they sought to legitimize their choices in the 1970s, as well as the pronatalist response to them.

Researchers were interested in capturing these voices. Those who were childless by choice were perceived more negatively than those who were involuntarily childless, as "less well-adjusted or as misguided," a perception that ran contrary to the published research on actual childless individuals.[54] Childless husbands, in particular, were judged as being more psychologically troubled than fathers.[55] Multiple studies from the 1970s and early 1980s found continuing animosity toward the voluntarily childless, who were considered to be selfish and individualistic, hedonist and maladjusted.[56] College students assumed that childlessness among couples was temporary; they could barely imagine childlessness as a voluntary, permanent status.[57] Parenthood was viewed as the normal, responsible, moral path, one that improved married life, prevented divorce, and helped make men, men and women, women.[58] Parenthood, most believed, was "crucial to the development of full emotional and sexual maturity."[59] Henry Greenbaum viewed childlessness as a sign of immaturity. Reluctance to have children, for Greenbaum, was a sign that adults had not developed a capacity for real intimacy: "People with a sense of pseudo-intimacy fail in marriage and shy away from parenthood because they have not reached in personality development the stage of generativity, which enables an individual to 'care for' somebody or something and to 'take care of' that which needs protection and attention."[60]

The European mainstream struggled to imagine a society in which childlessness was a normal expression of adulthood. Marriage and family textbooks published in the late twentieth century depicted childless adults negatively, especially those who had chosen childlessness.[61] Literature on evolutionary social biology explained that the voluntarily childless are viewed as defectors from the evolutionary imperative to promote genetic fitness.[62] It was also difficult for many to imagine late motherhood as an alternative; in the 1970s, American women tended to bear children within the first ten years of marriage, and median age at marriage for women was 20.8 years old.[63]

On the other side, the 1976 Ann Landers survey fueled the belief that many parents secretly disliked parenting and that the childless state was not deviant but desirable.[64] In the 1970s, the voluntarily childless viewed parents as wrong-headed and selfish, and, crucially, they spoke openly of their contempt. They sometimes used the nastiest language to describe pregnancy, childbirth, and childrearing. "Having seen labor once in all its glory with blood and everything—it turned my stomach," said one.[65] Another was "horrified" to watch her sister's trim figure turn into a "sock full of porridge."[66]

More devastatingly, the "childfree" (as they now styled themselves) viewed parenting as an all-or-nothing proposition. They defined parenting as a zero-sum game, only available by giving up on something else, and that something else was almost always called "freedom."[67] Having children, they reported, would come at the cost of just about everything they cared about: a job, a good marriage, financial solvency, even competence. Sociologist Jean Veevers, one of the first to systematically interview childless individuals and place them into a rich context, reported that many childless women viewed motherhood as "neither a significant achievement nor an especially creative act. It is contended that it is equally plausible that for some women a baby may compensate for the book they never wrote, the picture they never painted, or the degree they never finished."[68] Veevers also speculated, "If some women do not achieve professional recognition and success because they become mothers, it is also possible that others become mothers because they do not achieve professional recognition and success."[69] According to Veevers, childless people valued learning over teaching, self-development and novelty over shaping others.[70]

Furthermore, American child-free advocates began to argue that childlessness was not only an acceptable path but also a better choice than parenthood.[71] NON, founded in 1972—in California, of course—started off as aggressively in favor of the choice to remain child-free. Its founders, Ellen Peck and Shirley Radl, wrote books with titles, respectively, *The Baby Trap* and *Mother's Day Is Over*.[72] The organization grew to include two thousand members in sixty-one chapters, including in Canada, England, India, and South America. While the reach of NON remained almost exclusively limited to white, middle-class, heterosexual members, it mobilized the media to promote its agenda. Early on, NON was linked to Zero Population Growth (Radl was the national executive director), but NON did not limit its objections to parenthood to the fear of overpopulation.[73]

NON targeted pronatalism through social networks of family and friends, through the media, and through academic research. Members wrote letters to corporations and publications criticizing advertisements that promoted child-rearing. They chided a Lipton's soup commercial that featured a little girl who said that "It's not soup 'til mother makes it." This advertisement, claimed NON activists, was "way out of line," given that nonmothers could also make soup without any trouble.[74] NON celebrated Non-Parents' Day every year on August 1 by crowning a Non-Father and Non-Mother of the Year. In 1974, NON went so far as to hold an "antifertility rite" in Central Park.

Predictably, NON's message was not received kindly. NON's image in mainstream America was not helped by Ellen Peck's focus on the vacations, freedom, and financial gains afforded by childlessness; these benefits just seemed selfish.[75] When Peck appeared on *The Tonight Show* with Johnny Carson on April 2, 1971, the audience reacted with hostility. "I thought the audience was going to lynch her before she got out of here," Carson recalled, "because she simply said, and it was an honest opinion, that there can be more to life than just getting married and raising babies."[76] Non-Father of the Year Dan Wakefield was amazed at the hostility he received, even from friends. One friend who read about the event reported, "You know what it was like, picking up the paper and reading about you accepting the award as Non-Parent of the Year? . . . It's like picking up the paper and reading that one of your dearest friends has become a Nazi."[77]

NON found critics among some second-wave feminists, too.[78] The National Organization for Women, for instance, sought to improve conditions for mothers and "identified motherhood as a fundamentally feminist issue."[79] Writing for *Ms.* magazine, Ellen Willis found Peck's antinatalism shortsighted, arguing that the right to have children under good conditions was related to the right not to have children. NON activists countered that the focus on daycare and motherhood in feminist magazines such as *Ms.* left them feeling alienated.[80]

After Peck's resignation from NON in 1977, the organization tried to re-brand itself as a source for information that would help potential parents make an informed choice.[81] Its members now accepted the notion that thoughtful, rational people can arrive at different fertility decisions. This kind of understanding lead to a leadership upheaval and, in 1978, a new name—the National Alliance for Optional Parenthood (NAOP).[82]

Despite its more moderate face, NAOP produced a "parent test" guaranteed to stoke animosity. In a brochure entitled, "Am I Parent Material? Some Thoughtful Questions about One of the Most Important Decisions You'll Ever Make," NAOP asked perfectly rational questions regarding the cost of child-rearing, such as "Can I afford to support a child? Do I know how much it takes to raise a child?" alongside blatantly antinatalist ones, such as "Would I be willing to give up the freedom to do what I want to do, when I want to do it?" The brochure did not include any questions to elicit the positive side of parenting.[83]

In Europe, there is some evidence that the 1970s were a crucial decade during which attitudes about childlessness edged toward the positive. In the Netherlands, approval of voluntarily childless couples leapt from 22.7 percent in 1965 to 89.8 percent in 1996.[84] The increase in favorability occurred in two stages, for two different reasons. Most (90 percent) of the rising acceptance of voluntary childlessness between 1965 and 1980 occurred within the generational cohorts: as they grew older, they became more accepting of the voluntarily childless. But, for the change between 1983 and 1996, cohort replacement was more important than changes in attitudes within the generations. Older, less tolerant individuals passed away (including the ones who hadn't change their minds during the 1970s), and younger, more tolerant individuals—those born in or after 1940—grew into adulthood.[85] In the 1970s, in other words, people were willing to change their minds about childlessness, in a way that didn't happen in the decades before or after.

Into the Twenty-First Century

In 1976, there were 580,000 childless American women aged forty to forty-four. By 2008, there were 1.9 million.[86] Their presence in terms of the total population more than doubled. What has changed since the 1970s?

The pathways to childlessness continue to be complex. Age at marriage is now as late or later than it has been over most of the past five hundred years. It's particularly striking in contrast to the baby boom, when American men married at age twenty-two or twenty-three, and women, at age twenty or twenty-one, and they started having children within a few years. As late as 1976, 90 percent of first-born children were born to parents within their first five years of marriage.[87] Since 1975, however, the median age of marriage has risen by six years for both men and women, to age twenty-nine for men and twenty-seven for women.[88] This later age at marriage means that the same pathways to childlessness that occurred in the 1600s exist today: many women prioritize jobs and education over having children, at least for a while, and this prioritization leads many to lifelong childlessness.

Just like 150 years ago, in the time of Beatrice Webb, childless women in the twenty-first century are more highly educated, less religious, more committed to their careers, less traditional in gender roles, and more urban than mothers. Nearly 30 percent of French women with a college degree who were born in the 1960s remained childless.[89] In Germany, 38.5 percent of college graduates born in 1965 do not have children.[90] A similar pattern holds for women in the highest-earning jobs.[91] Women are more likely than men to cite opportunity costs as a reason to remain childless.[92] For men, the educational pattern is not nearly so stark, though highly educated men are more likely to be childless.[93] Childless women are more likely to see parenting as a burden and motherhood as an option, not a duty.[94]

But education and socioeconomic status alone do not explain rates of childlessness. The education gap between childless and parents has been narrowing. White women in the United States without a high school degree in 2002 were more likely to be childless than the high-school graduates of 1982.[95] In France, the socio-economic gap in childlessness has diminished but not disappeared since the 1960s, as the percentage of executives and other professionals without children has decreased and the percentage of childlessness among farm and wage workers has increased.[96]

Economic trade-offs still influence rates of childlessness. France maintains one of the most robust set of pro-family policies in the world. Families now receive allowances starting with the second child.[97] In addition, France offers a wide variety of measures that both support families and help women balance work and family. Nurseries care for babies as young as two or three months old and operate from as early as 7:00 in the morning to 7:00 in the evening. Free, high-quality écoles maternelles serve children from age two.[98] Furthermore, the government provides subsidies, allowances, and tax deductions for child care for families with children up to age six.[99] But if a parent—typically the mother, in practice—prefers to devote herself to child-rearing, she will receive a monetary allocation.[100] French family policy supports mothers whether they continue to work or leave the workforce to raise the child. The various messages presented by family policy allow French women to exercise a range of choices and, in general, fosters positive attitudes toward fertility.[101] Both the right and the left promote state support for families, though the left favors more help directed at the poor, whereas the right sees family support as separate from social policy. In France, women tend to postpone childbearing, but ultimately they do have children. The delay is just a delay.[102] Childlessness is low.

Still, economic incentives are not the only factor at work. Researchers now have conceptual tools to study childlessness as a gendered behavior.

For example, Ursula Henz found two pathways to childlessness in West Germany: the first in in households with a traditional division of labor and the second in households in which household tasks are split more evenly *and* in which children are viewed more favorably. Attitudes come into play when the division of labor is more equal.[103] Henz adds the crucial gender analysis: it's not just that people do what they want or that people maximize their options, but that these things happen in a context. Historian Mary Hartman places the division of biology from destiny since the Pill into a much longer history. She argues that reproductive freedom has led women to undergo the same transformation that men did ten thousand years ago, when the dawn of agriculture transformed the nature of men's work: their bodies—and perceptions about their bodies—no longer determined their destinies.[104]

And what about attitudes toward the voluntarily childless? Pronatalists continue to couch concerns about fertility rates in emotionally charged language. Australian Treasurer Peter Costello declared in 2004 that each couple should have three children: "One for your husband, one for your wife and one for the country."[105] Nicholas Eberstadt of the American Enterprise Institute decries the "world-wide flight from family" as "a significant victory for self-actualization over self-sacrifice."[106] In this view, self-actualization and the exercise of choice are negative, in and of themselves, and fall in opposition to integrity and the best of human behavior. In the twenty-first century, it's still hard to be single and, with sex viewed as "essential for health and happiness," perhaps even harder to be single and celibate.[107]

Outrage and anxiety still shape attitudes toward the childless, but the dynamics have softened. By the mid-1980s, positive attitudes toward the voluntarily childfree slowly began to seep in. In one poll, 82 percent of American women did not feel that children were an essential ingredient for a happy marriage.[108] In 1990, 65 percent of American adults said that children are very important for a successful marriage, but by 2007 only 41 percent said so.[109] And by 2002, the majority of adults (58 percent) disagreed with the statement that people without children "lead empty lives."[110] In 2009, 38 percent reported that the increase of childlessness among women is bad for society.[111] At the same time, about half of Americans (46 percent) said that childlessness makes no difference to society. In a 2017 study, voluntarily childless individuals were viewed by college students as psychologically less fulfilled than those who had two children. The author, Leslie Ashburn-Nardo, framed these negative beliefs as a form of backlash against individuals who fail to conform to social expectations. Ashburn-Nardo found that a sense of moral outrage—anger, distrust, disapproval—accompanied and explains much of the belief that the voluntarily childless are less fulfilled. Still, the median for moral outrage was 1.37 on a scale of 1 to 5, with 1 being "not at all" and a standard deviation of 0.57. While these findings are significant, the study hardly suggests that these college students are ready with pitchforks.[112]

The long history of childlessness provides a deep, complicated reservoir of experiences to draw on as we contemplate childlessness in the twenty-first century. The pathways to childlessness are many and complex. Over the centuries, individuals and families sought to complete an education or achieve economic stability before marriage, to weigh the direct and opportunity costs of having a child, and to become the person they believed they could be. Increasingly, some childless individuals expressed a preference against raising children at all, even within marriage.

Yet the history of childlessness also reminds us that framing childlessness as "voluntary" or as a "choice" may not offer the full picture. First, our lives unfold within constraints: economic circumstances, social norms, biological limitations—including infertility and aging—and the cultural assumptions we make about our bodies and our families.

Second, humans are imperfect actors. Mistakes, errors, lack of planning, and uncertainty all play their parts. There is no ideal situation in which we freely and accurately exercise our will. "Choice" implies black and white, one or the other, and a command over one's life that seems out of step with the reality of context, whim, and accident. It also tends to call forth our less generous selves and pit one side against the other. "Preference" might be a better word, one that implies a spectrum of desirability, flexible tendencies, and a willingness to entertain alternatives.

Third, "choice" may be liberating, but it isn't the only rhetoric available. When we're talking about childlessness, it's not as simple as self-actualization's "you do you" attitude or an economic calculation that reflects only a person's particular opportunities costs. Values are at stake: our visions for the good life and for what our bodies are here on earth to do. We need to figure out what those values might be and how they might be expressed in childless lives. Historical women can help us to collectively navigate how to be childless.

5

Flourishing

When I was thirty-six, I had a conversation on a subject that I thought I'd left behind years earlier. I was at a conference in Chicago. It was a clear, buoyant afternoon, the kind of day that makes even an introvert like me willing to reach out to others. During a break, I started chatting with two women I'd just met, both of them well along in their professional lives. They were discussing the upcoming wedding of one of their offspring. In an effort to include me in the conversation, one woman asked if I had children. Upon hearing my answer—a polite but clear "no"—she had a ready response: "Well, you never know! A lot of people in their forties have children, or adopt, or fall in love with someone who has children. That's what happened to my niece—she swore she'd never have children, but then she married a man with two kids."

I thought I'd heard the last of these kinds of conversations. My interlocutors might mean well, but their comments leave a sour taste. In my twenties, I'd been told, "Wait until you're thirty. Then you'll want to have children." In my early thirties: "Wait until you're thirty-five." Now, everyone seems to know someone who's become a mother one way or another after age forty. These conversations might continue indefinitely; my fiftysomething childless friends tell me that acquaintances have now begun to assume that they have grown children. At some point they'll start thinking that I have grandchildren, too.[1]

I'm not alone in experiencing these awkward conversations. They are common fodder for blogs and columns written by childless women.[2] Part of the trick is that childlessness is not visible; it is a condition that comes to light through inquiry and conversation. And so the childless person of the twenty-first century learns to how to negotiate conversations to preserve her sense of self. What may be revealed, and when, and to whom, inform these strategies.

The objections to these conversations are many. First, these exchanges suggest that there is only one path to happiness, and it requires raising children. Any other life will lead to regret. A second objection to the "you'll change your mind" conversation has to do with privacy. "I don't care who you are," writes blogger Jamie Berube, "unless you are my husband, doctor, or my best friend of fourteen years, do not ask me or make jokes about my pregnancy status. Or lack thereof. It's not funny, cute, or kind. In fact, it's the exact opposite, and depending on whatever my circumstances might be that you likely don't know about, it could be absolutely devastating." Childless women should not have to delve into their struggles with infertility, failed marriages, or miscarriages. Berube frames these conversations as an invasion of a woman's fundamental right to privacy.

A third objection to these conversations is related to dignity. In the *Huffington Post,* Ashley Grof argues that this conversation "automatically presumes that someone knows me better than I know myself, or that I don't know how the world works." These acquaintances assume that the childless person will eventually feel an inevitable urge to motherhood, against her own experiences and ideas. They deny the childless person's capacity to take responsibility and reflect upon her actions. The only personal growth these acquaintances foresee for the childless is an acceptance of motherhood, a return to the fold.

A fourth objection has to do with personal value. Having children requires a large investment of bodies, time, and resources; it places extensive restrictions on all of these limited goods. The assumption that a childless person should have children implies a devaluation of her current use of her body, time, and resources, whatever they might be. It suggests that the childless person is selfish, making the wrong decision about what to do with her life, failing to contribute to the good of society, or even actively harming society. It claims that there is just one path to living a good life—not just a happy life, but one that is worth living.

In fact, all of these reasons—arguments about happiness, privacy, dignity, and one's personal value—relate to our notion of the good life. When we talk about childlessness, then, we are discussing more than the pathways to childlessness or the freedom to choose one's path. We are debating more than a person's self-actualization or the opportunity costs of raising a family. At heart, we are also talking about what is good. When we talk about childlessness, we engage a conversation about the fundamental purpose of our lives and how we flourish.

And so we must consider just what it means to flourish as human beings, as individuals embedded in a society with responsibilities toward and with others. On the personal level, the question is, *How can lifelong childlessness be part of a good life?* and on the societal level, the question is, *How can it be good for the whole if some people remain childless?* These are questions whose answers reside in both the practical and the imaginative. For it is not simply a matter of figuring out how to navigate awkward conversations or find companionship in old age. It is a matter of promoting human lives that are most worthy of humanity. To borrow the words of Lauren Berlant, we must imagine "how to detach from lives that don't work" and move "toward flourishing not later but in the ongoing now."[3] How do we free ourselves from a world in which childlessness is stigmatized or shameful or just plain weird? And how do we cultivate the imagination toward lives that will serve humanity well? The stories of childless women from the past will help us to answer these questions.

Ages of Woman

Paris, 1964. Violette Farge stepped out onto the Avenue des Ternes. In her trendy miniskirt, the thirty-four-year-old felt almost naked. This was more than the typical early '60s experimentation. Farge was starting a new life: ten years earlier, at the age when many of her contemporaries had married and given birth to the baby boom, Farge had joined a convent and become a nun.

After some years, Farge came to believe, however, that she had not joined the convent due to a calling or a religious devotion but out of pride and perhaps out of fear of adulthood. Now she left behind her modest religious garments and reinvented herself in Paris, "going from the long habit to a skirt—surely a short one; how long in '64? (very short)."[4]

Farge's unusual life did not end here. At age thirty-eight, she decided that she wanted to marry. She soon met and married Jacques-Louis, a divorcé with custody of his two young children. The marriage ended twelve years later when he developed schizophrenia, but she remained in the lives of Jacques-Louis and his children. Farge retired from her work at a Catholic private school at age sixty-two but soon took on a one-year teaching position in Hungary. Ten years later, she undertook a mission to Burkina Faso.

Farge's decades are measured by moments of rupture. Twenty-four: enter the convent. Thirty-four: leave the convent. Thirty-eight: marry Jacques-Louis. Forty-nine: leave Jacques-Louis. Sixty-two: Hungary. Seventy-two: Burkina Faso. Her major life moments, the ones she chose to highlight in her unpublished autobiography, look quite different from those of a life dominated by child-rearing. The milestones that come with parenthood—birth, first steps, first day of school, leaving the house, and all of the joys and obligations that come with these transitions—simply don't apply.

When we consider the characteristics of a good life, we might be tempted to assign it strict stages, as in Erik Erikson's theory of psychosocial needs or, more quaintly, like the "ages of woman" evoked in Figure 5.1. From cradle to grave, according to this mid-nineteenth-century American print, woman follows prescribed stages, including marriage and child-rearing.

Of course, we must acknowledge that human needs change over the course of the lifetime and that these are partly shaped by biology. Flourishing means one thing at age eighteen, something quite different at thirty-five, and different again at sixty-five and ninety-five. Yet the biological facts of typical human development—a time to be born, a time to walk, a time to mature—become so easily encased in a set of cultural expectations

Figure 5.1 *The life and age of woman, stages of woman's life from the cradle to the grave*, circa 1848. New York: James Baillie. Photograph. https://www.loc. gov/item/2006686266/. Library of Congress, Prints & Photographs Division, LC-DIG-ppmsca-12817.

regarding child-rearing that it may be difficult to envision a life history apart from the arc of parenting.

Farge helps us to see alternatives. Her life suggests that we should not overly rely on such a developmental, age-related structure. The movement away from culturally and biologically imposed life stage is important because it adds flexibility to the timing of when certain developments "ought" to happen. Specifically in this context, it means that "generativity"—which for Erikson is supposed to occur in middle age—could happen at other times.

Farge's life also highlights the idiosyncratic quality of the childless life history. Of course, parents could certainly also mark their lives in terms of divorce, retirement, volunteering abroad, or any number of other milestones, but a childless life brings these moments into sharper relief.

The loosening of the screws on the iron arc of life is also conducive to a certain level of *autonomy*. Farge embodied a certain post-1960s style of liberty. She chose her path from country to country; she reinvented herself professionally, physically, and sexually; and she took on whole new identities as part of the quest for *authenticity*. Farge pushed ostensible limitations to quit a job, a town, or a way of life that was no longer working.[5] The order in which these identities unfolded was not preset; indeed, it would have been impossible to predict. We aren't like honeybees, whose path as queen or worker is set for life. We humans enjoy flexibility. We take on different roles as opportunities arise, from supportive auntie, to mother, to stepmother, to friend, within our very same phenotype, our very same body.[6] They do not exist in a hierarchy, with each identity neatly building off the previous one. And at no point does Farge attempt or claim to "have it all," the fraught adage that is more a threat than a promise.

Furthermore, Farge's story underscores a key difference between mothers and the childless in terms of how and when identities are formed. In her autobiography, Farge expressed many identities—nun, teacher, wife, stepmother—but did not particularly discuss the fact of her childlessness. Perhaps this is because of the difference in process between becoming a mother and remaining childless. Everyone starts off childless by default, but most people lose that quality. Becoming "someone's mom," the startling and unsettling realization that one's self is bound to this other person of one's own creation, unfolds in a relatively compressed span of time. Embodiment of the identity of motherhood comes early and fierce: pregnancy, childbirth, nursing, holding; the deft skills of rolling up a full diaper with one hand

and securely braiding baby hair with the other. Taking on the identity of a childless person is usually uncertain, unacknowledged, and perhaps even inappropriate, for years or even decades. For those without children, the conversation about bodies comes much later in life: Who's going to take care of you when you are old and weak? Even once it is settled, a childless identity is far from the dominant identity most of the time; it resides in the background except at salient moments, such as when conversation drifts into talk of children or at significant moments within the life of a couple.

That said, for some, the childless identity bursts forth bold and exposed. A public art installation I once spotted in Louisville's NuLu district invited passersby to respond to the prompt "Before I Die, I Want To _____." Louisville's denizens had responded in chalk with predictable statements of desire ("travel around the world," "be happy again"). No surprise that one person wrote, "be a mother." Then, at the bottom, I spotted something I'd never quite seen before: "Before I Die, I Want To Never Have Children." Childlessness here was a goal, not a lack. This anonymous contributor conceived remaining childless as a destination, a challenge, an identity to savor, and even a source of pride.[7]

Worthy Work

Quimper, 1734. For the first time, Louise Le Mace appeared in the tax rolls of her town, a community in Brittany on the furthest outstretched arm of northwestern France. Le Mace worked as a "mistress tailor," a member of the guild in her own right, with the training and accomplishments that earned her the title. She could have settled for the less-skilled "seamstress," or she could have worked for someone else. Instead, Le Mace completed a formal apprenticeship and fulfilled the requirements of her trade. In later years, she took on apprentices of her own. For decades, through at least 1763, Le Mace was always listed on the tax rolls as a mistress tailor. And she was never listed with a husband or a child.

In other words, Le Mace earned her place in the guild not because of a husband or father but because of her own skills, training, and professional success. She could pay her guild dues and was entrusted by others with training their children. She developed an identity distinct from her parents, even though she lived in their household. Her father, a shoemaker, kept a different trade. Le Mace paid heftier taxes as a mistress tailor than she would have if she had accepted a tax declaration as a daughter with no declared occupation. While we don't have access to her own words or ideas about her life—she left none—we can glean a strong sense of a professional, productive identity honored by her town and guild.

Louise Le Mace was not alone. Many early modern women worked independently of their husbands in a wide variety of professions. They collected taxes, managed shops, sold food, ran inns, taught dancing, designed interiors, translated books, and owned billiard halls.[8] These women defy the notion of women's work as piecemeal, impermanent, ancillary, and dependent.[9] In their economic capacities, they experienced some degree of *security* and *autonomy*.

But more is at stake here. As we imagine Le Mace laying out her fabric, marking the pattern and cutting out those unnatural shapes that under her careful eye became sleeves and vests and bodices, we might reflect upon the purpose and nature of work. Productive capacity is not the same as fostering a career of just any kind. It is not simply about earning a salary or paying off debt or securing money for leisure, but rather about developing our capacity to make something, a mastery that cannot be learned in a short period of time. It does not take the market as the ultimate arbiter of our worth. Women like Le Mace remind us to strive for a certain kind of work: a craft in which skills, materials, and artistry combine into the production of beautiful and useful things. Creative work like this requires a process of gestation and nurturing, followed by an uncertain launch into the world. Poet Anna Seward, a British contemporary of Le Mace, expressed just such an investment in her work. In a letter to her patron, William Hayley, she thanked him for his praise of her work: "And now, my dear bard. . . . Suffer me, then, to express my gratitude for the kind attention and ardent welcome with which my poetical offspring has been received in its lovely precincts . . . and for the generous, the discriminating approbation which has so highly gratified their parent."[10]

Le Mace and Seward, each in her own way, offer insights about the trade-offs between work and family and, therefore, about the ways that we might flourish. We will never know the true opportunity cost of our life paths, whether or not we would have launched that business or written that book or gotten that degree if we'd had the additional responsibility of parenting. Without accepting that children and work are necessarily at odds with each other, though, it's plausible to believe that childless people have a different set of energies to give to their productive lives than they would if they had

had children. This kind of work can prove a comfort during the inevitable moments of doubt about one's life and choices. The challenge remains, however, to channel it into work worth doing.

Virtuous Lives

London, 1694. At age twenty-eight, Mary Astell held a distinct vision for the life well lived. In her *Serious Proposal to the Ladies*, Astell proposed that unmarried women seek their spiritual and intellectual improvement in dedicated institutions.[11] Astell, a transplant to London from Newcastle-upon-Tyne, hoped to persuade women to stop focusing on their physical beauty and turn inward, to transfer comeliness "from a corruptible Body to an immortal Mind."[12]

Astell focused on the perils of defining oneself through the quest for a man. Sin was on her mind. "Your *Glass* will not do you half so much service as a serious reflection with your own Minds," she wrote.[13] Astell urged women to develop capacities other than those that are attractive to men. "We value *them* too much, and our *selves* to little, if we place any part of our worth in their Opinion; and do not think our selves capable of Nobler Things than the pitiful Conquest of some worthless heart."[14] Astell claimed for herself and her sex a higher standard of *dignity*.

Astell's proposal offers a firm and ringing rebuttal to the notion that child-rearing is somehow necessary to virtue. For Astell, the ultimate aim is moral development to secure "the love and admiration of GOD and Angels" not "vain insignificant men."[15] Piety could not take root without intellectual consideration of the theology undergirding belief.[16] Astell envisioned learning for the improvement of both the individual and the betterment of society: "Learning is therefore necessary to render [women] more agreeable and useful in company, and to furnish them with becoming entertainments when alone."[17] The ladies of the place would serve as an example for the rest of womankind, "that Women may no longer pass for those useless and impertinent Animals, which the ill conduct of too many has caused them to be mistaken for."[18]

Mary Astell understood that women needed alternatives that would support them not just prior to marriage, but for the indefinite future.[19] Astell hoped to build these places for "religious retirement" where women could either stay at the house until they chose to marry or remain for their entire lives. In this way, women could avoid a hasty marriage simply to avoid the moniker "old maid."[20]

In Protestant England, however, Astell's proposal smacked too much of a Catholic convent. Despite her protests that no vows would bind women to their retreats nor would they remain cut off from the world, no patron could be persuaded to support her work.[21] One interested donor of ten thousand pounds was convinced to retract the offer to avoid the stain of "popery."[22] Astell herself lived to the age of sixty-five and never married.

Bordeaux, 1761. Marie and Marianne de Lamothe were busy cultivating their own life stories. Coming of age in pre-Revolutionary France, the sisters were not given the same educational opportunities as their five brothers, who became lawyers, a doctor, and a priest.[23] Unlike Louise Le Mace, they did not become independent craftspeople supporting themselves with their own labor.

Yet they were able to shape their own lives in other ways. Most notably, the Lamothes were selective in their choice of companions. They frequently visited with friends, cousins, and neighbors but explicitly eschewed frivolous entertainment. In their rejection of an invitation to a ball in 1761, the sisters explained that "to spend maybe a night, dine, go to the ball of a stranger . . . that would hardly be according to our way of thinking." And in a later letter, they reported, "Thanks be to God, for five or six years, we have not gone to balls . . . nor have we curled our hair, nor have we been to the fair except when forced." These were not women to be easily led.[24]

For the Lamothe sisters, religious engagement provided a pathway toward *practical wisdom*, the ability to deal with life's challenges, limitations, and losses and toward *transcendence*, the experience of awe in the contemplation of life's mysteries. To that end, they spent their time in the companionship of clergy and female religious, notably the Sisters of Saint-Michel. They made their home a place for quiet prayer and meditation, while also participating in communal forms of worship at Mass, vespers, and religious retreats.[25]

Astell and the Lamothe sisters remind us that we should not simply pit career women against mothers. Of course, women have not and do not always have the opportunity to pursue fulfilling work or economic latitude, and that is an injustice. The point here is that a good life does not require certain specific actions or identities. There are many kinds of identities we can take on—religious contemplative, teacher, stepmother, wife, volunteer, craftsperson, poet—to break us out of the binary of "parent" versus "employee."

These life stories encourage us to see the variety of ways that women can find *personal fulfillment*, both inside and outside of societal norms.

Moreover, they suggest that there are many different approaches to living a good life. We can seek a life of liberty, as Violette Farge does when she trades her habit for a miniskirt. We can focus on securing our welfare through the careful application of work, as Louise Le Mace does when she becomes a mistress tailor. We can cultivate a life of virtue, as Marie and Marianne Lamothe do when they intentionally select their acquaintances. These three choices map (imperfectly) onto three avenues that philosophers have proposed over the centuries for how to live well: safeguarding freedom, maximizing welfare, and cultivating virtue.

Instead of requiring ourselves to pick from among these three traditions, however, we might consider an approach that allows us to acknowledge the complexities of how we actually move through the world. After all, Farge sought more than just liberty; she thought carefully about the efficacy of her actions, and she put years into the service of others. Astell wanted women to live both virtuously and independently.

Things get even more complicated when we think seriously about how tightly interconnected we are with the people and institutions that surround us.

Ourselves and Others

London, 1894. In the years after her marriage, Beatrice Webb toyed with regret over her choices. As early as age thirty-six, motherhood seemed closed to her, even though four of her sisters had, by this point, given birth after that age. Sidney simply remained unthinkable as the father of her children. Instead, she vowed to maintain her focus on writing and researching for the commonweal. But in moments of reflection, doubt crept in. On holiday at the sea, nestled among rocks near the pink and white chalk cliffs, the juxtaposition of "heat and coolness, motion and rest, sun and water, tide and rock" brought to mind another contrast: "Are the books we have written together worth (to the community) the babies we might have had? Then again, I dream over the problem of whether one would marry the same man, in order to have his babies, that one would select as joint author?"[26]

In the end, however, Beatrice Webb did not regret her childless marriage. It allowed her to continue spending her days "in unraveling ideas and attempting to clear issues" while sustaining her "in a frame of loving companionship and constant sympathy."[27] For Webb, a good life included *civic engagement*, a contribution to the wider world beyond her own social circles. In particular, Webb sought to promote *fairness* through the study of social and economic conditions and through the promotion of good government policy.

And she grew to love Sidney. "I see my boy's blue eyes resting on me with love as he grasps my bicycle to push it up a hard bit of hill, I hear his voice praising me for some rearrangement of our chapter, I see him writing page after page, hour after hour. . . . I decide that the answer is: one lover, not only in the letter but in the spirit."[28] And "On the whole, then, I would advise the brainworking woman to marry—if only she can find her Sidney!"[29] Webb valued and required deep *interpersonal connectedness* with someone else and felt *positive emotion* from the relationship.

For Suzanne Voilquin, these connections ran more broadly. Voilquin, born in Paris in 1801, discovered her vocation as a midwife in her mid-thirties, during her travels to Egypt. She earned a diploma in midwifery in Paris and practiced her profession in France, Russia, and the United States. She wrote, "I strongly feel that God did not take away from me my dear little angel"—her daughter who had died just two weeks after birth—"and save me from the plague so that I could spend the years he still gave me doing nothing."[30] Family duties would not suffice. "My old father and my sister can count on me, but this narrow life alone is not enough for me; it would soon smother me."[31] Compelled to serve something bigger than herself, she created the Maternal Society Founded in Favor of Unwed Mothers, which provided free childbirth services, and spent decades tirelessly crusading for the support of women during and after childbirth.

Webb and Voilquin invite us to consider the connection between an individual's personal thriving and a wider set of social relationships. Individual, free self-actualization, to use the language of Maslow and the Second Demographic Transition, is a limited concept. It may allow us to separate ourselves form the roles tradition has predetermined for us, including the role of parent, but it's not the only motivation in our lives. We thrive not only in our relations to others, but also through fulfilling our obligations to others. We don't live in an individually encased mold in which our choices reflect only our own desires and wants and freedom.

Philosopher Michael Sandel claims that we have three areas of obligation: natural duties, voluntary obligations, and obligations of solidarity.[32]

Natural duties include honoring the life and dignity of every human person. They are universal duties that do not require us to give our consent. Morally speaking, I am not permitted to kill another person, even though I never agreed that I would not kill anyone. Voluntary obligations include particular contracts and promises that we have freely taken on. If I agree to mow your lawn, I am morally obliged to complete the task. Obligations of solidarity, argues Sandel, are obligations due to our shared history or membership in a group. These include family, nation, religious tradition, city, and perhaps even profession. Like voluntary obligations, they are particular to a person or group; they are not universal. But unlike voluntary obligations, they do not require us to give our consent. I feel special obligations toward certain people, such as my parents or fellow citizens, even though I didn't choose them.

And so our understanding of flourishing can't be limited to individual dimensions. We've got to consider how the individual and the social are intertwined.

A Proposal

Childless women of the past remind us that a good life encompasses a range of experiences. Before we dig into specific issues related to childlessness—such as, Will I die alone?—let's pause to consider the elements of human flourishing discussed so far. Here I'm borrowing from a framework developed by Michael Bess in his fascinating book *Our Grandchildren Redesigned*. Bess proposes ten elements of human flourishing.[33] Here's how I understand them:

- *Security* refers to food, shelter, and a basic level of safety, all of which are of crucial importance to our individual selves and also signal our interdependence.
- *Dignity* includes respect for one's person and life and to make possible for others lives that are consistent with a human being's inalienable human dignity. It also requires that we make an effort to see the world from the perspective of others and to respect that they have the capacity to reflect about their positions and therefore may come to different conclusions about the world than we do.
- *Autonomy* refers to the ability to exercise separate control over one's thoughts and action, to navigate the world effectively and exert some

measure of control over one's life circumstances, even as we are shaped by the society around us.[34]

- *Personal fulfillment* comes from Aristotle's notion that we should be able to freely develop and use our talents, our curiosity, our imagination, our virtue, our appreciation of beauty. Nobody can tell us what this personal fulfillment must be; it is something we cultivate for ourselves.

- *Authenticity* is the characteristic of being true to oneself. We thrive when we know ourselves, own who we are, and more perfectly become the person we are for ourselves, even as we recognize that we are shaped by others. "Authenticity requires that we be critically aware of this slippery, dual nature of our personhood," Bess writes, "and that we aspire to be more than just a chameleon-like creature, constantly adapting our identity to conform to external norms or models."[35] Cultivating the true self, the real me, is a challenge for all humans.

- *The pursuit of practical wisdom* entails learning from one's experiences, growing from adversity, and coping with change and loss. Perhaps the most important piece of practical wisdom a person can acquire is the acceptance of limits and mortality.

- *Fairness* demands equity and reciprocity in human affairs.

- *Interpersonal connectedness* is the requirement that we have social standing and meaningful close relationships.

- *Civic engagement* encompasses the ways in which we contribute to and interact with those outside our immediate circles. At both the personal and civic levels, we are shaped by the people we know and the histories we find ourselves in.

- *Transcendence* is a connection to something greater than ourselves that may take the form of a spiritual orientation, a religious or faith tradition, or an experience of wonder and awe in the face the universe around us.

- To this list, I'd like to add an explicit mention of *positive emotion*, our ability to experience happiness and joy, pride and serenity, peace and love.

In developing this list, Bess draws on a variety of contemporary intellectual currents regarding human well-being, including the capabilities approach developed by economist Amartya Sen and philosopher Martha C. Nussbaum and the work in positive psychology of Martin E. P. Seligman,

Christopher Peterson, and Jonathan Haidt, among others.[36] Like many of these authors, Bess offers this framework as a work in progress that should be debated and discussed, and so I am adopting it here in the spirit of experimentation rather than commandment.[37]

One attraction of this framework is that it acknowledges that our sense of flourishing exists not only in a disembodied mind capable of reflecting on, say, *autonomy* and *personal fulfillment*, but also in our bodies themselves; it's obvious that *security* entails our embodied well-being, but so does *civic engagement* as we work together with others, as well as *practical wisdom*, which asks us to accept the physical cycles of our lives. We don't leave our bodies aside when we consider whether we are treating someone with *fairness* or are developing our own *authenticity*. Our embodied selves matter, whether we are parents or childless.

This framework insists that the states, institutions, and culture in which we live matters, too. To live a life that is *worthy of human dignity*, Nussbaum emphasizes, requires structural and political intervention to ensure that all members of a country or society can get above a certain threshold level (her list of capabilities include life, bodily health, and control over one's political and material environment).[38] The ultimate political goal, she writes, ought to be that "all should get above a certain threshold level of combined capability, in the sense of not coerced functioning but of substantial freedom to choose and act."[39]

At the same time, this framework borrows from ancient and contemporary claims—from Aristotle to Peterson and Seligman—that human flourishing entails the cultivation and expression of virtue. Good policies and just institutions are not enough. Using empirical research and documenting the virtues listed in the world's wisdom traditions, Peterson and Seligman have identified six virtues: wisdom and knowledge, courage, humanity, justice, temperance, and transcendence. They have also identified twenty-four character traits that are pathways toward expressing or cultivating those virtues; for instance, the virtue of humanity might be practiced through love, kindness, or social intelligence. While certain character traits may be more prized in some cultures than in others, the overarching virtue is present in all or most traditions.

Yet this framework doesn't lay down laws from on high about what ought to be done. It honors the fact that human beings must cultivate flourishing for themselves, alongside and with others, anew in every life. Rather than seek rational abstract rules for how to live, we should foster a "virtuous garden of excellences" that helps us to thrive in the rich and messy particularity of our situation.[40] The framework doesn't put the elements in a hierarchy. In this way, it is distinct from Abraham Maslow's hierarchy of needs, in which basic safety needs must be fulfilled for individuals to have access to higher-order needs such as love.[41] Getting away from the hierarchy of needs doesn't absolve us of responsibility for the security and dignity of others, but it relieves us of the temptation to equate individuals' human flourishing with their country's economic development or political stability, or even worse, with some level of civilizational achievement. Unlike schemas that rely on a single number—such as gross domestic product—this framework refuses to average out the experiences of millions into a few data points.[42] Instead, it recognizes the vast range of possibilities for human experience. It attempts to provide both a threshold of requirements to live a life worthy of human dignity as well as guidance for our aspirations to flourish by developing our strengths.

In the context of childlessness, this framework suggests that we ought not to assume that having children, or not having children, is a requirement of human flourishing. To be in possession of a capability includes the freedom to choose whether and how to exercise that capability—not a requirement that one exercise that capability. While Nussbaum includes bodily health on her list of ten central capabilities—"including reproductive health"—she does not require us to exercise that capability.[43]

One risk of using this framework is that I will impose our twenty-first-century understanding of human flourishing on the women of the past. But the rewards outweigh this risk. Rather than judge the lives of women in the past with a stamp of "flourishing" or "not," I will present their lives as examples to help us all think through complex issues. This framework will allow us to examine five questions that are of particular interest to childless women in the twenty-first century:

> Will I regret not having children?
> What makes for a meaningful household?
> How can I contribute to a better world?
> What will my life be like in old age?
> What is my connection to future generations?

I have chosen issues that, on the face of it, seem to affect parents and childless individuals quite differently. But often, issues that start off pitting the childless against parents turn out to be issues of importance to both. Childless lives often reveal issues that we might otherwise paper over.

Together, these elements provide us with a flexible framework for exploring the lives of childless individuals: how they might thrive, the lacunas that they might need to fill, and how their experiences can help all of us—parents and childless alike—to expand our range of possibilities for the good life.

6

Regret

A few days after my thirty-eighth birthday, I attended a college reunion. Toward the end of the evening, I chatted with a classmate I hadn't seen in sixteen years. Jane had just taken a job in a new city. After over a decade of marriage, she and her husband were professionally comfortable and personally satisfied. Now they debated whether or not to bear a child. "I would be a better mother now than I would have been at age twenty-four," Jane confided, "but I am struggling with the decision." She looked at me intensely and asked the question we've all wondered about: "Do you ever find that childless people feel regret?"

Many women like Jane—financially secure, healthy, empowered to make decisions, and close to age forty—can't help but view childlessness, with some urgency, as a choice. Whatever pathway they may have taken to this point, whatever philosophy of flourishing they might embrace, whatever faith they might have in fertility technology, the fact remains that "someday, maybe" has turned into "now or never." While there are many women who never doubt their decision to remain childless, there are many others for whom serious questions begin to arise. And so, after decades of postponement, a woman in Jane's position might ponder what it would be like for her to have a child: whether she would like to care for a child, whether she is ready to make sacrifices for the child, whether she thinks the child will make her feel more complete. And she asks herself whether she would regret not having children.

It is only natural, of course, that we should feel regret about any number of decisions. If we define regret as disappointment over an unattained goal, an unfulfilled intention, or an infelicitous action, then we can't help but accumulate regrets as life spins by.[1] Only those with the very lowest ambitions or the keenest ability to live in the present can avoid it. In fact, in the context of decision-making, regret is the second most frequently reported emotion, after anxiety.[2] The benefit of regret is that it can help us to proactively shape our decisions. We can resolve to do something to avoid the unpleasantness of regret later.[3] Indeed, much of the process of decision-making is in the service of avoiding regret.

It's a steep challenge. Regrets arise not only about the decision itself—in this case, whether to have children—but also about the process one takes to come to that decision. If we feel rushed, pressured, or uninformed, we might regret our lack of due diligence, even if we would have come to that same decision in the end. Yet we can also feel regret about something over which we really had little or no control. In addition, we might regret or feel bad about the secondary outcomes of the decision, such as growing old without children to care for us. We can regret both action and inaction. We can anticipate the future or gaze bitterly at the past. Regret, in other words, is related to both *positive emotion* and *practical wisdom*. Human flourishing entails feeling joy, happiness, and satisfaction, and it includes the ability to manage life's disappointments and changes with grace and acceptance.

Furthermore, regret is both cognitive and emotional. It involves memory, analysis, imagination, and judgment, as well as feelings of sadness or pain. Because regret involves cognitive judgments and analyses, it is shaped not just by our personal emotional experiences, but also by the social context in which we live. Regret is not framed by an individual alone, but by a culture.[4] It is a profoundly social phenomenon, shaped by the goals and desires of those around us. And so regret is governed by culturally constructed "feeling rules" that tell us when certain emotions are allowed and when they are not acceptable.[5] And yet, the focus on regret may lead us to focus on childlessness as an individual phenomenon rather than as something that is embedded in a community.

Regret is often taken to be a sign of personal dysfunction, as something to be overcome (unless it is accompanied by contrition as part of a repairing of past wrongs, as in legal contexts).[6] Yet in the case of childlessness, particularly for women, regret is couched as an inevitable stage that one must anticipate and grapple with.[7] The childless woman presents a rare case in which wallowing in regret is seen as natural, expected, and indeed normal. This holds true whether the woman is childless by choice or due to circumstances or infertility.

Here, I'm particularly interested in addressing the concern that by not having children, women will miss out on one of life's fundamental joys, and they will struggle to cope with this disappointment. Holding your own child, feeling her move in your arms, feeding her of your own body— these experiences, many believe, are blissful and irreplaceable. Women like

Jane fear that Bulgarian poet Blaga Dimitrova is right: "It is painful to be a woman. When you become a woman, it hurts. When you become beloved, it hurts. When you become a mother, it hurts. But the most intolerable pain in the world is that of the woman who has not experienced all these pains, down to the very last."[8] The anticipation of regret is the fear that in the end there is some kind of essential quality that impels a woman to become a mother, that there is no compensation for the lack of a child of one's own.

Worst of all is the thought that we, through our own choices, might bring this suffering upon ourselves. The anticipation of regret becomes particularly salient when our subjective preferences play into the decision, such as when we believe that we are independent arbiters over the creation (or not) of a new human being. For Jane, the "choiciness" of childlessness had become more immediate as she reached her late thirties—and so too did the possibility that she might make the wrong choice.

When we fear future regret, we mistrust ourselves; we believe that we cannot make rational choices that will help us to fully realize our best selves. According to philosopher L. A. Paul, the phenomenon of having a child of one's very own is so different from any other experience that we cannot rationally assign value to it. We can't anticipate the feelings, desires, beliefs or actions that would result from having a child, and therefore we have no rational grounds for making the decision. The experience is *epistemically transformative*: no matter what our previous experiences around children have been, we cannot know what it is like to have a child of our own without having actually experienced it. For Paul, having a child leads to a personal transformation that changes our core values and what it is like to be ourselves, what makes us happy and fulfilled.[9] The experiences of bearing and raising a child may be intensely positive or intensely negative, and we may assign positive or negative values to these experiences, but we cannot know ahead of time what they will be.

I suspect that a version of Paul's argument lurks behind many women's fears of future regret: the notion that they do not know themselves, that their current lives and preferences do not provide grounds for knowing what they will want in the future. Perhaps we simply can't know what it would be like for us to have a child. Perhaps we would be lucky parents and find child-rearing to be an intensely positive experience that outweighs any trade-off. Perhaps the scenario that scholar Tamar Hager recounts would actually come to pass: "If you don't feel it now, they said, it will come with pregnancy and birth and along with it, the feeling of responsibility which is natural, and the love, and then, your priorities will suddenly change. Although your life will be completely different, it won't matter to you."[10] Perhaps by choosing childlessness, we are cutting ourselves off from this blissful future and instead choosing a life of loneliness, solitude, and crippling regret.

Happiness

We could try to address Jane's question by asking who's happier: parents or childless individuals? Gertrude Savile (1697–1758), a British lifelong childless single woman, had no doubt of her own unpleasant situation. "I must thank my mother that I am grown so much into the love of cards, having nothing to please me or amuse me. I fear I shall grow more into it, and that it will become my whole pleasure. 'Tis the only one for a friendless, forsaken old maid."[11] Savile sunk into depression over her lonely existence. But should Savile's experience suggest that the same is in store for childless people in the twenty-first century? Do childless people experience fewer positive emotions and more negative emotions than parents?

Some research suggests that childless people feel fewer positive emotions than parents do. In a recent study, researchers asked participants to respond five times a day to a questionnaire on how much they were feeling each of nineteen emotions (eight positive emotions, such as joy and pride, and eleven negative ones, such as disgust and anxiety). As it turned out, from moment to moment, mothers felt fewer negative feelings and "marginally more daily positive emotion" than did childless women.[12] The same held true for men; fathers in particular reported better well-being than childless men. Another study, a meta-analysis of 152 published studies, found that new parents experienced an overall increase of positive feelings in the months following the specific event of childbirth.[13]

The picture looks different, however, if we expand our understanding of personal well-being to include more than just emotional state. Over the past several decades, psychologists have developed a variety of measures of well-being. They study not only the presence of positive emotions and the absence of negatives emotions, but also quality of life, autonomy, and the ability to shape the world around them.

These various measures may sound similar, but "happiness," "life satisfaction," and "quality of life" are in fact distinct and measurably different. They are quantifiable using various reliable surveys, and they are not perfectly related. For instance, "happiness" and "life satisfaction" have only a 25 percent common variance.[14] That is, if you know someone's happiness (their emotional state, their positive feelings, and the absence of negative feelings), you have only 25 percent of the information you need to precisely determine the person's life satisfaction (how they feel about their lives in general).

And so, in the same meta-analysis of 152 studies, those who became parents experienced a decrease in life satisfaction at the very same time that they reported an increase in positive feelings. The analysis suggests that couples who become parents suffer from a decline in their relationship, and this diminishes their overall life satisfaction.[15]

Another meta-analysis took a different approach. Rather than examine the specific event of childbirth, it combined studies around the globe that asked parents and nonparents to report on their life satisfaction in general. This analysis looked at both cross-sectional studies (parents vs. nonparents at one moment in time) and longitudinal studies (the same individuals over time). It also had the benefit of generating a cross-cultural analysis. Like the other meta-analysis, this study found that, globally speaking, parents have lower life satisfaction than childless individuals, especially in the first four or five years after the birth of a child.

Let's look at some more specific findings. One longitudinal study found that parents feel more socially integrated with relatives, friends, and neighbors than do the childless, but their sense of being able to achieve their own goals—their self-efficacy—decreases.[16] New mothers report more hours of housework and more marital strain, though they are less vulnerable to depression than new fathers (especially unmarried men).[17] And then there is the cost to couples' ability to talk and maintain intimacy. Childless couples spend more time alone together than those with children. In 2003, childless couples spent twenty-six hours per week together, compared with only nine hours for those with children. In both cases, time together had declined by 25 to 30 percent since 1975, but for different reasons: the childless were working more, whereas the parents were spending more time on their children.[18] Another study found that those with children in the house report more negative feelings—sadness, loneliness, restlessness, and fear—than nonparents.[19] Those whose children do not live with them fare even worse. Indeed, unlike just about any other change in adult status, parenthood in the United States is not associated with enhanced emotional well-being.[20]

Researchers tend to agree that many factors shape the experience of both parenting and being childless. The negative effects of parenting are more evident among women, those with lower socio-economic status, and those who are single parents.[21] And the negative effects of childlessness are more evident among individuals who identify themselves as involuntarily childless. In a large, representative study, American women who self-identified as voluntarily childless rated themselves about the same as mothers did in terms of happiness, satisfaction with life, and depression; in all of these measures, voluntarily childless women and mothers had more positive experiences compared with those who identified as involuntarily childless.[22] Another cross-sectional study found that women who were voluntarily childless rated themselves more highly than women who were involuntarily childless in terms of their autonomy and ability to navigate the complexities of the world around them. They felt close to their ideal of autonomy.[23]

Furthermore, the culture and policies of the country in which people live matters. One meta-analysis found that parents in the United States and Australia were far less satisfied than parents in Nordic countries.[24] In Nordic countries, single parents are no unhappier than married parents.[25] Perhaps, the author argues, parents find their situation more challenging—and their lives less satisfying—in countries that are less supportive of childcare.

Contrary to Gertrude Savile's experience, then, childless people have some grounds for reasoning that they are not, in fact, missing out on life's joys. The received wisdom about childlessness as an unhappy and lonely state does not map onto empirical evidence. Overall, there is no consistent finding that parenting in and of itself provides an emotional boost. But neither does childlessness necessarily lead to heightened well-being. While for many parenting is, indeed, a path to a happy and meaningful life, childless individuals, too, find meaning and satisfaction in their lives.[26] Often, any relationship between childlessness and psychological well-being is shaped by context, especially whether or not they have the social and cultural support for raising children. Childlessness in and of itself is not the key factor.[27]

Happiness as Older Adults

Are the childless more content at an older age? Or are parents happier and more satisfied once their children have grown and might offer support?

Perhaps parents reap the emotional rewards of parenting once their children have left the house. As it turns out, there is no strong reason to believe that parents of grown children enjoy an emotional boost compared with childless individuals of the same age.[28] In study after study, parents and childless older adults fare about the same, with a few nuances. Most of these studies do not distinguish between voluntary and involuntary childlessness, which only highlights the fact that older childless women were no different from older mothers in terms of depression, loneliness, happiness, and family and life satisfaction.

One study found that American parents aged sixty-three and over fared about the same as nonparents (whereas parents aged seventeen to twenty-five were less satisfied with their lives than their childless counterparts, and parents aged twenty-six to sixty-two were more satisfied than the childless of that age).[29] A different study based on two large, representative surveys of American women in their fifties found that there was no psychological disadvantage to childlessness, not even among women who had come of age during the baby boom (cohorts born 1928 to 1941), who might be expected to have been particularly susceptible to negative interpretations of their childless state.[30] Another study argues that, overall, parental status is not nearly as important to psychological well-being among older adults as physical health and marital status (including divorced, never-married, widowed, etc.), though both of these are complex factors.[31]

Let's turn now to Europe. A study of adults aged fifty-five to seventy-five in thirteen European countries found that childlessness significantly and independently predicts lower depressive mood. Only those who were separated or divorced as well as childless had higher scores for depressive mood.[32] However, childlessness did not significantly predict quality of life for older people—either for better or for worse. A study of Dutch and German older adults found little difference in life satisfaction between mothers and women who never had children.[33] A study in Norway of adults aged forty to eighty found no differences in affective well-being—that is, positive and negative affect, depression, and loneliness—between those with children and those without, for both women and men, and regardless of marital status, but it did find that women without children had a lower life satisfaction and self-esteem than those with children, whether those children still lived at home or not; however, this study could not differentiate between voluntary and involuntary childlessness.[34] Another study, drawing on fifteen countries across Europe, found that childlessness did not predict lower well-being for adults over aged sixty-five—whether social, affective, or economic.[35]

All together, these studies suggest that childlessness in and of itself does not matter as much to quality of life as an older adult as other factors; better economic variables, more education, and more social engagement all predicted a higher quality of life.[36] As older adults, the childless seem to do all right in terms of psychological well-being, especially if they remain socially engaged.

Again, the context is key. In a different study, when researchers broke down the results of twenty-four countries, they found that the association between psychological well-being (depression, loneliness, sleeplessness, happiness) and childlessness depended on the country, especially among women. In countries that tolerated childlessness, as well as countries with high levels of social contacts, childlessness did not weigh as heavily on women aged forty and over.[37]

So much for the general story. But what about me, myself? I know myself, don't I? Can't I predict how I would feel? Psychological research provides a surprising answer. We humans are good at worrying about how we might feel the future. But we are bad at predicting our feelings with any accuracy. When we anticipate how possible future events will make us feel, we overestimate the happiness we'll feel from the good ones and the sadness and regret from the bad.[38] We forget that if that future imagined event were to happen, we would have many other things on our minds. We even discount our own personality traits—our inclinations toward optimism, happiness, neuroticism—when we make predictions about our future feelings.[39] Happy people tend to be happy in the long run, and unhappy people tend to be unhappy.

These findings suggest that if we would only pay attention, we might realize that we *can* know, perhaps all too well, what it would be like to never have a child: our emotional experience would be about the same as it is now.

However, other psychological research suggests that we might be able to shift the baseline of our expectations and therefore experience greater happiness.[40] According to Sonja Lyubomirsky, we can purposely undertake interventions to help us appreciate good events longer and boost our happiness. Interventions include generating surprising and variable events (e.g., by doing acts of kindness that are not the same from day to day), increasing positive emotions (e.g., through exercises in gratitude and by *not* making logical sense out of a good event), and keeping our aspirations in check for what the next good event should be like.[41]

These interventions are available to many of us, whether we are trying to keep the positive feelings after good events or recover from the bad ones—and they are not dependent on parenting or childless status. In this perspective, to ask whether one is happier as a parent or as a childless person is the wrong question. The right question is, How might one develop the capacity to cope with events (both positive and negative) and how supportive is one's culture and lived context?

All together, these studies should reassure Jane: they suggest that having children—or not—is not necessarily a source of greater happiness and life satisfaction. To better anticipate whether she will feel regret, she might reflect on her experiences of looking back on past choices, uncertainties, and disappointments to see how she has reacted to such moments, and she should develop cognitive tools that might boost her happiness. The examples of older women looking back on their lives may also provide some insight.

Looking Back

London, 1857. Pauline Craven lay in illness and solitude. Such a state called forth reflection on her life, on "every impression, real and imaginary, which could most disturb me and throw me into a state of depression as humiliating as it was miserable."[42] Her husband was away on business and she, at age forty-nine, felt herself pass from youth to old age in a few short weeks. She crossed the threshold from anticipating regret to feeling regret retrospectively.

Although Craven did not explain the nature of her illness, her age, her sense of passage, and her relief at "the end of many vexations" suggest that it may have involved her reproductive organs. A lifelong ardent Catholic, the daughter of a French royalist family who lived much of her life in England and Italy, Pauline had married Augustus Craven at age twenty-six. She desperately wanted children; the explanation for their childlessness is unclear, but it's likely that either she or her husband were infertile. Yet she framed her childlessness as "regret," as though her actions had in some way been to blame. She now entered into a period of reflection. In her illness, she could not draw on consoling thoughts and wallowed instead in the "desires and the miscalculations of my life. Above all, I felt in all its old keenness the poignant regret of being childless, a regret proportionate to the love I bear children. It is the strongest of which my heart is capable, and it is spent, whether I will it or not, on every child who nestles in my arms. I love children, and I weep for those whose place has remained empty. May God's will be obeyed and loved! It is easy to say so to-day, but in my hours of storm that voice of the past has not been mute."[43]

Craven focused on her lack of children during this dark time of illness and loneliness. Other moments, too, might elicit regret. When a parent falls ill or passes away, when we no longer have the ceiling of the older generation above us, we might re-evaluate our place in the family and experience regret.[44]

But it's important to place regrets over childlessness within the context of all the regrets one might feel later in life. Studies that pick at the scab of childlessness, unsurprisingly, find more regret over that condition. But when women are asked more generally about their regrets, without specific mention of children, there are no differences in the total number of regrets between mothers, voluntarily childless, and involuntarily childless women. Even among the involuntarily childless, women asked about their general regrets in life are not likely to spontaneously mention their regret for not having children. They mention regret for not having children only when specifically asked.[45]

At this point, it's worth recalling the important distinction among three categories of childless individuals: those who self-identified as "involuntary," those who might seem to outsiders to be "involuntary" but who self-identify as "voluntary," and those who are "voluntary" both in their own eyes and in the eyes of others.

Those who self-identified as involuntarily childless were more likely to experience regret (71 percent) and characterize their regrets as significant. In particular, those with biomedical barriers to pregnancy and childbirth had the most concerns about childlessness—more than those who were child-free or who had situational barriers to bearing children—particularly if they placed a strong importance on becoming a mother. A 1992 study of American women who were involuntarily childless—either because they never married, they or their husbands were infertile, or they married too late to have children—expressed deep regrets. Often these regrets became stronger, they reported, later in life. Ms. Stewart never felt regret during the years when she was working. "I was always busy. I never truly regretted it when I was in business. I never did, but now I do, I do."[46] Ms. Newton, a sixty-seven-year-old widow, had married too late to have children. She advised young people to have children: "I would say definitely have children. Yes, definitely because it's something you do regret later on. You have the regrets. As I said, I have—a great deal."[47]

Women like Newton internalized the expectation of child-rearing that dominated during her youth. Born in the mid-1930s, Newton's cohort gave birth to the baby boom. Ideas about the normal pattern of child-rearing came early and frequent. A high school teacher had told Ms. Bennett, "The reason for marriage is procreation. And to live on through your children." It was a lesson she never forgot, but could never fulfill.[48] Furthermore, she belonged to a cohort that lived longer than any previous one; unlike her own mother, she could expect to live for a decade or more after menopause, yet without the benefit of a large number of childless companions.[49] And Newton's statement suggests that she herself was to blame for her lack of children, when in fact any number of factors might have contributed to her late marriage: no suitable partners, need to care for parents, unemployment.

Women who self-identified as involuntarily childless felt that they missed out on life events, from giving birth to birthday parties to grandchildren. Particularly during holidays or family gatherings, they felt sad or left out. Ms. Grant said, "I feel like you miss somebody never calling you Mom. You don't know what it is to give birth. You never can plan for a wedding or anything for your child. . . . I can't go to school for a meeting and be with the other mothers."[50] The women in this study did not report the opportunities and experiences that they enjoyed because of the time and energy they did not spend on raising children.[51] Rather, they felt excluded from their friends when the photos of grandchildren came out. They felt marginalized when their church held a mother–daughter banquet.[52] In addition, the involuntarily childless reported uneasiness due to feeling cut off from future generations.

In the second group are those women who were categorized by researchers as involuntarily childless but self-identified as childless by choice. Fewer of these women expressed regret—only one in three—and they deemed their regrets "transitory" or "not important." Claiming the label of "voluntarily childless" allowed them to exert some control in a part of their lives in which they did not have much control.[53]

While it is simplistic and unfair to suggest that women who struggle with infertility should just get over it and put on a happy face, this study suggests that we can exercise some power over our narratives. We can grow wiser about life's limitations. Psychological research finds that we are better at coping with disappointment than we expect. We are constantly doing emotional work to make sense out of unexpected positive events and cope with negative ones.[54] Particularly when we make binding decisions, we are motivated to rationalize that decision—to engage our "psychological immune system." This coping mechanism comes at the cost of clarity; we employ self-serving, overly positive illusions to cope with disappointment or the unexpected.[55] But whatever happens, we do whatever we can to feel good about it.

Finally, let's turn to the third group of women, those who clearly had chosen childlessness. These women tended not to report regret. Instead, they were proud of their childless identity and relished building relationships at work, in volunteer settings, and with extended family.[56] In a study of women at midlife—born in the 1950s and 1960s and interviewed at age forty-two to sixty—voluntarily childless women reported few regrets about forgoing children.[57] When asked about menopause, they again expressed few regrets. "No, I didn't get all emotional and say 'Now I am not going to have children.'" Responded another: "Any regrets? Not really. I can't think of any." And another: "I thought I would be regretful, but I'm not."[58] In a separate study, only two out of twenty-three voluntarily childless women reported deep regrets, and these were primarily regrets related to byproducts of childlessness (what researchers call "outcome" regret) rather than about childlessness itself. The others expressed regrets that were "fleeting," "minor," or "more of a curiosity than a regret."[59] Perhaps we might say that these women simply rationalized away their regrets, but, if so, they did this emotional work more successfully than either of the other two groups of women.

Regret is not, in the end, a boogeyman that might jump out at unexpected moments. It is a stance that emerges out of a relationship between us and our society, a negative emotion that is encouraged and fostered in childless women taught to fear a future of lamentation, guilt, and loneliness.[60]

And so we can't take at face value the belief that childlessness leads to regret. The assumption that childless women should go through a period of anguish over the decision is itself a "feeling rule" that enforces the notion that childlessness is universally undesirable and that motherhood is so natural as to lie beyond the realm of critical thought.

The Nightmare of My Life

Of course, one very well might regret having children. Researcher Orna Donath recently interviewed Israeli women who spoke frankly about their regrets. For some women, the regret is existential. Tirtza, aged fifty-seven, mother of two and a grandmother, recalled "I immediately saw that it is not for me. And not only that it is not for me, it is the nightmare of my life."[61]

A second woman, Antalya, expanded on the disjuncture between her experience and the myths of motherhood: "The truth is that I can't see any benefit. Honestly, nothing. I can't find . . . from my personal point of view . . . all these things that people are talking about are not appealing to me at all. I don't understand what they are talking about when they talk about the next generation, and when we'll grow old. . . . From my personal perspective? No. For me it is only an unbearable burden."[62]

Most of the women in Donath's study separated their love for their actual children from the experience of maternity. Charlotte, aged forty-four and the divorced mother of two reported, "Look, it's complicated because I regret becoming a mother, but I don't regret *them*, who they are, their personality. I love these people. Even though I married that imbecile, I don't regret it because if I'd married someone else I'd have different children and I love them, so it's really paradoxical. I regret having had children and becoming a mother, but I love the children that I've got. So yes, it's not something you can really explain. . . . I wouldn't want them not to be here, I just don't want to be a mother."[63]

Still, it's conceivable that we also might resent raising a child whose personality conflicts with our own or who frustrates, disappoints us, or causes suffering. The chorus in Euripides's *Medea* reminds us of the regrets that might come from having children:

> And I say this. Those who miss out
> On the experience,
> Who never have children,
> They're the lucky ones.
> They never know, the childless—
> They never have the chance—
> What a child may bring.
> Joy or grief, grief or joy.
> The childless never see

> That first sweet enchantment
> Shrivel with time into despair.
> How to bring them up.
> How to have something leave them.
> Will they turn out frivolous?
> Will they turn out decent?
> There's no predicting; and no end to it.

The first brief bliss of infancy can turn sour, for one never knows the path a child might take. As eighteenth-century political economist Jean-Baptiste Moheau reflected, children present the risk that after all our efforts for their education and formation, they will grow up to disappoint us with their "disorderly conduct and their vices."[64] Or as my friend Kyle puts it: "You don't parent the child you want; you parent the child you have." Some women, even among involuntarily childless women, reframe their experience in light of the disappointments of parents. "I have heard so many cases where children have disappointed their parents in so many ways," said Ms. Newton. "So I was glad in a way . . . that I didn't have that."[65]

It's possible, of course, to take this concern about regretting children to a further extreme. The chorus in *Medea* raises a dark possibility:

> But worst, the worst
> Of any human experience.
> You become prosperous: they grow—
> Good children, fine young people—
> And then some accident . . .
> Death steals them away,
> Spirits them underground.
> How does anyone survive that?
> Why make yourself vulnerable,
> Mortals to be toyed with by gods?[66]

Even if all goes well and the child develops into a decent and happy adult, says the chorus, the whims of life make us ever prey to unbearable loss. This is an extreme reaction, a paralyzing anticipation of future regret. Surely most of us would disagree; we would not decide against having children solely out of the fear that we might be vulnerable to their deaths. We would say, instead, that we can't live a life in which we seek only to avoid pain.

The same consideration should be extended to the decision to remain child-less: we can't allow the fear of regret to guide our lives.

Beyond Regret

Bath, 1734. At age forty-seven, Mary Chandler, a poet and a business woman, sat down to compose her own epitaph. Like many literary women of her time, she undertook this exercise as a way to articulate her values and tell her story. Perhaps she entered this particularly reflective mood due to her recent success with the poem *The Description of Bath* (1733), which made her name as author and went through six editions during her lifetime. Born in 1687 to an upstanding family—her father and brother Samuel were Dissenting ministers, and brother John was a doctor—Chandler early in life developed a curve in her spine that made her a difficult match on the marriage market. For thirty years, she supported herself with a milliner's shop that became a local fixture.[67] The focus of her epitaph, however, lay elsewhere:

> Here lies a true maid, deformed and old;
> who, that she never was handsome, ne'er needed be told.
> Tho' she ne'er had a lover, much friendship had met;
> and thought all mankind quite out of her debt.
> She ne'er could forgive, for she ne'er had resented,
> as she ne'er had deny'd, so she never repented.
> She lov'd the whole species, but some had distinguish'd;
> Tho' not fond of her station, content with her lot;
> a favour receiv'd she had never forgot.
> She rejoice'd in the Good that her Neighbour possess'd,
> and Piety, Purity, Truth she profess'd.
> She liv'd in much Peace, but ne'er courted pleasure;
> her book and her pen had her moments of leisure.
> Pleas'd with Life, fond health, yet fearless of death;
> believing she lost not her soul with her breath.[68]

A friend, a believer, a neighbor, and a writer, Chandler defined herself without recourse to the traditional definitions of mother, wife, and daughter.[69] She knew that she had missed satisfactions that others enjoyed, yet she portrayed herself on an even keel through life, undisturbed by emotional waves of resentment. Chandler's clear-eyed comprehension also appears in her poetic response to the suggestion by friends that she needed to marry:

> . . . Thus far in mirth. But now for steady truth,
> I'm climbed above the scale of fickle youth.
> From pain of love I'm perfectly at ease,
> my person nature never formed to please.
> Friendship's the sweetest joy in human life,
> 'tis that I wish—and not to be a wife.[70]

Resignation and contentment lived side by side in Chandler. She valued "Piety, Purity, Truth" and "Peace" over base pleasures and self-pity and remained unwavering in her commitment to her Christian faith. Upon reflection about the friendships and values she had cultivated over the decades, she hoped to be remembered for living a good life.

Chandler's poetry compels us to question whether the fear of regret ought to be the most important focus of our attention. To dwell on the question of regret may draw us too much into ourselves and the things that we lack. And it suggests as well that perhaps there is just one way to achieve personal happiness—children—and that if we do not meet that condition, then we are doomed to feel unfulfilled. This idea lurking behind the fear of regret offers a dishearteningly narrow vision of what it means to be human. Chandler reminds us, however, that despite the disappointments that life may bring, regardless of our situation, we can actively strive to cultivate the good in ourselves and others.

About four hundred pages into *War and Peace*, during the last lingering days of a Russian winter, Prince Andrei—bitter, alienated, and disappointed—passes an ancient, gnarled oak tree. He nods in recognition. The oak appears dead to the flowers and birches awaking all around; "It alone did not want to submit to the charm of spring and did not want to see either the springtime or the sun."[71] Some weeks later, however, Prince Andrei encounters this oak again, its vitality awakened, its leaves pushing directly through the bark: "Suddenly a causeless springtime feeling of joy and renewal came over him. All the best moments of his life suddenly recalled themselves to him at the same time. Austerlitz with the lofty sky, and the dead, reproachful face of his wife, and Pierre on the ferry, and a girl excited by the beauty of the night, and that night itself, and the moon—all of it suddenly recalled itself to him."[72]

We don't have to know the story of *War and Peace* to recognize these moments. It is not the happiest moments, but rather the "best" ones, bathed in beauty as well as sorrow, life in the teeth of its pain, that recall us to spring and allow us to grow. Life is not just about the avoidance of suffering. The experience of sadness and loss is fundamental to the human condition.

The shadow of regret for not having children suggests that our only driving concern is our own satisfaction. But if we only inquire about happiness, life satisfaction, and regret, then we are missing an important piece of the puzzle: Just what is it that makes us happy and satisfied? Are some regrets more legitimate than others? Experience cautions us that happiness is not the measure of all good; we can take pleasure and satisfaction in selfish, indulgent, and self-deluding behavior. The absence of sadness and pain is not enough. For all their rigor and careful discernment, the previously cited studies take us only so far. They present no overt judgment of these subjective ratings, no measure against which to calibrate them.

Fear of future regret suggests that we will not figure out how to cope with life's disappointments, that our older selves will not be wiser than we are now, or that the wisdom of age entails a rejection of the person we are today rather than compassion for our present selves. It is the wish, perhaps, that life will be tied up with a bow, a comedic ending in the classic sense—a satisfying transfer of knowledge from one generation to the next, all conflict smoothed over by a fortuitous birth. It is a longing for a clearer path. It's fear of the tragic ending, the heroine taken down by her fatal flaw: her own nonmothering success. Our very sense of self is threatened by the possibility that childlessness will turn out to go against our best interests. Acute anticipation of regret is hoping for immortality—that if we get it right, we'll avoid life's pain and suffering and maybe we'll never have to die.

But why should we get to have everything? Wisdom traditions remind us that we should remain in the present, rather than imagine all the potential roads to pain. Life as a recluse without vulnerability toward loss is contrary to thriving. "It's not about avoiding regret," says my partner John. "You'll feel regret no matter what." Maximizing happiness and life satisfaction, then, is not the only aim of our decisions. Despite the overwhelming cultural imperative in the West since at least the Enlightenment that demands that we can and should be happy, our happiness is not the only driver of our actions.[73]

Our decisions bear consequences, and some of them will carry sadness. We won't avoid regrets, but we might shape the landscape of regret. We might become better attuned to the social pressures informing our regrets and our stance toward the very concept of regret. The alternative lives that we might imagine are not missed opportunities but rather support for our reality; in the words of Robert Pogue Harrison, the "vast ocean of potentiality on which actuality drifts like a single glass wave gives buoyancy and depth to our experience of the real."[74] This decision should not overshadow the rich complexity of what came before or the decades unfolding after. Instead of worrying about making the right choice, we ought to make the most of our choices.

7

Home and Hearth

Down the block from my house is a familiar sight. Affixed to the rear window of my neighbors' SUV is a set of stickers, stick figures of a family: dad, mom, pets, and the specified number and gender of kids. In response to such advertisements of self-contained family joy, some couples have begun to display stick figures of their own: man, woman, and bags of money. EpicFamilyDecals, one company that sells these snarky designs on Etsy, markets them in this way: "Are you and your spouse saving your money and not spending it on diapers, toddler shoes and college??? Want to shove it in that family of 6's face?? This is the sticker for you!"[1]

The moneybags decal celebrates the fact that childless people don't have to make the same cold hard trade-offs of time and money as parents do. Raising a child is expensive and costs more now than it did fifty years ago. In 1960, the annual outlay for a middle-income family to raise a child to age eighteen was $11,031 (in 2013 dollars). By 2013, increased costs of health-care and child care pushed the price tag up nearly 24 percent to $13,630.[2] Why wouldn't the childfree be pleased to have cut such a deal?

Of course, this smug stick couple is exactly the kind of image that gives parents the suspicion that childless people just might be a little self-absorbed—shallow, perhaps. The image of DINKS (dual-income, no kids) rolling about in cash instead of investing it in their progeny brings to the forefront the financial opportunity cost of child-rearing.

The money bags family crudely suggests as well that the childless couple is no more than a pair of consumers. With piles of gold bars and stacks of cash at their disposal, they enjoy elaborate vacations, fine dining, and expensive clothes. After all, childless women earn more money than mothers at almost all income levels, with the exception of partnered mothers earning in the top 10 percent of women's incomes.[3] Fathers, it is well established, out-earn both childless women and mothers. Even if we stretch the imagination to view these smiling twigs as prudent savers or generous donors to worthy causes, their only mode of being, it's suggested, is to interact with the market, to see everything, even children, as something with a price.

But it's not just the childless who might be characterized as unabashed consumers. When I visit the home of someone with children, I'm immediately struck by the overflow of stuff: toys, puzzles, stray socks, and a whole manner of objects made out of plastic. A trip to the kitchen reveals a parallel universe of children's food and drinks. "Kids are unbiased allies of capitalism," writes social critic Corinne Maier, and it's hard not to agree.[4] In fact, we could describe the childless household in terms of an absence of certain consumer goods: a lack of sippy cups and maternity clothes, of dolls and diapers.

The wagon loads of stuff accompanying the birth of a child is the ultimate example of the phenomenon that economists call the Diderot effect. Historian Jan de Vries explains that it comes from Denis Diderot's essay "Regrets on Parting with My Old Dressing Gown":

> Soon after the *philosophe* had replaced his old dressing gown with a splendid new one, he looked about his study and found it somehow deficient. His desk appeared shabby as he sat before it in his new gown, and after he replaced it with a grand new one, the wall tapestry appeared rather threadbare. New draperies were ordered, and in this way, soon everything in the study was replaced with new things. . . . Diderot had not set out to remodel his study, but a sense of style and coherence had led him to this result nonetheless.[5]

The Diderot effect suggests that certain consumer goods seem to fit together even if they are not intrinsically linked: a dressing gown and a desk, or tea and sugar, or baby bottles and plastic toys. These consumer clusters shape our identities and even, some say, our values. We move from one consumer cluster to another in purposeful leaps, not through gradual steps or an unconscious drift. Having children works in just this way: it entails a sudden, deliberate shift to a new consumer cluster.

So it is easy to think of the household as a site of consumption, whether it contains children or not. The moneybags stickers and the avalanche of child-centered purchases both encourage us to view household members primarily as consumers. The house itself becomes nothing more than a container for our stuff.

This interpretation does not necessarily reduce households to mindless consumption. Economic historians like De Vries contribute the useful idea that household members are active seekers making choices rather than passive consumers victimized by advertisements and corporations. For De Vries, the family is not a backward-looking institution destined to be defeated by market forces. Instead, the family looks forward to the future to achieve new goals. It drives societal change, rather than clinging to old ways.[6] In this view, family members strategize and specialize to use their time, skills, and money to the best possible advantage to secure what they really want: health, independence, pleasure, or other ultimate commodities. When they buy stuff, they are expressing and forming their values.

Critics of this market-oriented view of the household contend that the ultimate goals of a household cannot be described in terms of commodities, however abstract and worthy these commodities may be. Philosopher Michael Sandel argues that commodification masks important values and questions that we should ask, particularly when dealing with issues so fraught as reproduction and our homes. Economic utility—maximizing market efficiency, perfecting the incentive structure—is often assumed to be the goal, but that distracts us from other goods, other benchmarks or reasons to make decisions. Sandel asks,

> If some people like opera and others like dogfights or mud wrestling, must we really be nonjudgmental and give these preferences equal weight in the utilitarian calculus? When market reasoning is concerned with material goods, such as cars, toasters, and flat-screen televisions, the objection doesn't loom large; it's reasonable to assume that the value of the goods is simply a matter of consumer preference. But when market reasoning is applied to sex, procreation, child rearing, education, health, criminal punishment, immigration policy, and environmental protection, it's less plausible to assume that everyone's preferences are equally worthwhile.[7]

In other words, following Sandel's logic, market reasoning encourages the wrong way to think about having children or not having children and the wrong way to think about the households in which we live and develop as moral agents. The household and its members are not just members of an economic chain, producing and consuming, motivated only by economic incentives. They are also ethical agents capable of seeking values that cannot and should not be commodified. If we attempt to put a price on health, independence, or pleasure (whether that price is expressed in currency, time, or skills), then we cheapen and degrade them.[8]

Furthermore, according to Sandel, we should not think about children as something that can be traded on a market, or as a "major commodity." We shouldn't think about our bodies in that way, either. And we should not consider the childless lives that we live as something that can be entirely summed up with an equation and traded for. A serious engagement in determining the price of having a child corrupts the very notion of a life cultivated alongside family, friends, and colleagues. We exist in a complicated world, one in which our bodies matter; we are social creatures who *use* markets to make decisions and assign value, but we are not, either as individuals or collectively, *only* a market.

So, if we view children as an opportunity cost, as the moneybags sticker does, then we corrupt our understanding of children and we damage our ideas about what we do with our lives and resources. The original stickers, the ones proudly displayed by parents, might objectify children, but at least they don't turn them into commodities.

Both childless people and parents face the challenge of creating a household that is not just a site of consumption, one in which doing and talking and being—not buying—are at the center. In this chapter, then, I'm less interested in the actual stuff that flows in and out of the childless household and more interested in thinking about what the household is and does. I'm interested in the household's many roles, not just as a market actor or as a container of goods, but as a place for rest and reflection, for solitude and community, for performing rituals, and for making plans. I'm also interested in thinking about who makes up a household—a single person, a couple, or a completely different arrangement—and the power dynamics that shape the negotiations among these household members and with the world outside.[9] In all of these explorations, we will again consider how the childless person might thrive and the contributions that childless experiences might add to our understanding of human flourishing.

A critical view of the market-oriented interpretation of the household does not mean a rejection of the importance of the household's materiality. We are not just abstract souls floating about and yearning for freedom, but embodied existences rooted in a time and place. If we are lucky, we return day after day to the same place, to a bed in a room in a household. "To last," writes Wendell Berry, "love must enflesh itself in the materiality of the world—produce food, shelter, warmth or shade, surround itself with careful acts, well-made things."[10] These are not consumer goods, but material manifestations of care and connection.

Alone

London, 1794. At age thirty-nine, Mary Capper finally had her chance. She had spent decades taking care of her family of merchants and clergymen. Twelve years earlier, she had moved in with her newly married brother to help run his household. The following year, she moved in with another brother in London as his housekeeper. A few years later, after the death of her father, Capper moved again, this time to care for her widowed mother. Around this time, she considered marriage to a fellow Quaker but had to break off the relationship, perhaps because he was insufficiently dedicated to the Quakers, perhaps as well because of her need to look after her mother. Only after her mother died did Capper feel free from family duties and able to follow her passion: to become a Quaker minister, a position that enabled her to travel extensively and develop her talents. For the next fifty years, she followed her vocation while living alone in Birmingham.[11]

Singlewomen of Capper's time struggled to set up house on their own, largely due to the expense of supporting oneself alone, but also because of the social opprobrium that singlewomen living alone would face. Very few managed to pull it off as young women. If they did not live with parents or siblings, as Capper did, they might support themselves as a servant or stay as a lodger in another household. There was no specified moment at which they could set out on their own, no set age of acceptability, no sharp ritual break. For married couples, the wedding signaled the establishment of a separate household; singlewomen did so with no official fanfare.

However, if their parents had passed away, if they enjoyed some wealth or status, and if they had reached a respectable and postmenopausal age, singlewomen could live alone without arousing suspicion.[12] Historian Amy Froide reports that "in a sample of eighteenth-century communities in Staffordshire and Dorset, only between 4.5 and 5.9 percent of singlewomen under 45 years of age headed their own households. But between 36.4 and 40 percent of singlewomen age 45 and older headed their own households."[13]

After decades of dependency, early modern singlewomen had to judge for themselves when living alone would be accepted. Living alone, making a household of their own, in other words, represented a claim of autonomy and security, a sharp calculation of one's standing and reputation, not a sign of disconnection.

Rantigny, 1937. In her sixty-seventh year, Anne Panneton began a long-distance correspondence with cousins she had never met. She sketched out her early years as a way of introduction. She was born in 1870 in a small town forty miles north of Paris. A sad childhood due to the long illness of her father gave way to a studious youth and a fulfilling career as a teacher, a pathway that had recently opened to young women of promise as new laws requiring universal schooling led to a demand for teachers. Panneton served for twenty-five years as director of the school in Rantigny, the town adjacent to her birthplace, and retired at age sixty after forty years of service in the same schoolhouse. She reported to her cousins the crucial dates in her life: her father's death (aged twelve), the Great War (her late forties), her mother's death (aged fifty-five). The reproductive years barely merited a mention; Panneton did not provide any explanation or comment about remaining single and childless. It's not clear whether her memories of that time were too painful, too much of a blur, or just not important to her.

Anne Panneton situated her lifelong singleness within a dense web of association and responsibility. She was pleased with her situation, living alone yet surrounded by friends and former students. In her late sixties, she managed the house for herself, with hired help only for the heaviest of tasks.[14] She suffered from heart problems, and winter nights could be cold enough to freeze a cup of coffee, but she laughed off hardship: "If I'd put sugar in it, it would have made a proper coffee ice cream."[15] Although Panneton herself stayed in one spot, the world came to her through books, the mail, and the radio. In her retirement, she especially enjoyed reading published literary talks from the Sorbonne and listening to religious radio programs "of all confessions" and classical music programs, "for, in art, I am hardly modern."[16]

In her tidy, simple house, Panneton lived out the experience prescribed by German feminist Louise Otto in her a short article "'Small–Clean–Alone': The Joys of Living Alone" (1881). Otto presented an affirmation of women who, by necessity or by choice, keep their own household: "Be her home ever so small—as long as it is clean, not only clean of dirt and unpleasant odors but also free of distracting problems which bring with them burdensome and unsympathetic people–it is better to be alone than with such things and people even though it is nice to be in the vicinity of those we enjoy, appreciate and love."[17]

Anne Panneton's town had not always been so quiet. During the Great War, she lived just thirty miles from the Western Front. She witnessed the invasion of 1914 and, during bombardments, shepherded her two hundred students into cellars. French soldiers billeted in her school's outlying buildings, and during vacation periods they took over the classrooms as well. In over four years of war, Panneton never missed a day of class, remaining a firm presence amid the turmoil.[18] Afterward, her former students repaid her fortitude with regular visits during her retirement, bringing azaleas and roses to celebrate the new year.[19] Through her profession and the circumstances of war, Panneton maintained deep personal ties and stayed engaged in her community.

Then, in the late 1930s, the radio and the newspaper kept Panneton apprised of the renewed threat of war. When the Nazis invaded Poland and France declared war, Panneton was sixty-nine years old. Her physical strength worried her more than her morale: "I've regained my war mentality from 25 years ago, but not my 44 years."[20] Still, she vowed, "It's better to live and to die *chez soi*."[21]

When the Germans invaded France in May 1940, Rantigny became a target due to its factories and proximity to a major rail line. Panneton stayed for a week under daily bombardment until receiving the order to evacuate. She was able to secure a midnight ride on a truck to Paris and from there moved with friends to a house on the edge of the forest of Fontainebleau.[22] She was soon evacuated again, this time to Orleans, where bombardment forced her to take refuge with two wounded nuns. For thirty-six hours, the women sheltered without food or water. One of the nuns died two weeks later, "almost in my arms."[23] Her old friend, with whom she had traveled to Fontainebleau, returned to Paris three months later with an amputated arm. Panneton herself returned home after six weeks to a house that had been left open to all comers. During the harsh winter that followed she quartered a Pomeranian soldier.[24] Now she silenced her radio and only glanced at newspaper headlines. For four long years, Panneton found distraction from fear through books and through the intense and direct observation of her town.[25] After D-Day in June 1944, the bombardment returned, but she remained at home and managed to survive unscathed.[26] Panneton's last letters date from 1948.

Through the war, Panneton depended on friends and strangers and on the company of former students and books. She drew upon a lifetime of mental fortitude and intellectual resources and monitored the amount of news she took in to retain her morale. Her singleton household without children took on many qualities over the years, from a pleasant harbor to a place of refuge, with a fragility brought home by war. She was sustained through friendship and deep roots.

Studies of singletons in the United States of the twenty-first century confirm Panneton's experience. Singletons have increased social contacts as compared to married people, not less. They remain connected with others, yet cherish the benefits of solitude, including the opportunity to reflect quietly on one's decisions, to grow spiritually and creatively, to enjoy space for anonymity.[27] While we might be tempted to view the rise of the singleton household as evidence of atomization and social isolation, single women of the past and present have not always have that experience. They remind us that we can flourish and grow in a household for one.

In Community

Paris, 1831. It's Friday night, and Suzanne Voilquin and her husband Eugène are busily balancing wooden planks across boxes to create enough seats for the thirty or forty friends they expect that evening. Their home is a gathering spot for Saint-Simonians, believers in the improvement of society through science, the promotion of useful work, and ideal living communities. They are followers of Prosper Enfantin, who leads the movement from his estate a few miles away in Ménilmontant. On Fridays, the Voilquins create a study hall where Eugène leads sessions for reading and debating Saint-Simonian ideas. On Wednesdays, they move the furniture aside: for Suzanne's evening, dancing is as important as discussion.[28] In their modest apartment on rue Cadet, "luxury, comfort even were banned," but Suzanne embraced the simple decor. She was building a group of like-minded comrades through her alternative household. For her, the home provided more than shelter and food and a place for connection. It was also a place in which to experiment, to imagine, to hatch plans, and to carry them out.

To join the Saint-Simonians, Suzanne Voilquin had moved across Paris, leaving behind the working-class neighborhood of her youth. She was born at the turn of the nineteenth century in Paris's third arrondissement, in the parish of Saint-Merri. Until in her early thirties, she lived in this area of the Right Bank between Les Halles and the Marais, north of the Place de Grève. She and her brothers and sister grew up absorbing the revolutionary tales of their father while attending church alongside their devout mother. It was in many ways a typical household of the time: a nuclear family in which all the members contributed to the household economy through earning wages and splitting household tasks. As Suzanne grew, she too contributed to the household. At the age of nine, her mother entrusted Suzanne with the care of her younger sister Adrienne, saying, "This is not a sister that I give you but a daughter; from this moment on she belongs to you."[29]

When Suzanne was about twenty, disaster befell her family. First, her mother died from cancer, a loss that left Suzanne almost disconsolate. Then, her father's naive business dealings met with a cyclical downturn. When the business collapsed, the family split apart.

In its disintegration, too, Suzanne's parental household was typical of the nuclear household: it was inherently weak. As compared with households in which extended families span the generations, common in early-marriage societies, the nuclear household possesses few resources to keep it afloat when trouble strikes. Yes, the nuclear family can ask for help from extended family, friends, and neighbors. But household success ultimately rests on the rickety fortunes of just two adults—the marital couple. Famine, unemployment, illness, or ordinary incompetence could destroy a household. In Voilquin's case, the mother's death and the father's insolvency caused Suzanne's nuclear family to fall apart.

Over the years that followed, Suzanne lived in a variety of households. After a period of staying with her brother—and an ill-fated romance with a medical student called Stanislaus—Suzanne and her sister Adrienne took up needlework and lived together on rue Michel-le-Comte. Suzanne lived alone after Adrienne's marriage. Then, after her own marriage, Suzanne and her husband Eugène set up house with Adrienne and her husband. They later lived in and near various large households of Saint-Simonians. It was during this period that Suzanne and Eugène Voilquin hosted gatherings in their small apartment in a new neighborhood.

Over the following years, through many ups and downs, Suzanne Voilquin constantly shifted the number and gender of her household companions while pursuing a bewildering number of unconventional choices. After Suzanne's "moral divorce" from Eugène Voilquin—he wanted to try his luck with another woman, and she complied—Suzanne moved briefly into a sixth-floor apartment on the Left Bank, before gaining the financial support of a bourgeois Saint-Simonian and his mother, which allowed her to move into the neighborhood known as the Marais.

Meanwhile, Suzanne sought new ways to improve the lives of women and the poor. She edited the first all-female newspaper, *La tribune des femmes*.

She worked for a sympathetic bourgeois family three days a week, an arrangement that allowed her four days to write for the newspaper and organize meetings.[30] As on rue Cadet, Suzanne held an animated weekly salon that attracted several dozen like-minded people.[31] And she built her alternative community. Even during Enfantin's imprisonment (and even though women had been excluded from the leadership at his house), she and her associates sang and danced to violins at Enfantin's house and strolled home happily singing along the boulevards—this in the Paris that Balzac described as filthy and unwalkable.[32]

A life-longer searcher, in 1834 Voilquin traveled to Egypt with other Saint-Simonians, where she found her calling as a midwife. In later decades, she labored in pre-emancipation Russia, and then moved to the United States—to New Orleans—before and during the Civil War. She witnessed and experienced oppression and poverty around the world. She was a hippy of the 1830s who lived communally and experimented with free love and even on one occasion used hallucinogenic drugs.

But, to her great disappointment, Suzanne Voilquin did not raise children. Within a few days of her marriage to Eugène Voilquin, she had exhibited signs of syphilis. Eugène was devastated; he had believed himself cured of the disease. During their first five years of marriage, Suzanne miscarried three times. Later, in Egypt, she bore a child who died two weeks after birth. Her profound disappointment resonated as she wrote nearly forty years later: "O! holy maternity, my dear ideal!! why did you always flee?"[33] Suzanne's childlessness was both involuntary and devastating.

Although Suzanne did not choose her life without raising children, her life provides us with a new way to imagine the childless household. In her memoirs of these years, Suzanne Voilquin doesn't tell us much about how she ate or slept or clothed herself. She says almost nothing about the goods she purchased. The few material objects she mentions are symbols of attachment and affection. They are all gifts, not purchases: the ring from Stanislas, later worn on a black ribbon around her neck; the clothing from a sympathetic friend; the gold watch from her father that she sold to pay for her passage to Egypt; the white burnoose from Enfantin that shielded her from the Egyptian sun and allowed her to pursue medical training dressed as a man.[34]

What about household furnishings? Whether in her own house or visiting others, Suzanne interprets the lack of luxury as a sign of happiness, or at least the possibility of happiness. She comments on the lack of material comforts in her homes, such as the house on rue Cadet in which she and Eugène hosted Saint-Simonian gatherings. Later, in Old Cairo, she is skeptical of the luxury she witnesses in the Bey's palace in Egypt. As for her own lodgings, she is able to afford a five-room apartment, yet the furnishings remained simple: a cotton mattress and mosquito netting, a table, a stool and her trunk for seats, and a simple rush mat as its sole ornament. But "every pioneer has started thus!"[35] Her households, in her view, were not sites of expenditure and consumption, not catalysts for the Diderot effect, but rather repositories for gifts and memory and workshops for community and dreams.

It is hard to see in Voilquin a hedonistic modern consumer seeking comfort, whether personal or social. She does seek pleasure, but derives it through relatively nonconsumptive activities, such as dancing, singing, and conversation. Even to adopt de Vries's view of the modern consumer as an "active, searching consumer" whose knowledge and experiences (her consumer capital) allows for the exploitation of "the combinatory possibilities of available goods"—that is to say, even if we view the consumer as an actor rather than an atomized victim of the market—it takes a willful act of diminishment to interpret Voilquin primarily as a consumer, rather than as a friend, a visionary, a midwife, a sister, a believer.[36] Voilquin repeatedly gave up material security to pursue ideals, companionship, and vocation. She found community wherever she traveled, even though she raised eyebrows traveling alone or in the company of women. She did not leap from one consumer cluster to another, and her ultimate goals of association, emancipation, and vocation were relatively unattached to the market. It is useful to think about her not just as an economic actor, but as an ethical actor, someone who recognizes that her actions belong to her and have consequences for the future.

Suzanne's adult households differed dramatically, then, from the nuclear household that characterized her age. Throughout the many stages of her life, Suzanne lived in and created alternative households; never in her adult life did she live in the typical European household centered on the nuclear family. Instead, she sought households with chosen companions for the exchange of ideas and the sharing of food, song, and dance. She demonstrates that we can stake out alternatives in how we construct our home life.

In this, Suzanne was not the first. Mary Astell's 1694 *Serious Proposal to the Ladies* embraced the communal household, as did nuns and beguines living together in community. Single women long had set up alternative households, sharing expenses and household tasks, seeking protection in numbers, as lodgers, co-renters, or companions.[37] Nor was Voilquin the last. In the 1990s, a survey of Northampton, England, found 330 distinct ways that people grouped together in a household.[38] Households with multiple generations, with an empty nest, with non-heteronormative structures all continue to evolve and shape how we live.

Yet Voilquin's households, like those of childless women before and after her, shared many characteristics in common with the nuclear household. They were weak, easily broken up by suspicious neighbors and crippling poverty. But this instability also led them to constantly evolve and become more resourceful. To survive a harsh and relentless world, with populations rising and the economy uncertain, members of a nuclear household from the 1500s on had to make adjustments, to calculate advantage, to take responsibility and imagine alternatives.[39] Historian Mary Hartman writes, "Families at every social level were teeming with plans."[40] Over time, these proactive householders began to fashion institutions, such as civil courts and insurance companies, that provided additional security. They marshaled their resources to make small but frequent purchases. The buying power of young men and women earning cash and buying pipes, ribbons, and watches created the demand that launched the industrial revolution. For Hartman, even the power of the Reformation can be linked to increasing household religiosity, a buffer against the slings and arrows barraging the precarious nuclear family.[41]

The scheming and planning nuclear household is tied to the later age at marriage that, we have seen, has been a key pathway to childlessness over the past several centuries. In the words of demographer John Hajnal, "In societies where the household is the principal unit of economic production as well as consumption . . . the marriage pattern is tied in very intimately with the performance of the economy as a whole. The emotional content of marriage, the relation between the couple and other relatives, the methods of choosing or allocating marriage partners—all this and many other things cannot be the same in a society where a bride is usually a girl of 16 and one in which she is typically a woman of 24."[42] Smaller, experimental, ad hoc households were both a cause and a consequence of later marriage and therefore of childlessness, and they continue to remind us that homes are constructed and negotiated, not timeless and monolithic.

Suzanne Voilquin and her traveling band of companions sought to create households that better developed the individual as a member of a supportive community. They show us that the household, with or without children, can be a laboratory for the working out of ideas.

The Generalist

Bordeaux, 1758. Marie Lamothe is managing the family budget. The price of cod has become prohibitive, and eggs are scarce, but cuttlefish and peas are affordable given the wholesale price for the wine they produced this year. Marie knows all the details and judges for herself what to buy and when to sell.[43] Marie and her sister Marianne Lamothe spent their lives managing the households of their parents and brothers. Although they had servants, as was typical for well-heeled families in eighteenth-century Bordeaux, the Lamothe sisters labored constantly. As historian Christine Adams recounts, "They selected and prepared the family's foods, such as the small delicacies that they sent to their brothers Victor and Alexandre, who lived in Paris. They knitted stockings and slippers. They sewed the family's sheets, handkerchiefs, *serviettes*, shirts, collars, night shirts and bonnets, and *souliers*. . . . They did the laundry. They went shopping for the family's needs, and searched for the best prices . . . [and] their help was considered essential at the family's country homes during the wine harvest."[44]

Many will argue that the Lamothe sisters embodied a stifling, coercive side of domesticity: the assumption that female family members are suitable only for domestic work and would gladly provide these services. And while household labor is in itself honorable and important, the presumption that women are uniquely qualified to perform it (and it alone) has posed a persistent threat to women's dignity, authenticity, and personal fulfillment. The expectation of female domesticity was elevated to the level of ideology by the Victorians. The breadwinner–homemaker household, in which the husband earns money through labor, trade, or profession and the wife runs the household, became an ideal by the mid 1800s and an economically feasible reality for many by the mid-1900s, the period of the baby boom.[45] For those with the resources to live comfortably, a burgeoning set of make-work tasks filled the time. It's easy enough to interpret later trends in household crafting as a continuation of this kind of entrapment (crocheted toilet paper covers, anyone?).

An alternative view argues that the Lamothe sisters were *generalists*, those amazing creatures who can handle just about any task, chore, or negotiation. When we imagine Marie and Marianne de Lamothe up to their elbows in a tub of laundry or eyeing a pattern for their niece's dress collar, we need not interpret this kind of labor as drudgery or busywork—so long as the tasks are properly understood as belonging to all, rather than to just one sex. Indeed, the loss of these skills might be detrimental to our overall well-being. When we use our hands to perform meaningful tasks, such as chopping vegetables or knitting, we support a neural rewards circuit that can help us to be more resilient against depression.[46] In this view, the Lamothe sisters remind us that we need not have children to expand our repertoire of craft and care.

In his seminal work *The Unsettling of America*, published in 1977, Wendell Berry takes this argument even further. He claims that without these domestic tasks, we risk abdicating responsibility for our households. Berry raises the specter of individuals stripped of the ability to do or care about anything but the one thing for which they have been trained. Instead of producing their own food, caring for their own health, or taking seriously their own education, modern Americans delegate these responsibilities to experts: businessmen, marketers, educators, doctors, sanitation professionals. Left only to make money and entertain themselves, Berry claims, they have lost the capacity to take care of their own most basic needs of shelter, food, and clothing: "From morning to night he does not touch anything that he has produced himself, in which he can take pride."[47]

This disintegration of action, argues Berry, has a deleterious effect on our health and independence. Moreover, specialization has undermined our character. "Specialization," he writes, "is thus seen to be a way of institutionalizing, justifying, and paying highly for a calamitous disintegration and scattering-out of the various functions of character: workmanship, care, conscience, responsibility."[48] In other words, we perform these actions not only to provide food and shelter to others and to ourselves, but also because the acts themselves are constitutive of our characters. *Doing* is important not just for the sake of the outcome—a nutritious meal or a mended fence—but because the act of sewing, canning, chopping, or painting forms us into responsible human beings. Berry's ideal household is a center for work, for play, and, ultimately, for building character.

Berry believes that the reliance on experts can explain the diffuse underlying anxiety experienced by so many modern Americans. The tension they feel results from their helpless dependence upon others to manage even the most basic of needs. Specialization makes for only the smallest margin of error, for if we can only do one thing, then we have only "*one chance*" in life: only our own "small specialty within a delicate, tense, everywhere-strained system of specialties."[49] Instead of focusing on our small segment of expertise, Berry enjoins us to increase the sphere of our responsibilities to expand our "capacities as a person."[50] An understanding of the flow of food from seed to soil to harvest to stovetop, for instance, can also help us to maintain contact with land and develop an environmental ethic.

Berry's view of the household privileges craft, hard work, and risk over absolute security and safety. Berry urges us to experiment in how we fashion and shape our homes. Whereas the domestic ideal prevalent from the mid-nineteenth century onward viewed the home as a haven, a place of rest and safety, Berry's household might be a place of trial and error, of difficult negotiation among household members, even exhaustion; for him, these characteristics of a household are a value, not a flaw.

The piece missing in Berry, however, is an explicit acknowledgement that the responsibilities for domestic care ought to fall equitably on both women and men according to the needs, interests, and talents of household members. Missing as well is a model for a functioning household of one. If we can reimagine household labor that is more gender equitable and can encompass a wide variety of household variations, then his view of domestic labor as caring and responsible becomes much more palatable, and, indeed, empowering.

Commitment to domestic tasks, to being a generalist, need not mean a rejection of modern life and technology. Albert Borgmann explains that we ought not to strive for self-sufficiency only for its own sake, a quest that will "draw a narrow and impermeable boundary" around the household and its tightly knit inhabitants. If we give ourselves over to domestic labor, abandoning all technologies that help us to find ease and comfort, then we risk losing our civic engagement in the wider world, for in such a household "there is no time to be a citizen of the cultural and political world at large and no possibility of assuming one's responsibility in it." Technology allows us to pursue our human excellences, to escape the bitterness of knowing that our talents lay fallow under the burden of repetitive labor. And so we must choose our technologies wisely and "gratefully accept the disburdenment from daily and time-consuming chores" but, in exchange, "allow celebration and world citizenship to prosper in the time that has been gained."[51]

A childless household attunes us to the fact that domestic tasks serve the needs not only of children, but of adults as well. In such a household, labor and leisure revolve around adults rather than children. We get up as our bodies and our work demand. We prepare only one meal for our adult tastes and systems, rather than special food for young palates, teeth, and digestion. Household labor might, therefore, take on a more sustainable balance between repetition and creativity, between the comforting sameness of cyclical tasks and the experimentation that elevates and inspires. The household can be engaging not through stifling make-work but through stimulating innovation. At the same time, the concept of the generalist suggests that childless individuals might borrow from the activities and traditions of families with children to develop their autonomy, personal fulfillment, and interpersonal connectedness.

If we could liberate the notion of domestic work from the straightjacket of predefined gender roles, we might better appreciate the contribution that it makes to human flourishing. Working with one's hands to feed and care for ourselves and others enhances our interpersonal connectedness. Every household with more than one member must take up the essential question of who does what and when and how; those who live alone still often care for others.[52] The household is the site of care for its inhabitants, the place where we secure food, shelter, and clothing. It is the place that provides the conditions for rest and leisure, for intellectual stimulation and emotional support. The household is where we restore our capacity to contribute productively to the human experiment.

The Hearth

In all of Suzanne Voilquin's years of travel, one particularly memorable meal stands out. In Marseilles, on her way to Egypt, Voilquin visits political prisoners on behalf of republican friends. Under the watchful guards, she joins them for an evening featuring a dilapidated chair and iron utensils, but she reflects that "one is not in prison to have every comfort."[53] Good conversation draws them together, and bouillabaisse, a local delicacy, brings them back for another festive meal.

This meal invites a number of different interpretations. We could, I suppose, emphasize the economic forces at work: local women purchase the fish, the onions, and garlic; their human capital makes the soup delicious, while their social capital allows them to imbue the dish with local culture and to invite Suzanne to the table. The meal also suggests a gendered analysis of tasks, given the fact that the women are the cooks and the men are the political prisoners.

Here, however, I prefer to emphasize the concept of the *hearth*, a central focus for human activity that brings people together in a household and gives meaning. Like the notion of being a generalist, the health suggest ways that childless individuals might borrow from traditional childful families to enhance their sense of interpersonal connectedness.

Albert Borgmann argues that the hearth, which may or may not be a literal hearth, provides a spatial and emotional center to the house. It engages us physically and brings all members of the household together with their appointed tasks:

> Thus a stove used to furnish more than mere warmth. It was a *focus*, a hearth, a place that gathered the work and leisure of a family and gave the house a center. Its coldness marked the morning, and the spreading of its warmth the beginning of the day. It assigned to the different family members tasks that defined their place in the household. The mother built the fire, the children keep the firebox filled, and the father cut the firewood. It provided for the entire family a regular and bodily engagement with the rhythm of the seasons that was woven together of the threat of cold and the solace of warmth, the smell of wood smoke, the exertion of sawing and of carrying, the teaching of skills, and the fidelity to daily tasks.[54]

The hearth thus provides security and anchoring through physical embodiment and responsible commitment to the common task. Fire makes eating a matter of a fixed time and place and, therefore, binds households together, over and over again.[55] The hearth can also come of the form of annual holidays that you feel in your bones as the seasons change. It could be a sport or a garden, or bedtime or music, or anything that brings the household together, that we clear the time and space for, that we protect from technological clutter and outside demands.

On special occasions, feasting and hospitality are a hearth: markers of human belonging and an expression of power. A feast must be organized and the provisions supplied; the guests reciprocate with loyalty.[56] The ritual of the feast, writes Borgmann, requires "an order and discipline that challenges and ennobles the participants."[57] Suzanne and her companions created together a shared meal worthy enough to be captured in her memoirs many decades and many adventures later.

It's easy to imagine the hearth of a household with children, the rituals of the daily bedtimes and meals. For Borgmann, the hearth sustains the traditional family. "Families, I have found, that we are willing to call healthy, close, or warm turn out, on closer inspection, to be centered on a focal concern."[58] Borgmann's description of the hearth celebrates traditional roles ("the mother built the fire, the children keep the firebox filled, and the father cut firewood"). Mary Capper, the Quaker minister, spoke of something akin to a hearth during her visit to a family during one of her many travels. In a diary entry from July 1826 she wrote, "A day of some rest, grateful to body and mind. My lot is in a kind, amiable family; the daily care of little children, and the well-regulated exertions of parents, may evidently be so ordered as to harmonize a whole family, and to cultivate that watchful frame of spirit which manifests our dependence on a superior Power to teach and guide us; a Power that keeps us from evil, and promotes a sweet union and affectionate accordance, when met in families or social companies."[59] For Capper, the hearth of the household was the tender working together of daily life in the service of a higher ideal.

It takes a different kind of intentionality, then, to develop a hearth in a childless household. A household without children has fewer inherited scripts to follow, more scope for negotiation, and a different set of power relations among family members. Debates over where and how to celebrate holidays can become perilous without the ballast of children to shape our practices, but can also lead to unanticipated new traditions.[60] The daily ritual of preparing cooked food can connect household members through their habitual tasks. In my house, as in Suzanne Voilquin's, dinner focuses the household. Prepared with skill and care, each meal recombines a set of common ingredients in some slightly different way. I brush humus off the mushrooms and into our metal compost bowl. John designs the meal. We negotiate the amount of garlic as he prepares his side dish of jalapeños. The hearth need not require two people, either; single people create their own ritual spaces as they develop the meals that make their house a home. Empty nesters must re-establish their habits and patterns when children leave the home. Childless lives remind us that such rituals are not timeless or unquestioned.

We come into ourselves not only through rites of passage, but also through everyday interactions and conversations—through intersubjectivity. When we realize that other people possess minds and think, only then do we realize that we have minds, too—that we think. The first encounter with someone else with a mind, who thinks, is usually between a parent and child. As infants, we require such human interaction. We're knitted together through neurochemical messaging transmitted from one person to the next that reaches right into our neurons.[61] Whether or not we have children, we are reminded of this need for intersubjectivity day by day, minute by minute, in our everyday encounters and in the special daily rituals we carve out for ourselves and those closest to us.

The household is not a self-contained pod, receiving input and then mindlessly engaging in market pursuits, as the car with moneybags suggests. Household members are not just active consumers searching for the products that secure their ultimate commodities, but the shapers of institutions and values and human lives that are not reducible to a commodity. Materiality is not the same as the market. Households are important locations for the development and engagement of individuals who have struck out in life together. Collectively, these households shape the world around them. Suzanne Voilquin, Mary Capper, Anne Panneton, and the Lamothe sisters remind us that if we are going to fully understand and embrace childless individuals, we ought to continually reinvent and reimagine the concrete structures—the households—in which the self is embodied.

8

A Better World

In *The Woman in White* (1860), Wilkie Collins invented one of the great childless characters of British popular fiction, the self-absorbed Uncle Fairlie. From his pampered hideaway, Uncle Fairlie complains to a visitor about the voices of children that he imagines might be playing in the gardens. "Such brats—oh, dear me, such brats! Shall I confess it, Mr. Hartright?—I sadly want a reform in the construction of children. Nature's only idea seems to be to make them machines for the production of incessant noise."[1] The distasteful, lethargic Uncle Fairlie is responsible for much unhappiness due to his inability to watch out for his nieces, a failing inextricably linked to his childless state.

In that same decade, Parisian seamstress and activist Suzanne Voilquin recorded in her memoir her impressions of the doctor who had broken the news that her mother ways dying. "He was a learned and charitable man, but he was a bachelor," she recalled. "If he had had children, he would not have added to my distress by this brutality of language; he would have left me with hope."[2]

Uncle Fairlie and the unnamed doctor embody the caricature of childless individuals that rose to prominence in the late nineteenth century and grew ever more insistent as the decades passed: the childless are selfish, ambitious, individualistic, pleasure-loving and nonconforming. They do not know, and cannot know, how to become more giving toward others, more attuned to the needs of society, or more deeply appreciative of life's limits and challenges. Childlessness is a state of stagnant being, a state of arrested development.

To this tired argument, childless individuals counter with their own set of stereotypes. *We're* not the selfish ones; it is parents who create their own little versions of themselves. *We're* not the unreflective ones; it is parents who fail to think through the costs and demands of parenting, or even whether they like children.[3] *We're* not the immature ones; it is parents who tap into their most primitive impulses to reproduce and discipline.[4] In my twenties, as I was sorting out my path and committing myself to childlessness, I engaged in this kind of conversation on a regular basis. It felt important to justify why I was not making the same sacrifices for children that my parents and grandparents had made.

I hope I have become wiser with age. Clearly, neither parenthood nor childlessness automatically confer morality, nor do they always imply selfishness. Let's turn away from this defensive and unproductive exchange regarding personal characteristics and shift toward a more fruitful conversation. Part of human flourishing is attention to our responsibilities to others, to the stories of which we are a part, whether we have chosen them or not.

Pronatalists understand this idea well. Over the years, those who promote childbearing have offered many arguments for why having children supports the greater good, ranging from scriptural admonition ("Be fruitful and multiply") to the continuation of family tradition to the need to produce young workers who can support the welfare state. In this chapter, by contrast, I am interested in exploring arguments in favor of childlessness. Can childlessness benefit the greater good and alleviate suffering on the large scale? How can childlessness contribute to a better world?

In this chapter, I'll focus on two proposals for how childlessness might benefit the greater good and the human experiment. The first are arguments against bearing children due to the unhappiness of human existence. The second are arguments for slowing population growth due to limitations on the world's resources. Both of these arguments are controversial and some might say completely misguided. It's one thing to entertain the notion that one's own childlessness might contribute to the greater good; it's a further and darker step to imply that certain other people *should* be childless. I am in no way proposing policies to enforce childlessness. I deeply distrust any suggestion that governments should exert this kind of power.[5] That said, it's worth examining arguments that challenge our received wisdom to better understand our core beliefs and further our understanding of human flourishing. And so I am exploring here a question that makes us human, that no other animal can ask: Would it be better for everyone if I didn't have children?

Wish You Weren't Here

Critics of childbearing as detrimental to human flourishing began with the earliest philosophers, many of whom did not hesitate to take a polemical tone. Thales of Mitelus, a pre-Socratic Greek philosopher, wrote, "Who truly finds reality sufficiently desirable to introduce their son or daughter to the inevitability of death, to the treachery of man's dealings with man, to the self-interest that fuels the world, to the burden of being forced to do tiring work for pay, if not to precarious unemployment? How could parents be so naïve, stupid and short-sighted as to love misery, illness, destitution, poverty, old age and misery enough to want to pass them on to their offspring?"[6] Montesquieu argued, "Men should be bewailed at their birth and not at their death."[7] For Gustave Flaubert, the critic of bourgeois complacency, life is just too tedious to subject to a new person. "The idea of bringing someone into this world fills me with *horror*. . . . May my flesh perish utterly! May I never transmit to anyone the boredom and ignominies of existence!"[8]

Philosopher Seana Valentine Shiffrin brings these intentionally heated arguments to a calmer moral plane. She claims that procreation always involves moral trade-offs. "By being caused to exist as persons," she reasons,

> children are forced to assume moral agency, to face various demanding and sometimes wrenching moral questions, and to discharge taxing moral duties. They must endure the fairly substantial amount of pain, suffering, difficulty, significant disappointment, distress, and significant loss that occur within the typical life. They must face and undergo the fear and harm of death. Finally, they must bear the result of imposed risks that their lives may go terribly wrong in a variety of ways.[9]

Most of the time—that is, when we're not discussing procreation—we object to placing burdens on people without their consent, unless the burden will avert a greater harm. Yet the burdens and risks inherent in life itself occur without the consent of the person being harmed—the new child—because they are imposed before birth and without averting a greater harm.[10]

Of course, the vast majority of people experience their existence as a benefit that far outweighs these burdens and risks. The burden of existence makes possible a greater good—the joys, loves, and accomplishments of our own lives—and so it is a justifiable burden. Some potential parents may well reason that if they commit to help shoulder their children's burdens, their moral obligations will be met.

Philosopher David Benatar disagrees. He argues that such a commitment is insufficient to overcome the moral difficulty presented by procreation.

In a deliberately provocative argument, he claims that coming into existence is always a harm to that person, and therefore it is morally wrong to reproduce.

The core of Benatar's argument lies in the asymmetry between the good and the bad in life: "The absence of bad things, such as pain, is good even if there is nobody to enjoy that good, whereas the absence of good things, such as pleasure, is bad only if there is somebody who is deprived of these good things."[11] We would not miss the good things if we had never existed. But even those of us with the luckiest and happiest of lives suffer greatly, merely from the fact of existing. Existence itself, according to Benatar, is an assault on human flourishing.

Therefore, claims Benatar, we would be better off if we had never been born. Our primary moral obligation ought to be toward the unborn person. We do not regret that our unborn child never got to experience the good things in life, he says, any more than we regret that nonexistent Martians never get the chance to fall in love, prosper, and have baby Martians of their own.[12] But we very well might regret, Benatar says, having brought into existence a child with an unhappy or unfortunate life.[13]

Prospective parents might hope that their child will join the ranks of the lucky, but there is no guarantee. And even if the child should be so happy, she will nevertheless suffer from daily disappointments, the frustration of goals, the loss of her loved ones, and her own eventual death. Our state of constant striving, as philosopher Arthur Schopenhauer recognized, brings us only discontent.[14] The conclusion, to him, is plain: "If the act of procreation were neither the outcome of a desire nor accompanied by feelings of pleasure, but a matter to be decided on the basis of purely rational considerations, is it likely the human race would still exist? Would each of us not rather have felt so much pity for the coming generation as to prefer to spare it the burden of existence, or at least not wish to take it upon himself to impose that burden upon it in cold blood?"[15]

In light of this suffering, Benatar argues that we are morally obligated not to procreate. Ever. The human race should allow itself to go extinct. We should take all precaution against pregnancy and abort those that accidentally occur.

The only possible exception, Benatar acknowledges, is that we should minimize the physical and mental anguish of the final generation of humans, and so we should implement phased extinction so that the final generation is relatively small. Indeed, Benatar recognizes that existing humans have many good reasons to want to keep living. His argument only applies *before* an individual has come into existence, and he does not advocate suicide.

For Benatar, we must choose childlessness not to achieve a liberating, higher-order level of self-actualization, but out of a deep and clear-eyed pessimism about human existence. The predilections of those who dislike children or who want to pad their own pocketbooks or live unfettered lives have no play here. He prefers to face squarely the sadness and frustrations of life head on rather than shunt them to the side. He decries the "smug macho tone" of those who admonish him to "grin and bear it" as "an indifference to or inappropriate denial of suffering, whether one's own or that of others."[16] He certainly does not embrace suffering as the point of human existence.

Benatar urges instead a hard look at our common experience of suffering. He knows that most of us won't accept it; we tend toward optimism. We adapt, we accommodate, we habituate to the bad.[17] And we are unwilling to think rationally about the harm we are doing to our children simply by bringing them into life. In reality, "one can never have a child for that child's sake"—it is always done for the sake of the parents, the state, the nation, or done without much thought at all.[18]

A lack of regret about one's own suffering makes it easy for people to unthinkingly procreate and spread the misery to the next generation. Such parents "may be happier than others," Benatar stresses, "but that does not make them right."[19] Those who cheerfully procreate "play Russian roulette with a *fully* loaded gun—aimed, of course, not at their own heads, but at those of their future offspring."[20]

Overpopulation

My partner John vehemently opposes Benatar's argument to end the species: "Benatar is double-bookkeeping, but he's cheating on one side. We should count the pleasures, satisfactions, and happiness that life can bring in our calculation on whether or not to procreate." John, the father of four grown children, describes himself as "childful" as a counterweight to those (like me) who are "childless." For him, Benatar's utilitarian argument to minimize suffering ignores the virtues of a life well led. In this regard, Benatar's position is akin to the economic approach to procreation that assumes that all decisions can be reduced to a cost–benefit analysis. In John's view, the measure of a good society is not its amount of misery, and its joys and pains should not be weighed in the balance. Instead of seeking a lack of suffering, we should aspire for justice to redress wrongs and practical wisdom to cope with existential suffering; justice and wisdom aren't simply a poor compensation for our suffering, not simply a bandage on a fundamental human flaw, but rather the greatest good to which humans can aspire, a noble outcome of human experience and reflection and one that both childfree and childful can foster.

Let's say that you, like John, reject Benatar's argument. Perhaps you happen to think that the human experiment is worth continuing, whether or not you yourself will raise a child. Do there have to be so many of us? Maybe childlessness can alleviate misery by lessening the burden on an overpopulated planet.

Concern about overpopulation is a relatively recent phenomenon. Prior to the 1700s, global annual population growth rates were low, probably below 0.1 percent.[21] Locally, of course, demographic growth might have exceeded these rates for a short time, but overpopulation tended to lead to famine and disease and migration and, therefore, to small growth overall. It's a pattern that extends back to our earliest human ancestors.

In these low-growth societies, population growth reflected the prosperity and power of the rulers, whereas childlessness led to a diminished status for families and individuals. Rulers long favored population growth as a blunt measure of their prosperity, a driver of economic growth—as both producers and consumers of goods and services—and a supply of fresh soldiers to fight and die in war. In this view, children are not only a private good, but a public good.

Rulers therefore tried to spur faster population growth by marshalling resources and occasionally by passing laws to influence behavior. In 3 CE, the Roman Empire adopted Augustus's infamous laws encouraging marriage and children. The unmarried were subject to taxes, passed over for public offices, and unable to inherit unless they were closely related to the testator. Childless married women could only receive one tenth of the amount her husband left to her. Whereas men only needed one child to remove this penalty, women required three (and freedwomen four); at this point the woman was also free of her husband or father's guardianship. Despite these restrictions, the law had little effect on the birth rate.[22]

Much later, in seventeenth-century France, Louis XIV's advisors believed that population growth would create loyal subjects and stabilize the country under its metaphorical father.[23] Louis XIV's Edict on Marriage (1666) offered tax incentives to encourage men to marry at younger ages and rewarded the fathers of large families.[24] A related law regulated the foundation of monasteries and convents, in an effort to curtail monastic professions. Significantly, mothers did not appear in the law, other than as the wives of fathers; the law elided their role in reproduction. Again, these policies appear to have done little to change behavior. In fact, they were implemented just as French couples began to deliberately limit their family size.[25]

Between 1700 and 1820, demographic growth increased to 0.4 percent, which meant that the global population increased from about six hundred million to just over one billion.[26] In addition, the development of consumer societies, industrialization, and global finance created new wealth. The same young women who postponed marriage and childbearing to secure their household finances also worked to produce some of the consumer goods—fabric, ribbons, lace—that fueled economic growth. They also consumed tea and sugar (often produced by enslaved people thousands of miles away in the colonies), burned coal, and purchased pocket watches, all of which supported a global economy.

Early political economists of the 1700s struggled to understand this growth economy, to wrap their heads around the notion that wealth could be created; it was not just a zero-sum game in which growth in one country meant contraction in another. With the rise of industry and its ability to create new wealth (fitfully, unevenly), political economists examined the relationship between wealth, population, agriculture, and colonial possessions. The link between economic prosperity and large populations became more complex.

For Adam Smith, economic growth and population growth were positively linked, and both were desirable. He believed that the demand for labor—the market for labor, the real wages for labor—directly influenced the population of a country and therefore its economic growth. Workers ought to be paid high wages—a "liberal reward for labor"—to increase wealth and population. For while the rich were able to raise healthy children, he wrote, the children of the poor died young.[27] Like most population theorists before him, Smith viewed the population increase as a good. "To complain of it," he wrote, "is to lament over the necessary effect and cause of the greatest public prosperity."[28]

For Thomas Robert Malthus, however, demographic growth spelled disaster. He famously argued in his 1798 *Essay on Population* that economic development stimulates demographic growth. Left to our own devices, our exponential reproduction will outstrip the increase in agricultural production. Economic development stimulates fertility: two by two becomes four by four, which inexorably leads to eight by eight. Eventually, population growth leads to economic strain—starvation, war, disease—and the population collapses. Malthus combined an apocalyptic vision of exponential growth with a more traditional notion of the natural unending cycle that could not be overcome. Our best hope, the only peaceful hope for those too poor to support a family, lay in the virtuous delay of marriage. Our security and dignity depended on it.

Malthus won many supporters. Overpopulation and starvation appeared too frequently to be ignored, and Malthus provided a clear solution. By the 1820s, Malthus's ideas led him into the public eye. He advised Parliament on Irish emigration, won academic prizes, and helped to establish the Statistical Society of London. Well after his death in 1834, his *Essay* continued to inform conversation and policy related to population, both at home and on the continent.[29] "Happy the country where public and private wisdom unite to prevent the population from growing too rapidly," read the Académie Française essay contest topic in 1851.[30] In Germany, liberals and authoritarians alike embraced Malthus, as he provided a way out of the overpopulation and lack of natural resources that they feared.[31] Malthus's insights regarding the importance of population and of data remained the current in which population thinkers swam, even as new developments changed the way they were used.

In Praise of Old Maids

Malthus was one of the first people, and certainly the most famous, to recognize that one might choose not to have children for the sake of the greater good.[32] This insight had the potential to raise the status of childless women. The old maid, wrote Malthus, deserves our praise far more than the matron of a burgeoning brood. In the 1803 edition of his *Essay*, Malthus—a thirty-seven-year-old bachelor clergyman living with his parents—opined that "the conduct of the old maid had contributed more to the happiness of the society than that of the matron."[33] These unmarried women had spared the country the burden of feeding a dozen more mouths, while virtuously remaining chaste. Their own restraint had allowed others to partake in motherhood's bounty. By contrast, the matron had acted as "a monopolist" whose marriage had prevented another woman from enjoying a similar happiness. Even if her sons were dying in the name of Britain on some Caribbean island, the mother ought not to claim any special consideration, for "there is no particular reason for supposing that her sons would fight better for their country than the sons of other women."[34]

Such Spartan sentiments notwithstanding, Malthus offered balm to the unmarried soul. These childless women deserved honors, yet they suffered the indignity of dependence and the expectation of deference to their married sisters. Why should "a giddy girl of sixteen" who had snagged an aging husband have the privilege of running the household, walking first into the room, and sitting at the head of the table, while her unmarried aunt was always required follow behind?[35] Indeed, it was the fear of this embarrassment, he claimed, that led many women to enter loveless unions that "to every delicate mind appear little better than legal prostitutions."[36] We ought to accord "a greater degree of respect and of personal liberty to single women" as a dissuasion from empty marriages and useless overpopulation.[37]

Malthus apparently did not realize that among the less well-to-do, celibate singleness had been the common lot for women for centuries. The old maid was already part of a system. He did not imagine that a woman might enter marriage without having children, let alone that sexuality outside of marriage might be acceptable. It would take later neo-Malthusians to turn his ideas into the promotion of contraceptives. Yet Malthus was rather romantic about the "passion between the sexes," though he was quick to couch them, as all things, in the laws of nature: "The passion between the sexes has appeared in every age to be so nearly the same that it may be considered, in algebraic language, as a given quantity."[38] For Malthus, this passion ought to be expressed only within marriage, a delayed marriage that will produce fewer children. A supporter of companionate marriage, Malthus saw little of value in the loveless match between a young bride and an older man "agreeable neither in mind or person."[39] Better to go childless than to enter a miserable marriage. Instead, a virtuous unmarried and childless woman should be honored.

Malthus and his successors had a point: the personal was, and still is, political. Motherhood and economics intertwined in an awkward dance in which now one, and now the other, took the lead. Malthus attempted to address the burning issue at the heart of the new field of political economy: how to handle globally unprecedented rates of growth. His answer offered data, mathematical models, and a superhuman standard of virtue to address the issue of overpopulation in an economy of scarcity. He believed that we could choose to embrace preventative checks to avoid the more devastating checks of war or famine. The natural balance would be achieved; we could choose how painful the process would be. But Malthus's conclusions were draconian: abstinence and the virtuous delay of marriage for the poor provided the only nonviolent way out of rampant demographic growth. The burden of alleviating misery fell squarely on the poor themselves.

Lord Byron pointed out that Malthus had "preached celibacy and happily married on the proceeds."[40] Indeed, after his marriage in 1804, in subsequent editions of his *Essay*, Malthus excised the section in praise of old maids.

Structure or Virtue?

Malthus soon attracted a chorus of critics. Americans decried British curtailment of liberty and aligned population increase with democracy and expansion.[41] Religious authorities objected to Malthus's cruel and disinterested God. And Romantics cringed at his stifling sexuality.[42]

Most insistently and steadily, commentators criticized Malthus as tone deaf to the problem of structural inequality. Poverty, he wrote, stemmed not from the avaricious rich, unjust institutions, or misfortune. No, poverty resulted from the poor man's own actions: his marriage and children. Marriage without the prospect of supporting the inevitable offspring was, for Malthus, immoral. No man has the "right to subsistence," and no state support should be admitted.[43] It would subvert the laws of nature: "It may appear to be hard that a mother and her children, who had been guilty of no particular crime themselves, should suffer for the ill-conduct of the father; but this is one of the invariable laws of nature"; therefore, we should not try to overturn it with ill-conceived charity or government policies.[44] The only blame to fall on the heads of the wealthy was their persistence in perpetuating the myth that all people are to raise children for the sake of king and country.[45] Like any true-believing rationalist, Malthus argued that once the laws have been revealed, one must follow them to the death (or at least, to the deaths of millions of others).

Early on, critics of Malthus across the political field roundly rejected his reasoning. Socialists of all stripes, including Pierre-Joseph Proudhon, Karl Marx, and many others, despised Malthus for complacently accepting the socio-economic and political order. It wasn't nature that created the population "problem," they argued, but rather the capitalist economy that relied upon cycles of boom and bust and required periods of low employment.[46] In *Progress and Poverty* (1879), a book that sold two million copies, American Henry George wrote that Malthus's ideas were "eminently soothing and reassuring to the [ruling] classes," for they (wrongly) made poverty and destitution "the inevitable results of universal laws with which . . . it were as hopeless to quarrel as with the law of gravitation."[47] Socialists believed that Malthus's solution dehumanized workers and isolated them from the possibility of love and family life, while ignoring the root causes of misery in monopolies and nascent industrial capitalism.[48] In their eyes, Malthus had completely misunderstood the kinds of obligations we have to each other. If we think of our social commitments as a way of honoring the stories of which we are a part, Malthus had misread the story.

French early feminists also argued that Malthus had missed a crucial perspective in his story: the view of women. In their eyes, Malthus's praise of the old maid did not read as empowering, but as demeaning and ignorant of the laws and prejudices that enforced poverty and impeded women. An anonymous woman, possibly Désirée Veret, writing in 1834 in the *Tribune des femmes*—the first female-run newspaper—sarcastically portrayed a Malthusian bourgeois male voice called "egotistical man." Malthus represented a typical man who feared women's reproductive powers and assaulted her dignity. Not content merely to denigrate her work, tame her sons, and exploit her daughters, "egotistical man" whips himself into a frenzy over her contribution to population growth, "for I am truly afraid of those starving slaves. Almshouses, prisons, and penal colonies are not enough, and the cannons no longer destroy them since *war has become civilized!*—Oh WOMAN, your fertility is a scourge! WOMAN, *be cautious!*"[49] ("Egotistical man" also says to woman, "besides, you aren't tormented by *great ideas!*"[50])

Ever since Malthus's infamous admonition that impoverished laborers ought to remain celibate, one essential issue has dominated population debates: Is overpopulation a natural problem requiring the multitudes to exercise restraint and deprive themselves of parenting? Or is it a structural problem that can be addressed by rethinking the laws and practices that govern our economy? Malthus argued that going childless can help save the world, but his critics saw childlessness as a degrading punishment that was undeserved by the victims of industrial capitalism.

A Time Bomb

The tension between individual childlessness and structural forces became all the more powerful a century later, when a period of unprecedented growth pushed Malthusian ideas to the fore. Between 1950 and 1970, the global population grew at its fastest rate on record: 1.9 percent annually.[51] The postwar baby boom occurred in countries that had already experienced the demographic transition, while many other countries enjoyed lower mortality rates but not yet significantly lower fertility. During this period, economic growth, too, reached its peak, spurred by global catching-up to the technology frontier and by rebuilding after the destructive world wars. All together the average total global growth rate (economic and demographic growth together) reached their historic peak of 4 percent.[52]

Concern about population growth grew apace, expressed through both popular books and the muscle of the United Nations, powerful foundations, and private associations. In 1964, economist Kenneth Boulding proposed a system in which the right to reproduce is bartered on a marketplace.[53] Books including Philip Appleman's *The Silent Explosion* (1965) and Edward Stockwell's *Population and People* (1968) focused on the threat of overpopulation in impoverished nations, whereas Paul Ehrlich's influential *The Population Bomb* (1968) warned that overpopulation was an environmental threat at home as well as abroad.[54] The organization Zero Population Growth enjoyed a bright, brief period of influence, too, with its call for Americans to have not more than two children through the use of contraception, abortion, and sterilization.[55] In April 1972, the Nixon-appointed Committee on Population Growth and the American Future "denounced the outmoded tradition of American pronatalism and encouraged all Americans to embrace fertility control."[56]

On the global scale, Malthusian fears of overpopulation led to policies from coerced sterilization in the United States to China's one-child policy to quotas for inserting IUDs in India, supported by big money from Western foundations and governments.[57] Structural forces targeted individuals and their bodies in East and South Asia. The emerging demographic transition theory was not just an explanatory mechanism for declining mortality and declining fertility, but also a tool for measuring and spurring "modernization" in countries around the world.[58] These actions, which are a far bigger story than I am able to discuss here, affected millions of lives.

Critics argue that these efforts tended to ignore qualitative evidence emerging as early as the late 1950s showing that fertility could be better stabilized through a different mechanism all together: women's education.[59] Women with better education—that is, more autonomy, more knowledge of the outside world, better communication skills—are more able to exert standing within their families. In a cross-region comparison within India, the only variables with a statistically significant effect on fertility rates were female literacy rates and female employment.[60] These studies made the case that population growth might be better addressed indirectly by changing structural inequality regarding female education rather than by targeting the bodies of poor people.

The same tension between individual reproduction and structural forces occurs in twenty-first-century discussions about climate change. Critics argue that with a population exceeding seven billion, the earth has now exceeded its carrying capacity in terms of arable land, fresh water, and forests. Nutrient-rich soil erodes faster than it can be regenerated through decomposition. We are drawing down on resources rather than letting them renew. In this view, Malthus's concern about population outstripping resources has finally come true, and the stakes are higher than ever. After all, average annual demographic growth for the global population has reached an astonishing 1.4 percent over the past century, leading the population to increase from less than two billion in 1913 to over seven billion by 2012.[61] Some people dread bringing into the world a child who will contribute to climate change and suffer from severe weather and social unrest. One academic ecologist argued that "in terms of saving on resource use [childlessness is] probably about the most significant thing I could do."[62] A 2009 study found that, under current conditions, having one child "adds about 9,441 metric tons of carbon dioxide to the carbon legacy of an average female."[63] By comparison, a lifetime of increased fuel economy from twenty to thirty miles per gallon saves 148 metric tons of carbon dioxide.[64]

Still, it is a tall order to expect individuals to take climate change into account as they weigh their reproductive decisions. Madeline Ostrander, who is sympathetic to this tension, argues that it is unjust to ask individual women to shoulder the blame for the world's environmental problems through their reproductive choices: "The average woman couldn't, by herself, wrench billions of barrels of oil and tons of coal out of North American soil and sell them overseas, or stonewall policies that might have steered the U.S. economy away from fossil fuels years ago."[65] John Seager, head of Population Connections, agrees: "Trust women," he says, a shorthand for his work to ensure that women have the education, opportunities, healthcare, and reproductive control to keep populations low.[66] In this view, Malthus and his intellectual descendants unfairly blame the poor and ordinary for larger structural forces that special interests have heatedly defended, from landowners to industrialists to oil companies.

The Spanish language differentiates between "children of my own" and "children in general": *hijo*, as in *una pareja sin hijos*—"a couple without children"—and *niño*, as in *¡ese maldito niño!*—"that wretched child!" In English, the two words are not distinguished. Our children and their children are expressed with the very same word. The conflation of both concepts into the word *children* parallels our consternation when it comes to making our own reproductive lives in light of the needs of the greater population. Population poses a devilish conundrum: people, you can't live with 'em, you can't live without 'em.

Childlessness raises the existential specter that humanity itself might be better off with fewer people. The existence of childless individuals helps us to imagine dramatic answers to the persistent problems of human suffering and limited resources. Yet not having children isn't a simple solution to climate change, poverty, inequality, or existential suffering. Assuming that, contrary to Benatar, we want some people to continue the human experiment, it is not sufficient to simply have fewer of them. Forcing childlessness on someone else is an assault on their dignity and security, and voluntary childlessness for the purpose of saving the world places burdens on individuals that might better be borne by laws as well as educational and economic structures.

How any structural changes might occur can and should be debated openly as part of a democratic process. After all, any incentives that the state might create—whether to have children or not to have children—are not just a matter of money, but also a statement of values and an expression of the rights and responsibilities of citizens.[67] Here, I simply want to bring this discussion to a few conclusions.

First, childlessness plays a role in long patterns of human demography. Low growth is far more common in human history than high growth, and high growth has never been as high as we might commonly believe. If we take a longer perspective, high growth seems less sustainable. World population growth surely must slow down. After all, if the global population were to increase at the rate that it has for the last three hundred years—about 0.8 percent—the world's population would be seventy billion by 2300. Low growth characterizes the deep history of our species, and it very well may also shape our future. By the early twenty-first century, half of the world's population lived in countries with subreplacement fertility.[68] The United Nations has issued several possibilities for the century to come. The central scenario predicts that the global demographic growth rate will fall to 0.4 percent in the 2030s and to 0.1 percent by the 2070s, with −0.1 percent growth in Europe and 0.06 percent growth in the United States between 2012 and 2050.[69] While this United Nations forecast does not necessarily entail a rise in childlessness, it certainly suggests that millions of women will be childless.

Second, critics of Malthus reveal a longer history of why choosing childlessness is so painful to the childful and why childlessness could become a shorthand for selfishness, including in a secular context. The tension between the personal and the macro has a long and contentious history that cuts into deeply held convictions about the value of human life. For anti-Malthusians, the responsibilities we have to other people could not be reducible to the crunching of numbers or to finger-wagging at women or the poor. When Malthus claimed the moral high ground for childless people, he blamed women and the poor for their own situation while ignoring structural causes of suffering. The consequences of childlessness and of having children are important; at the same time, the reduction of children and of empty wombs into statistics undermines their value. In addition, other stories—the story of growth, the story of the nation, the story of human progress—existed in tension with the Malthusian story. To many, a preference for childlessness might signal a stunted view of one's body and reproductive power. Childlessness, in this light, means withholding one's contribution to the greater good, to growth, to human possibility. After all, our current billions possess an astonishing wealth of talent and creativity, and each one is imbued with human dignity.[70] Rather than dismiss this perspective out of hand, child-free individuals might try to understand and respect it.

Third, given the resource imperative of slowing human population growth to two or fewer children per person (i.e., by holding at or just below replacement) and the inevitability that some people will have more than two children, it's important that some people have zero. And it's healthy for them and for our societies to view individuals with zero children as a normal part of human culture. We don't have to embrace all of Malthus's ideas to recognize that childlessness can be useful part of a global population matrix. The relationship between the childless and the childful is an issue not of separation but of interdependence. We would be wise, as a species, if we could recognize that both having children, and not, are legitimate contributions to our continued human experiment.

9

Old and Alone

Paris, 1908. After her husband passed away on Easter Monday, sixty-five-year-old Marguerite Babineaux withered into a bitter, lonely old woman. "I don't count much for anyone," she wrote in her diary. "Everyone has a superior affection to the one they hold for me, I am worthless for anything or anybody."[1] Despite her close relationship with her nieces and grand-nieces, she became convinced that she was worthless since she did not rank first in anyone's affections. Even the servants saw her as only someone who pays and commands.[2] She lived like a *vieille fille*, an old maid who has "lived isolated in life."[3] Her sense of worth had rested solely in her marriage, and now she had nothing.

Forty-seven years earlier, Marguerite's wedding with Jules had brought nothing but joy. At such a young age—only eighteen—she had expected many years to bear children. Instead, the couple proved to be infertile; although it's not clear whether the physical issue lay with herself or her husband, Marguerite Babineaux blamed herself entirely. To her, Jules could only be a source of delight. Any connection she had to a meaningful existence she attributed to her husband. "You opened me to intelligence and to ideas," she recalled in a diary entry addressed to him. "You developed good qualities in me, you were so good, so just, so perfect that I wanted to make myself a little like you."[4] Her memories of youth provided little of substance. Reflecting on the happiness of earlier days, she recalls "I've been young, I've lived, I have had fun, I have danced, I have desired pretty things: diamonds, jewels . . . you satisfied everything."[5]

Marguerite believed that the best way to honor Jules was to continually parse her sorrow. At night she dreamed of him, of holding his hands, in dreams so vivid that she believed he still lived and begged him to return.[6] She clung to a single photograph. Any consolation she felt from attending mass was washed away upon her return to an empty home, with no one to turn toward her and smile. For her, the afterlife became nothing more than a place where she would be reunited with Jules.[7] She always needed his attentions, and still she wrote, "Although I have aged, you know well that I have remained young, 'petite' as you would say," in this need for affection.[8]

For months, Marguerite was unable to find relief in her culture, her heritage, or her own ability to create something of lasting importance in the world, to make a positive difference in the lives of others, to envision a future that was larger than her sorrows. As she faced her own mortality, she confided her doubts to her dead husband. "All is incertitude, this 'beyond' that I understand so poorly; I don't know anything about the other life; if you could, my darling friend, come in my dreams, tell me a few words that I will remember when I wake."[9] The priest's advice failed to console or convince; she looked only for words from Jules, which never came.[10] She focused only on her personal afterlife, about which she knew nothing and could plan for nothing: "What awaits me when I cease to live—is it our reunion, is it nothingness, is it even worse, another life where we do not find each other."[11]

Paris, 2003. Her neighbors described eighty-eight-year-old Marie-France as polite but aloof, perfectly coiffed in make-up and blonde dyed hair, and private about the details of her life. Only after years of civil exchanges did she show neighbors the picture of her older brother, who had died during the Great War, or reveal information about her earlier marriage. She did not mention any children. After breaking her hip in June 2003, she stayed in her seventh-floor apartment overlooking the Bastille Opera. She rejected any offer of help from her neighbors and refused to register with the city for free assistance with her domestic tasks.[12]

In August, a heat wave settled over Paris, raising temperatures into the hundreds for days and causing the deaths of 14,802 French people.[13] On August 12, having refused help again, Marie-France died alone in her apartment. After her death, city officials found that much of her life story had been a lie. Marie-France was a foundling, raised in a state orphanage and given a patriotic name at the start of the Great War. She had never had a brother. She had never been married. The shame of these facts dug in so deeply that she refused state assistance to avoid public acknowledgement of her origins.[14]

Marguerite's experience of her early widowhood and Marie-France's death represent the nightmare scenario for childless women: that we will experience a profound sense of loneliness deepened by the frailty and dependence of old age, and eventually we will die alone. These anecdotes might give pause to even the most vehemently childfree.

And yet, they are merely anecdotes. After all, Marguerite's diary was preserved only for the months after her husband died, perhaps the only time in her life in which she felt the need for the solace of writing, and not at all representative of how she would have wanted to be remembered. Marie-France was one of many for whom the structures of poverty, poor housing, and social shame had contributed to isolation and death. Yet the account that neighbors gave of Marie-France emphasized her own complicity in her isolation and death. In the months that followed, snippets of stories about individual victims—what historian Richard Keller terms the "anecdotal life"—failed to fully tell the story of how the heat wave intersected with structural forces that left some individuals more vulnerable than others.

When we start the story of a person's life with their most painful moments or horrific death, it is difficult not to emphasize their own contributions to their isolation. These anecdotes serve to sketch a biography that, says Keller, makes the victims "responsible for their own alienation" and "leads inevitably to the victims' deaths in isolation."[15] The anecdotal life simplifies: it strips a full human existence down into a few stories, it erases the complexities of urban life, and it undercuts our own relationship with these individuals.[16]

The word *childless* can work in the same way, a shorthand for isolation. It can reduce a person's life into a single attribute, a single word. It can imply that the childless are complicit in their aging, that they are at fault for becoming socially marginalized, that childlessness will come to define their lives and even their deaths.

At times, childless individuals are told that only relevant question is, "Who will take care of you when you're old?" The lives of Marguerite and Marie-France remind us to tell a story about the childless that is more consistent with their inalienable human dignity. As we become older, all the dimensions of human flourishing still apply: positive emotion, security, dignity, autonomy, fulfillment, authenticity, fairness, interpersonal connectedness, civic engagement, transcendence—and the pursuit of practical wisdom to cope with the inevitabilities of old age. Childless lives may help us all to develop the wisdom to confront life's inevitable transitions with clear and open eyes.

When Is Old Age?

When Gertrude Savile (1697–1758) felt old age creep upon her, she started to contemplate her death. She declared in her diary that her tombstone should read "Gertrude Savile, spinster" and wrote her own epitaph, which began:

> Here Lyes a Maid; who only try'd that State,
> The easiest Lott perhaps assign'd by Fate

It ended with a plea for acceptance:

> Therefore I'm better here, and let me rest in peace;
> Rake not my Ashes; let your censure sease;
> Let this thought stop your Judging; she is gon
> To answer for her faults to Him alone
> Who knew them[17]

Savile wrote these lines when she was thirty years old.

For women, the inability to reproduce has often been linked to old age. It's a milestone that is both cultural and biological. In the early modern period, age twenty-five loomed over a young woman's existence. An age of little importance today—with the exception of access to car rentals—twenty-five appeared to unmarried women of earlier centuries as a threshold with "old maid" blazoned across it. For Gertrude Savile, a well-heeled daughter of an Anglican rector who eventually commanded a comfortable annual income of 335 pounds, age twenty-five augured "insults, scorns and the thousands ills" heaped upon an unmarried woman.[18] She recorded increasing anxiety and anger as the mantle of old maidenhood draped down upon her shoulders. "An old maid is the very butt for ridicule and insults," she continued. "Miserable are women at the best, but without a protector she's a boat upon a very stormy sea without a pilot; a very cat, who, if seen abroad is hunted and worried by all the curs in the town."[19]

In 1688, thirty-four-year-old poet Jane Barker wrote about facing down this transition:

> But in this happy life let me remain
> Fearless of twenty-five and all its train,
> Of slights or scorns, or being called Old Maid[20]

However courageous and content Barker remained about her own life, she could not help but recognize that twenty-five represented a turning point. After that age, regardless of biological fertility, she was considered unlikely to become a mother.

Still, in the early modern period as today, old age was a state of mind. Past and present, childlessness in old age is a social condition as well as a biological one. William Hayley's *Philosophical, Historical and Moral*

Essay on Old Maids (1786) refused to give a firm answer on the age at which one passes into "Old Madism." Hayley noted that those who were twenty placed the age of no return at thirty, those aged thirty looked to age forty-five, whereas some fifty-year-olds placed old age at sixty.[21] The debate itself suggested that there is no moment that designated permanent childlessness.[22]

Yet childless women are still taught to listen for the ticking of the clock. After all, only one in seventy-eight American women who are childless at age thirty-nine give birth after age forty.[23] In Europe, only 0.8 percent of all women become mothers after age forty, and only 2 percent of men become fathers for the first time at that age.[24] The well-publicized twenty-first century trend in later motherhood simply means that women now have their first child after forty about as often as they did in the late 1960s. "Having it all" still runs up against biology.

Of course, the horizon may shift. Freezing eggs is only the beginning. In 2015, a company called OvaScience announced a process in which it can cultivate new eggs from a woman's egg precursor cells, located in the ovary's outer cortex. Because precursor cells are stem cells, the eggs are young and more likely to be chromosomally viable. Challenges remain in terms of egg viability, and the treatment requires two invasive operations. But the process may eventually extend the window of fertility deep into a woman's forties or beyond. Arthur Tzianabos, OvaScience's president and chief science officer, says "This is outstanding in its potential to transform into happy endings for women."[25]

Scientists have also come far in the development of ectogenesis, that is, the technology of artificial wombs. This technology has helped premature babies to survive, even those born as early as twenty-one weeks with a birth weight of one pound, six ounces. While we are a long way from being able to both conceive and bring a child to term outside of a human body, the science is further down the road than we might think.[26]

Such treatments continue the long-term historical trend of pushing the horizon of fertility ever later into a woman's life. Just as women in the twenty-first century think nothing of postponing childbirth into their thirties—the age of twenty-five is no longer a threshold—so might women of the future view age fifty or sixty as a reasonable time to feel ready for children.[27]

Until the time when we can generate a baby through an external womb, however, the age of menopause is unlikely to change. Over the last century, average age at menopause for American women has remained around 51.5.[28]

At the same time, life expectancy continues its long rise. For childless women of the past, the problem wasn't securing a comfortable old age; the problem was surviving, period. In the Middle Ages, "old age" began at forty, for those who lived that long. By age fifty, farmers' bodies were broken, textile workers had gone blind, and artisans were poisoned by lead.[29] Workers found their fingers smashed by hammers or parboiled from picking silk threads out of their cocoons. Even intellectuals found their horizons pulled in quite close to hand. Erasmus judged he was old at age thirty-seven.[30] In England in the 1600s, when late marriage became common, parish records reveal that only about 8 to 16 percent of the population lived to be sixty.[31]

Only a century ago did life expectancy for American women first surpass the average age at menopause. Those born in the 1930s—the parents of the baby boom—could expect to live for a decade past menopause. And those born in the 1970s or 1980s might outlive their eggs by twenty, thirty, or even forty or more years. In 2015, the average age of marriage for women reached 27.1 years, menopause could be expected some twenty-four years later, and the end of life at least another thirty years later, at age eighty-one.[32] Over one-third of a woman's life now takes place after childbearing ceases to be an option. While childlessness has long been common, flourishing in a childless old age—by this I mean eighty-five or ninety-five years old—is a contemporary issue.

Parents and Childless

The distinction between childless people and parents in old age has become more salient over the past century. Before the 1900s, a high fertility rate provided no guarantee that a child would live long enough to support her parents. In a preindustrial, pre-demographic transition society with high fertility (say six children per couple) and high mortality (in which a child had only a one in three chance of outliving his father), the likelihood that a father would die without a living heir is at least one in six.[33] In Britain between 1330 and 1729, 27 percent of all married men and 23 percent of all married women died without surviving children. Even for noble families, in which marriage and the production of heirs were high-stakes obsessions, 16 percent of married men died without surviving children. In later periods, the pattern continued: between 1730 and 1829, 20 percent of ducal husbands and 18 percent of wives died without surviving children, and from 1830 to 1934, 20 percent of husbands and 13 percent of wives.[34]

Over the past few centuries, however, increased life expectancy has made it unlikely that parents will outlive their children. In the United States, out of two hundred women who gave birth to a son and a daughter, only one is childless by age eighty.[35] So a childless old age now likely occurs due to childlessness. In the 2020s, we should expect a rise in childless older adults as those who came of age in the 1970s reach retirement; due to women's longevity, childless older women outnumber childless older men two to one.[36]

For all these reasons, we might worry about the predicament of childless elders. After all, children can help their aging parents financially. They can house and care for their parents. They can help their parents transition from work to retirement. And in moments of crisis, they can advocate for their parents in the face of insurance companies, medical decisions, and housing.

The childless will not have children to fulfill these roles. The worry about who will care for them intensifies when they care for their own aging parents, when the ceiling above their own mortality is blown away. One childless woman relates, "It concerns me as a I get older. When my mother was ill, I did everything for her. I don't have someone to take care of me and it concerns me."[37] So, childless lives sharply attune us to the issues of old age.

Despite all this, childless or not, the elderly face common concerns: to secure shelter, clothing, and food and to participate in the household, politics, and religion. And as they face their final years, they want to insure that they will receive a proper burial.[38] All of us will (potentially) grow old, and old age affects all facets of experience. Old age is not just an economic issue, not just an issue about retirement and the dependency ratio; it is a social and biological condition whose quality is shaped by physical and mental health, money, meaningful activities, independent living, quality care-giving, companionship and family, and a full and rich personal life narrative. Elderly people must tread the fine line between acknowledging their physical and cognitive declines and embracing such stereotypes too quickly. To add to the confusion, brains, bodies, and spirits are heterochronic, all different ages at the same time. (I'm reminded of the 104-year-old who declared to his much-younger mistress, "Today, I ate like four men, drank like six, and made love like a young man!"[39]) While childlessness more firmly places the vulnerability of aging in the forefront, old age comes to us all, and having children is no guarantee of support. Childless lives help illuminate the problems of old age and provide different ways to think about it.

A Fulfilling Third Age

Mary Chandler, the eighteenth-century poet of Bath, envisioned a secure and cozy household for her older years:

> Would heaven indulgent grant my wish
> for future life, it should be this;
> health, peace, and friendship I would share
> a Mind from business free, and care . . .
> a fortune from encumbrance clear,
> about a hundred pounds a year;
> a house not small, built warm and neat,
> above a hut, below a seat . . .
> and near some neighbours wise and good . . .
> There should I spent my remnant days,
> review my life, and mend my ways . . .
> A friendly cleric should be near . . .
> My thoughts my own, my time I'd spend
> in writing to some faithful friend . . .
> delight me with some useful book . . .
> Some money still I'd keep in store,
> that I might have to give the poor . . .
> Thus calmly see my sun decline;
> my life and manners thus refine.
> And acting in my narrow sphere,
> in cheerful hope, without one care,
> I'd quit the world, nor wish a tear.[40]

For Chandler, a fulfilling old age need not include a husband or offspring, and life after work did not require visits from children. The desire to live to a healthy old age—the very notion that old age might be a stage in life—emerged in Chandler's century. Physicians and medical theories in the 1700s began to explore what constituted a good old age and to conceive of one's old age as more than just a time to prepare for death and the afterlife.[41]

They also recognized the difference between stages of old age. Before the inevitable time of dependency and fragility, the French conceived of the "Third Age" of retirement, freedom, and leisure, which became a reality for millions in the twentieth century and resonates today.[42]

Health

The very first wish that Mary Chandler put on her list was health. The rise in the number of people ages eighty-five and older in recent decades is attributable not just to advances in the health of infants and children but also to improvements in the health and mortality of older adults.[43] In addition, longer life does not necessarily indicate a longer period of disability or need for care. The percentage of years in which people can expect to live without severe disabilities has increased.[44] How does childlessness affect health in old age?

Some studies have found that childless women suffer worse health and earlier death that the childful, even controlling for marriage and wealth. It may be the daily stresses and the lack of access to support in old age. Or, it may be because they have not experienced pregnancy and the hormonal protection it offers to cancers of the breast, uterus, and ovary. Alternatively, we might place blame on the habits of childless individuals. One study (based in Finland and the Netherlands) found that childless older people are more likely than parents to smoke, drink, and avoid exercise, perhaps because they, unlike parents, have not experienced informal social pressure to internalize healthier behaviors that carry into old age. Childless men who have lost their wives are particularly prone to health difficulties, sleepless nights, and dispirited days.[45]

But it could be, as well, that less healthy women have fewer or no children and that these less healthy women account for the higher mortality. An Australian study found that childless women experienced poorer health in their thirties and early forties. This study wasn't able to differentiate among voluntarily and involuntarily childless women, so it could be that these childless women suffered from the inability to reproduce.[46]

Nevertheless, the trend reversed for those aged over forty-five. Never-married, childless women in particular experienced better physical health and less bodily pain than mothers, which suggests that they could create a meaningful and healthy life for themselves without children. Another study of never-married Australian older women found no evidence these women were in poor physical or emotional health.[47] Childless lives remind us that health in old age may be related to developing good habits earlier in life—whether they are for the sake of children, ourselves, or someone else.[48] The condition of childlessness in our thirties, forties, and fifties shape the older adults that we become.[49]

Wealth

Chandler also wished for a comfortable income, "a fortune from encumbrance clear / about a hundred pounds a year," enough to live independently and allow her the opportunity to share her fortune with "the poor." A hundred pounds far exceeded most family's incomes but was not considered enough for a genteel lady's dowry. Yet it could afford her a library subscription and a maidservant.[50] This level of income was not common in the eighteenth century, and childless women were particularly liable to precarious dependency. Chandler's vision remained a fantasy for many.

But the mere presence of biological children was no guarantee that they would support their parents financially. In the 1700s, some French parents concluded notarized agreements with their children, something like a retirement contract, a transfer of property from the older generation to the younger in exchange for a contractual obligation that the parents would be taken care of in their old age.[51] A peasant proverb from Provence and around the Mediterranean expressed the fear of abandonment: "One father can support one hundred children, but a hundred children wouldn't know how to support one father."[52]

In the twenty-first century, however, childless women control far more wealth than mothers do as they head into retirement. In the United States, unmarried childless women enjoy 12 to 31 percent more income and 33 percent more wealth than unmarried mothers; among married couples, childlessness is consistently associated with higher income.[53] In Australia, never-married women report fewer financial difficulties than those who are or have been married.[54]

In both West Germany and East Germany, for women born between 1928 and 1955, childless women worked more and had more income than did women with children. For each child born, women worked for fewer total years—in West Germany, about five fewer years per child, while in

communist East Germany, less than a year per child. Women with no children had more income from savings and government welfare than did
women with children. The more children a woman had, the lower the income, especially during childbearing years. In neither country did state-
provided benefits for parents make up for the gap in wages. As these women
face retirement and old age, they will have very different amounts of wealth
from which to draw.[55] Again, the condition of childlessness in our thirties,
forties, and fifties shapes our old age later.

Of course, meaningful work provides benefits far beyond income.
Childless women have long known the value of finding useful work in their
older decades. In the early modern period, with no specific guidelines on
the right age to retire, it was not unusual for even the relatively well off
to work until the end of life.[56] Retirement had little meaning. And if new
opportunities arose to open a shop, they could and did, even if they were
starting off in their forties, fifties, or sixties. After decades of assisting their
parents or their siblings' families, they may have been eager for a different
stage of life. Ann Goodridge inherited a house and a large sum of money
at age forty-eight; instead of living her life at ease, she opened a shop as an
independent glover. Elizabeth Shergold was forty years old in 1714 when
she and her sister Joanna, both unmarried, inherited their mother's estate,
which allowed the sisters to set up shop in their own names. Mary Sibron
became a tradeswoman for the first time at age sixty-eight.[57]

Care

Mary Chandler's poetic vision for old age included her living arrangements
in "a house not small, built warm and neat / above a hut, below a seat . . ."—
somewhere in that broad range between a hovel and a grand estate. It was
an aspiration that childless women could not always achieve. In an era with
widespread domestic service, many in the middle class could purchase day-
to-day support. Old age without children may not have been desirable, but
for many it was not disastrous.[58] For others, though, old age provided little
security; older domestic servants themselves faced the same difficulty with
fewer resources. Domestic servants that had worked for the same household for decades could not count on support in their old age. One woman
in an eighteenth-century German state simply received a letter of good conduct stating "that she had worked for our family as a children's maid for fifty

years, and always conducted herself honorably, truly, and uprightly; she has been let go for no other reason other than that her eyes have gone bad so that she can no longer carry out her duties."[59] The letter did not mention where the woman would go. In urban areas, impoverished childless older people might secure a spot for themselves in an overcrowded hospital. They petitioned for a space by emphasizing their own infirmities. The price of admission was the surrender of all their personal possessions. Death was the only way out.[60]

Chandler's desire to live independently resonates with twenty-first century culture. How to balance this desire with the eventual need for healthcare is one of the challenges of our time. Childlessness may help us to better anticipate the isolation that has historically been a difficulty for both parents and childless alike. Childless older adults are now more likely to live on their own or in institutions, as compared with parents who are more likely to live with spouses or children.[61] If they live at home, they are more likely to use home-help services. They enter retirement institutions at lower levels of disability.[62] The increase in elders living on their own might signal neglect, but it might also show their desire for privacy and independence. Or it may simply be a symptom of the increasing number of elderly individuals due to increased longevity.

Should childless individuals lament the lack of children to care for them in their old age? Elderly parents have, at times, tended to live with their children. In one nineteenth-century English town, for instance, 80 percent of those over sixty-five who had surviving children lived with them.[63] In France, families could and did pull together to care for each other in old age, even if they possessed little property and few resources.[64] Children remain the second most important source of emotional and physical support, after partners and spouses. The burden is likely to fall on one particular child—in fact, it matters more whether you have any children at all, rather than the number of children that you have.[65]

But there was no golden age of care for the elderly, at least not in late-marriage societies.[66] Vulnerability and social isolation are not problems unique to the childless. Children emigrate or migrate; they cope with their own economic stress, marital strife, addictions, and problems. They may have nothing to give. The young respected the staying power of their elders but disdained their weakness and infirmity. The idea of children caring for their elderly parents is—to quote one demographer—"overrated."[67]

You don't have to look long for evidence of parental neglect. By the late Middle Ages, as couples married at an older age and set up their own separate households, parents no longer counted on their children for care in their old age.[68] To ensure that they would be cared for, many aged adults wrote up contracts, including with their children, in medieval England.[69] Whether or not they had grown children, widows often paid others to care for them.[70] A study of rural England between 1599 and 1796 found that only 49 percent of men and 37 percent of women aged sixty-five and older lived with a child. The urban figures were a tad higher.[71] They weren't living with their spouses, either. In rural areas, only 26 percent of women aged sixty-five and older lived with a husband, and in the cities the figure was only 10 to 15 percent![72] For women, 8 to 16 percent lived alone, and 5 percent lived with other kin.[73] And fully a third of elderly women lived with nonkin: their employers, if they were domestic servants; their lodgers and servants; or, due to the Poor Law, they might have been placed in the homes of other poor community members.[74]

Three hundred years ago, Daniel Defoe complained about uncaring children who refused to help their parents.[75] Charles Fourier wrote in his *Theory of the Four Movements* (1808), "The elderly are scorned"; they are "troublesome, mocked behind their backs, and pushed into the grave."[76] The English Poor Law, from 1601 onward, identified impoverished and isolated elderly as a population of particular concern.[77] For centuries in England, "children were irrelevant to [parents'] long-term economic security."[78] And in the early 1960s, a poll of French citizens revealed that adult children did not want their elderly parents to move in with them, unless the parents provided some kind of a service, such as caring for the grandchildren or keeping house. While 72 percent of French adults praised the expansion of nursing homes and senior communities, only 22 percent could imagine living in one. Nursing homes were "brutal," "sad," and "demoralizing" places where "the old are treated too much like animals": this was the fate to which the younger generation consigned their parents.[79] In 1998 in Britain, over 80 percent of single or widowed older individuals lived alone (regardless of parent status), and, not surprisingly, the likelihood of living alone increased with age as spouses pass away. Forty-three percent of men, and 72 percent of women aged eighty-five and older lived alone.[80]

Companionship

For Mary Chandler, living alone did not seem a burden, so long as she stayed "near some neighbours wise and good," with a cleric nearby and friends available by letter. She hoped to live out her days independently in her own house, surrounded by books and friends, and a sympathetic ear. But other childless women might fear a lack of companionship; Gertrude Savile, who bickered with family and servants, worried "What must I do when I am very old woman? As I have done while young—keep out of the world."[81]

Early modern childlessness and singlehood left many in a state of precariousness. In her late forties, Agnes Porter began to employ new strategies to manage the specter of spinsterhood. She requested that a former pupil address her letters to *Mrs.* Porter, not *Miss.* "I know, my love, I am not yet an old woman, though I begin to be rather advanced in life for a Miss. Do not suppose that being styled Mrs. will spoil my marriage—on the contrary, I may be mistaken for a jolly little widow and pop off when you least expect it."[82] Better to be a widow than a spinster in the 1790s, long before the advent of "Ms." Porter strategized, too, to find someone to grow old with. When her friend Miss Mitchell married, her rejoicing was tempered by the realization that she could no longer count on "ending my evening of life with her."[83] She feared "the ills that singlewomen are exposed to, even at the hour of death, from being the property of no one."[84]

Poet Mary Masters did not regret love, nor a specific man, but perhaps missed companionship, social standing or a sense of belonging, or freedom from financial constraints. She wrote to a friend that "my circumstances do really require an addition to make my situation easy, and place me in the happy! happy! state of independency." Her requirements remained modest: "Were I a villager near some post-town in a peaceful retirement, I could live to God and myself, and enjoy the correspondence of two or three sincere friends. I think I should be then as happy as this world could make me: I should be as fond of my apartment as a hermit of his cell, and care seldom to quit it: There I would wait the last important hour with content and cheerfulness, while I was daily making a due preparation for it. This is the most ardent desire of . . . M. Masters."[85]

As it happened, early modern childless women like Chandler had a wide range of networks represented in their wills: parents, siblings, nieces, nephews, aunts, uncles, in-laws, cousins, pastors, employers, godchildren, friends, land-ladies, servants.[86] The same is true in recent decades. After forty years of marriage, Joséphine Bruyère, the poet and academic, reported that she and her husband "continue to walk on the path of life and we continue to share everything, as an old couple who loves each other."[87] She did not lack for family with which to share her legacy. She dedicated the memoir to Louis, to her sister, and to all her nieces, nephews, and grand-nieces and nephews. She wanted to share not just her career but her life, to let her family know "what the life of their aunt and great-aunt was before and after her marriage with their Uncle Louis."[88] The writing itself was a "salutary exercise" for her, as she focused on the essential in her life.[89] She continued to grow and to find new priorities. At age sixty-six, after a long period of reflection and conversation with a trusted cleric, she rejoined the Catholic Church.

Not surprisingly, many childless people strategize to avoid isolation long before old age arrives. While childless men and women have smaller social nets than parents do, they do not experience more loneliness or less life satisfaction.[90] Childless women in particular tend to be successful at creating alternative ties with family and friends.[91] They have closer ties with their siblings and more frequent ties to their nieces and nephews.[92] They are just as likely to volunteer as parents are. In fact, women who never married are more likely to volunteer or to be involved with church activities than are older married women with children.[93]

As we've seen already, childlessness doesn't seem to be a factor in the increasing depression and loneliness of old age; the decline in health and social interaction is enough to make old age difficult.[94] Childlessness doesn't make people happier, or less happy. Grandparents may certainly enjoy spending time with their grandchildren, but childless people also find joy and happiness in their relationships.[95] Aging is a process of social marginalization, but it need not be so stark. Some, whether they are childless or parents, have internalized the notion of elder marginalization, and therefore refuse help when it is available. An eighty-one-year-old man interviewed by social workers in the early 1960s, "not having any more family, nor any real friends, has become reclusive, hides his misery, and is humiliated at the thought of asking for anything."[96] By contrast, those with more close friends have more positive attitudes toward death.[97] Loneliness is cultural and spiritual, not simply a result of childlessness.

As with other issues, the difference between voluntary or involuntary childlessness affects perceptions of well-being. Involuntarily childless older women felt more vulnerable and alone than they had earlier in life, especially without children to care for them. A 1993 study in which women self-identified as either voluntarily or involuntarily childless found that women who self-identified as involuntarily childless rated their happiness and satisfaction with life lower, and their depression scores were higher.[98] Even those with siblings and nieces and nephews wished they had children to support them.[99] As Ms. Grant related "See, like when I was a young girl and I didn't have no children . . . it really didn't bother me that much. But as I got older it kind of hit me more. And now that my husband's gone, like, I do wish I had a like, somebody of my own."[100] That said, voluntarily childless women and mothers with close ties to their children had similar ratings for well-being. Once again, the difference between involuntary and voluntary childlessness was key.

So, parents and childless older adults may be able to cope with aging equally well. The childless may not have the children who will take on the responsibility of providing care over years or decades, but they have other social, emotional, and financial resources that they have cultivated for decades.[101] The notion that childlessness inevitably leads to a sad and lonely old age is just a myth.

Parting

A brick house in a small village in Hampshire in the coldest month of the year: February, 1938. Sidney Webb lay recovering from a stroke he had suffered two weeks earlier. In another corner of the house, Beatrice Webb reflected once more on a life well spent. Over and done were the days of uncovering the labyrinth of local government, of promoting trade unions and reimagining political systems. Beatrice's cramped handwriting recorded, "As a young woman of twenty-eight I heard around me a whispering, occasionally openly said: 'What a failure she has made of her life.' As an aged woman of eighty there is a tuneful chorus . . . singing of the successful achievement of the Webbs. When one is about to quit the stage of life, it is consoling to hear the applause of a great audience. Alas! for human vanity in its most hairless form of delight in flattery. Is it wrong or is it right?"[102] Webb ruminated on the problem of equating one's worth with one's accomplishments; one's soul risks dwelling in vanity of accomplishments whose worth has eroded with time.

In a brighter moments Webb wrote, "Today we have no reason for discouragement except the coming of old age, which being inevitable and universal it is cowardly to resent."[103] But in bleaker times she grappled with uncertainty over how to value her long and intensely engaged life. Over the course of her lifetime, moral and physical certitude had been shaken to the roots.

> How can the human mind acclimatize itself to the insecurity and uncertainty of this terrible doctrine of relativity, latent in all modern science long before Einstein applied it to the astronomical universe? It is a most disconcerting conclusion, that there is no absolute truth. . . . Is morality a question of taste, and truth a question of relative standpoints? And are all tasks and all standpoints equally valid? What, in fact, is my own standpoint from which I survey the world of the past and the future? For it is exactly these questions which I shall have to answer in the last chapter of my book! And it is this point in space and time—the exact point at which I stand—that seems to me so singularly bleak and bare, so featureless.[104]

As Webb's interest in the old causes waned, E. M. Forster's descriptions of an old woman in A Passage to India resonated: "The twilight of the double vision," "a spiritual muddle is set up."[105]

Visits to old places recalled only ghosts. In 1937, at age seventy-nine, she returned to the old family home, where she and her eight sisters had learned to read and where she had shepherded her father in his last illness, now a sanitarium sheltering 260 tuberculosis patients. She wandered freely through the house and garden, amid the beds of resting and restless patients. Webb felt the passage of time: "To outlive one's own generation, to realize that even the memory of these men and women has passed away—well, it adds to the melancholy of old age, to which is added, in our case, the consciousness of decay in our own civilization, our own race, our own class, of the beloved and oneself!"[106]

A visit to London that December left her similarly cold.

> To me, the old home with the roaring traffic, facing the Thames river with its barges and bridges, the old servant and the old friends and the old old gossip about the Labour world, was like ghost-land, and old Mrs Webb of eighty being the oldest ghost of the lot. I was glad to get back to our silent and comfortable cottage home with my old man. We too are ghosts of our

former selves haunting this mad century with its tragic happenings; but we are happy ghosts, loving each other and always with a job in hand, like two aged craftsmen.[107]

Two months later, Sidney had a stroke, and the partnership never resumed work. Beatrice passed away first, on April 30, 1943.

Eventually, at the cellular level, our bodies break down. Aging occurs in part due to the stresses and insults of everyday life and, in part, through "programmed senescence." Every day, we constantly encounter toxins, our cells turn abnormal, and we suffer from injuries. For decades, our bodies actively strive to repair this constant damage, and can do so remarkably well. Then, by our mid-twenties or early thirties, for reasons not fully understood, our bodies no longer retain the ability to fix themselves. Slowly, inexorably, the damages to our cells are no longer repaired. Our cells divide only so many times before they stop reproducing and eventually die. The countdown to a dying cell, made physical in the ever-shortening telomeres at the end of our chromosomes, occurs in each one of the sixty trillion cells in our human body.[108] Over time, we grow brittle and inflexible, and we deteriorate and die.

For our lives to have meaning, they must come to an end. We pass through fixed stages in life—infancy, childhood, adolescence, adulthood, menopause, old age—in which time is the ultimate scarce and therefore valued resource.[109] Childless lives, in which old age and mortality are frequent conversations, attune us all the more closely to this reality.

Beatrice Webb's reflections in old age provide the opposite of the anecdotes about Marguerite Babineaux's painful widowhood and Marie-France's lonely death: a good old age, an old age that we might hope for, childless or not, not because she was in perfect health (she was not), or never experienced loss and disappointment, or had an entirely attractive set of beliefs (decay of race!), but because she was a "happy ghost" ending life with Sidney "like two aged craftsmen," connected and yet disconnected with her times, comfortable and quiet, proud of her work and ready to let it go.

10

Legacy

One day a few years ago, I decided to show Grandma something new. We sat on her couch together. I held up the little magic box, slid my fingers across the screen, and considered which button to press. Email? Internet? These things didn't interest her. How about the camera? About half of her living space fit into the viewer: in the foreground a walking cane and brown recliner, toward the back a single bed, and on the wall, photographs of six generations. Foreground and background being distinct by about three feet. I took a picture to illustrate. But what if you press here? The screen swiveled around to show the two of us. "Mercy!" She laughed with astonishment and I immediately hit click. Now the screen showed her hand over her mouth, her brown eyes in squinted crescents, her whole being a little bit in motion. "You just press here?" she asked. *Click.* "Well I'll be." In the photo her face leans in close, mouth slightly open in study, in the corner her bright blurry finger.

I have been thinking a lot about legacy these days. My grandmother's passing and funeral have pushed such thoughts unavoidably to the front. Her simple, powerful lived philosophy offered an answer to David Benatar's claim that we are better off easing humanity out of existence. It came down to this: meet the love of your life, raise children, help out with the grandkids and great-grandkids, and accept the pain of life as part of something bigger than yourself. There is a lot of wisdom in this. It's a specific answer to a more general question: How do we create a bond between the living, the dead, and those not yet born? How do we love the world—and preserve it—even as we seek to renew it?

My grandmother's life also raises the question of how to carry on a legacy without having children. If part of human flourishing is our own experience of transcendence and the wisdom to grapple with our place in human history, we might consider the insights that childless lives provide to our ideas of legacy.

What Happens to Your Stuff When You Die?

By the time my grandmother died, she had given away most of her belongings. All that was left after ninety-five years fit into a one-room apartment. I claimed a pair of ornate brass lamps. They're hefty pieces, and as I gently laid one down in the back seat of my car, I noticed a sticky note on the bottom. The handwriting belonged to my Aunt Midge—my grandmother's eldest daughter—who had passed away eight years earlier. It read, "These are for Midge."

When I arrived back home and brought the lamps into the house, I realized that I had nowhere to put them. I already owned enough lighting, more than I ever used. Three solutions: add redundant stuff to my current collection, give away other perfectly good lamps, or discover dark places that needed more light. Determined not to add to the clutter, I took one lamp to my office and put the other in the basement by the laundry. Problem solved, stuff put in its place, connection preserved. But only temporarily. What will happen to these lamps when I die?

Montauban, France, 1787. Anne Silhes, a seamstress, wrote her will. With no children—at least none that survived her—she left her bed, curtains, and armoire to her elder sister Jeanne. Anne had inherited these pieces from her mother, who presumably had left other goods to Jeanne, perhaps a table. Anne stipulated that if Jeanne were to sell the armoire, she would need to give half of the proceeds to a younger sister named Guillamette.[1] Over the years, the sisters had probably exchanged loans of cash, food, and fuel during times of mismatched fortunes, when one was up and the other down.[2]

Most childless folks did not have the luxury of worrying about where their money would go. The stevedore unloading coal from a barge and the woman hawking cheese out of a basket that she hoisted on her shoulders were unlikely to possess property at the end of life. For those lucky ones who did, in Montauban as elsewhere, childless testators chose their heirs from a web of relations: their spouses, their siblings, their nephews or nieces. If they were rich, they might choose a godchild, a niece, or a younger nephew (the elder nephew already stood as heir to his own parents).[3] When potter Antoine Bescomes was conscripted into Napoleon's army, he made a will leaving his property to his nephew and godson.[4] Other departing soldiers chose their brothers or their friends—rarely their parents.[5] But when Catherine Pradel prepared to enter the order of St. Ursula, she gave her mother her rights in her father's estate.

In addition, childless individuals, far more frequently than those with children, often chose heirs who weren't related by blood: servants, employers, landlords. The childless in France could arrange, with the help of a notary, to transfer their wealth to a child that they adopted from friends, neighbors, or kin, even though the practice went counter to French customary law.[6] Even without these arrangements, those who were poor and unmarried were just as likely to leave their few belongings to a friend or a neighbor as to a family member.[7] In many cases, elderly and ill testators chose to repay their debt of dependency by leaving their savings to the people who had sheltered them. Jeanne Sauret, a widowed farm servant, spent her final illness bedridden in her employer's house. She left everything—probably some linens, possibly a watch—to her employer's children.[8] Marguerite Bessede made the arrangement even more explicit: she agreed to make her cousin her heir "on condition that [he] come to the aid of the said Bessede with food and care if she be in need of it."[9] In many cases, the land and property of a childless couple reverted back to the original family. In eighteenth-century France, Mathieu Baume brought land to his marriage with Elizabeth Bonnand, while she provided the house. When he died, she retained the use of the land until her death, when it returned to his brothers and sisters. The house reverted to her family—with the exception of one room, set aside for the shelter of his sister.[10] The young and the old had little to leave, but they used their wills to fulfill obligations, assert their independence, and shape their legacies.

In the 1700s as in centuries past, artisans crafted consumer goods intended to last for generations. Both rich and poor lived among material products that they had inherited and expected to survive beyond them.[11] In a family of scarcity, such gifts carried enormous weight. Jewelry was rare, watches easily pawned, photographs not invented yet. Furniture, by contrast, conferred a modicum of status and permanence.[12] Anne Silhes did not put provisos on the future selling of the bed—perhaps because it was so unlikely, the bed being the last thing a poor woman was likely to sell. She expected that her furniture would be welcome and needed, and transferred again after Jeanne's death.

Already in 1700s, however, goods were being made more cheaply and affordably, but wore out more quickly and went out of fashion sooner.[13] Consumers bought goods to use them, not to store value; consumption and investment became separated. Value came in appearance rather than the material's intrinsic worth. Consumers avidly purchased semi-luxuries, ones made out of cotton, steel, and varnish instead of silk, gold, and exotic wood.[14]

The flow of items through a house increased, as did the potential for self-fashioning through consumer goods. And as life expectancies lengthened, potential heirs bought their own stuff long before they could inherit. Prior to my grandmother's death, I had lived on my own for twenty years, and I had acquired eight lamps. "Today," writes historian Jan de Vries, "most people, after a lifetime of frenetic consumer activity and prodigious expenditures, die with personal possessions of inconsequential resale value."[15]

If these objects are worthless, then perhaps critical theorist Michael Cobb is right when he suggests that our desire to leave an inheritance is an extension of Karl Marx's idea of the fetishization of otherwise worthless commodities.[16] Perhaps as we drown in a tide of our own possessions we place too much value in material objects that came to us from beloved family members. Perhaps my grandmother's brass lamps are causing me to care too much about stuff and become distracted from the problems of a commodity-driven society. After all, if I were to let go of them (which, let's face it, aren't being used in any significant way), I'd still treasure my grandmother.

And yet, my grandmother's lamps seem to contain, somehow, her attention and solid characteristics.[17] I love bringing them into my spaces; their particular shape and glow remind me of the tidy apartment where we played cards and looked at photos. I wish that my Aunt Midge had lived to own them herself. The inconsequential resale value doesn't bother me.

For some objects, however mass produced and lacking in market value they may be, our relationships are complex. It is not only because they are intrinsically valuable that we treasure them. We care about what happens to our wealth and possessions, not always because of their material worth (though for some that is considerable), but because of our human need to be loved and remembered. Some physical objects are not ephemeral, but, in fact, are older than us and will outlast us. So it's only natural that we might wish to leave our possessions to someone who cares about us, whether or not it is our own child. We want to be valued and remembered.[18] I don't mind the mild fetishization of a reasonable number of objects. At the same time, securing legacy is not going to happen through the material objects I possess.

Kinship

My friend Sarah got a surprise when she saw her father and step-mother's annual Christmas card. They had decided to include a photograph of themselves surrounded not by their own children, but by their grandchildren, the offspring of her brother and step-sisters. No doubt they saw in these youngsters the promise of generations to come and a sign of their own continued prosperity—and who can blame them? Yet, for Sarah, who herself is childless, the photograph contained an undercurrent of sadness, for her own contributions to the emotional life of the family over the course of decades had been erased. It made her feel as though she didn't exist in her own family.

We humans are unique among primates in our ability to maintain ties to kin whom we do not see every day.[19] Kin provide an answer to the existential question, "Who are we?"[20] They show where we come from, whether we would choose it or not; they help us feel like we are part of something larger than ourselves. If we are lucky, they provide us with a history and a geography, they fill in the gaps. Through our kin, we can extend and compress our social networks; we know that we need not be a stranger when we arrive in a strange land.[21] Ever since our ancestors rapidly migrated across the globe tens of thousands of years ago, kin have allowed us to return to who we are. When we meet with our kin, we talk about how we are related and about those who are no longer here. We offer a meal and a place to rest, we tell our old stories and exchange our new ones, we invite them to join us on the next stage.[22] Far from a relic of our ancient heritage, kinship has shaped and continues to shape the structures of our economies, politics, education, and emotional lives.[23]

We often squeeze these rich relationships into a single metaphor: the family tree, the line stretching back through parents and grandparents with ourselves squarely planted at the bottom. The tree is as old as the Hebrew Bible. During the early modern period, western European families came to focus even more strongly on lineage, particularly paternal lineage, as a result of increased urban mobility, religious upheaval, and a greater emphasis on planning to achieve personal and family goals—and just as childlessness became more common.[24]

But I must admit, I chafe under the tree metaphor. The tree is not neutral: it presents a specific understanding of kinship. The tree overstates its claim. It appears sharply contained and unidirectional, adrift in time from the rest of humanity. It prunes away some relationships and fosters others.[25] It is a social fiction that denies instability and obscures moments of transition.[26] If we conceive of our relationship to each other as a single line, then we lose everything else. And the childless person spells the end of the line.

I resist the tree analogy both because I know that it is false and because I fear that it is true. The danger is not just metaphorical. Eighty-three-year-old involuntarily childless Ms. Ernst worried, "I don't think I made that much of an impression [in life]. Now, that's one case where, if you had children, you'd feel like your children are carrying on your thoughts and all, but if you don't have children, who else will care about what I thought?"[27] Who indeed will care about my ideas, my papers, my scribbles? And more than that: perhaps Ms. Riggs stated the problem most clearly when she lamented, "What's happening is our group is gradually dying off. Whereas family goes on, doesn't it? There is a continuity and a love and a warmth. When you have children and grandchildren, families go vertically. The interests remain like a tree. And it's the vertical aspect of the family which helps to perpetuate it."[28]

I can't help but wonder, What will happen to my accumulated family knowledge, like the story of my Russian great-grandmother who sailed to America with "Chicago" pinned to her dress? And what about the tangible reminders (which I still can't let go of), like the trunk she brought with her on a steamer from the Old World that sits now, over a hundred years later, in my entryway? My siblings and I are three unique combinations of our family strands, all childless (to date). The familiar traces—my mother's smile, my grandfather's ears, my grandmother's goofball trait—will melt away.

Moreover, ending the family line may also feel like a rejection of what our ancestors endured and sacrificed so that we could exist. For many women of color, the choice to remain childless conflicts with the legacy of women who, for generations, exercised little or no choice over their reproduction. Enslaved women were raped or coerced into having children to suit the demands of their owners and raised these children while also suffering in the fields and under the whip of white owners.[29] Over the years, women of color have raised their daughters with survival skills to navigate discrimination, low-paying work, and sexual harassment.[30] Choosing childlessness raises the question of how to best honor one's own ancestors.

Fear of ending the line is ancient and widespread. As we have seen, prior to the twentieth century, parents could easily outlive all of their children. In Britain between 1330 and 1729, as many as one in four parents died without surviving children.[31] If we take into account the high percentage who never married, the specter of childlessness reaches deeply into family genealogies, snatching away real and imagined heirs, complicating hopes of a family legacy. Only a timely intervention—remarriage, polygamy, adoption, or an inheritance strategy that included brothers as well as sons—could preserve the linear chain.[32] Otherwise, the family line ended.

Some flexibility and imagination is in order, then, when we contemplate the family tree of the childless. Fortunately, humans have developed many systems for managing kin—through male lines, through female lines, through male and female simultaneously, back and forth across gender lines.[33] For some—including English speakers, the Khoisan of southern Africa, and the Eskimos of the Arctic—nearness of kin depends more rigorously on the linear tree. Parents, siblings, and children are near; aunts and uncles, cousins, and nieces and nephews are further out. But many societies around the world sort relations into a pattern called *crossness*, with parallel and cross kin, as illustrated in Figure 10.1. The rules—who is close and who is far—apply differently. In certain Crow and Omaha family systems, the father's brothers are called *father* and the mother's sisters are called *mother*; the children of all of our mothers and all of our fathers are our sisters and brothers. And, if we are female, then the children of our all of sisters (whether they'd be considered sisters or female cousins to English speakers)—well, they are our sons and daughters, too.[34]

So, we do not need to focus on lineage and descent. We could visualize families as part of a many-limbed tree, one that includes branches backward to include the line of mothers as well as fathers, a thickening set of ancestors that doubles every generation. Add in aunts and uncles, and the ancestors grow into a dense grove of kin. Our kin extend laterally, through siblings and cousins, not just through a generational chain.[35] The childless person entwines with brothers, sisters, cousins, nieces, and nephews, embraced in a sinuous vine with no beginning and no end.

Lest we romanticize this branching tree, we'd do well to recall a saying among the peasants of Montauban: *A qui Diu nou da maynadyes, la disable qy'ou da nebouts*—"To whom God does not give children, the devil gives nephews."[36] Kinship is both a biological relationship and a social act. It is embedded our brains as well as our bodies, for it requires language and abstract concepts to imagine a relationship with someone living far away or in the distant past or future.[37] Blood ties are not enough.

Anyone who has ever attended a family reunion knows that we enact kinship differently with different people. In 1928, at age seventy, Beatrice Webb attended a gathering hosted by her sister Kate, along with some 150 nieces,

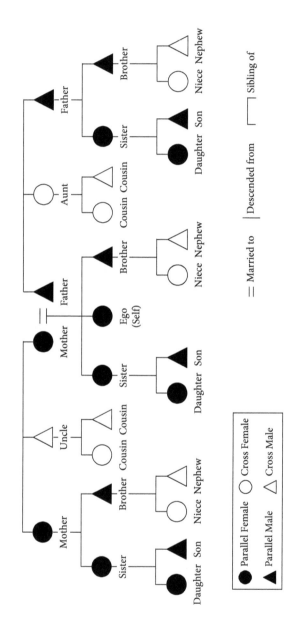

Figure 10.1 Cross and parallel kin. Note that in this system, the childless ego (self) may have daughters and sons.

nephews, and grand- and great-grand nieces and nephews, most of whom she barely knew:

> Among the lot there is an ex-chorus girl, an ex-duchess, half a dozen peers' sons, a baronet, an out-of-work actor, a shorthand typist, an old curiosity dealer. . . . But there is no great personal distinction—not so much as in the group of parents, the nine Potter girls and their ten mates. . . . My relation to all of them is "dutiful," not affectionate, and unless they want to see us, or I think they do, I certainly don't want to see them. Kate is the real centre of the Richard Potter family life, in so far as it has a centre. . . . Kate is loved, I am liked and Rosy is tolerated. So fare the remnant of the Richard Potter sisters in the minds of their descendants.[38]

Kinship makes a relationship possible, but it doesn't offer any guarantees. It is, historian Judith Bennett writes, "a gentle web with some strong strands and others weak or broken."[39]

Kinship also encompasses nonblood relations, notably spouses, in-laws, and adopted children. The Western rise in childlessness requires more deliberate practices of developing kin, of creating relationships in which sharing extends not just to those who are "near" in sense of the Western system of kin—for we lack not only children but often siblings as well, and therefore have fewer nieces, nephews and cousins—but to those who share other bonds. But this is not new. After all, chimps, too, often lack maternal siblings and form alliances with nonkin for the purpose of sharing food, helping in fights, and grooming.[40] We humans adeptly modify our definitions of kin to suit circumstance and overlay social kin on official systems; we can do so now to provide the family we need, even without children.[41]

We could complement the image of the tree with the predominant metaphor of our times: the web. The edges connecting the vertices in the web can capture the variability in the intensity and emotionally complexity of relationships. And the *digitized* web can capture the fact that our network develops rapidly over time. We foster some connections and allow others to lapse. New connections emerge when we change location, discover new friends, or reproduce. And they end, or at least they transform, as we move away, focus on others, or confront death. This metaphor loses some of the hierarchical clarity of the tree, but it diminishes the impact of any one gap and envisions instead a growing, pulsating, multicolored network of relations, its nodes winking on and off.

The Child

Of course, we might wish to leave behind on earth something greater than a legacy of goods or relations. For many, raising children provides a pathway to the transcendent, a connection to someone outside of oneself, and a commitment to ensure the health of the world in which that child will grow up and grow old.

Not so fast, protests my friend Simon. For too many people, he says, raising children is an all-to-easy shortcut to transcendence, a way to avoid thinking about life's ultimate meaning. We have a child, and connection to the future will continue: what other spiritual growth is needed? Indeed, this is one reason that older parents find it so hard to swallow their children's decision not to have children. Without grandchildren (and so on), their own access to, or investment in, transcendence may seem to be cut off. The state of childlessness forces us to confront the issue of transcendence with greater deliberation.

No doubt, the impulse to secure a legacy contains more than a little hubris. When we try to preserve the things we value for the sake of the future, we rail against our physical limitations. As philosopher Samuel Scheffler puts it, valuing something is "a way of trying to control time," to fight against mortality and fortune.[42] In the act of preservation we defiantly claim, "things may come and things may go, but *we* decide what matters."[43] And what, exactly, is worth preserving?

Wendell Berry critiques the "strange, almost occult yearning for the future" evident in so much of our daily lives.[44] "Politicians understand very well the power of the promise to build a better or more prosperous or more secure future. Parents characteristically strive and sacrifice to make a better or more secure future for their children. Workers work toward a secure future in which they will retire and enjoy themselves. Our obsession with security is a measure of the power we have granted the future to hold over us."[45] For Berry, this obsession ironically blinds us to the true needs, physical and spiritual, of those who will follow us. As written in the Tao, "Chase after money and security / and your heart will never unclench."[46] It's a truncated future that looks only, at best, to the next generation or two and speaks to our deepest fears rather than our greatest aspirations.

In this light, the imagined child of the future reflects our own weaknesses for hubris, security, and even greed. It is all too tempting, argues literary critic and queer theorist Lee Edelman, to spin visions of future children that unquestioningly and narcissistically affirm our own ideas and power structures. Edelman provocatively suggests that this kind of "reproductive futurism," is (in Andrew J. Counter's formulation) "the master-ideology of Western civilization, the very ground upon which the social and political order stands."[47] Edelman argues forcefully against the "reproductive futurism" bound up in any political vision that focuses on the image of the Child. The "Ponzi scheme of reproductive futurism" embodied in politics both left and right "remains, at its core, conservative insofar as it works to *affirm* a structure, to *authenticate* social order" through its "pious sentimentality" toward the Child, which is not to be confused with attentiveness to the needs of actual children.[48] For Edelman, pronatalists are narcissists who misplace their self-regard as love for their state, their nation, their family.[49] The Child is a fantasy that shapes the logic of political thought in the public discourse.

For instance, Counter argues, the bourgeois cult of the Child that arose in early nineteenth-century French literature, "in which affectionate domestic relations between parents and children came to be understood as the ultimate horizon of human happiness," celebrated the Child and the affection and virtue that came with family life.[50] In addition to the aesthetic soppiness, the bourgeois cult of the Child contained a political edge, a dagger aimed at the breast of the aristocracy, which in the postrevolutionary era seemed incapable of parental care or of true concern for the French nation.[51] For Counter, reproductive futurism is anti-elitist, rooted in anti-aristocratic origins formed in the revolutionary era.[52] Politically, the enemy of reproductive futurism was embodied in the Bourbon line, which struggled to produce a male heir.

All this changed, however, in 1820, with the birth of the "miracle child," Henri, whose father, the Duc de Berry (a nephew of Louis XVI), had been assassinated seven months earlier. This specific child was celebrated just as the abstract Child became a figure of hope for the Bourbon line after decades of revolutionary upheaval. The celebration of the Duc de Bordeaux represents the Bourbon regime's bid to claim the bourgeois ideal for itself, not just in having a child (which, of course, had been a celebrated event in monarchies for many centuries), but also in the representation of the Child as part of the domestic tableau. The poetry celebrating the birth of Henri was hackneyed and trite, but that very banality masked the attempted reassertion of power: "By pointing to a presumptively universal good with no precise content, the words *espérance* and *avenir* contribute to that illusory sense of postpolitical unanimity."[53]

Edelman and Counter's critique of the clichéd yet potent image of the Child deployed across the political spectrum is intended to provoke. (Edelman also characterizes the claim "It takes a village to raise a child" as a "terroristic adage.")[54] For Edelman, it is a dangerous fantasy that justifies violence and exclusion toward those who do not participate.[55] In a deliberately confrontational argument, he interprets the 1998 murder of Matthew Shepard, killed for being homosexual, as the outcome of reproductive futurism. With the Child as our political lodestar, "somewhere, someone else will be savagely beaten and left to die—sacrificed to a future whose beat goes on, like a pulse or a heart—and another corpse will be left like a mangled scarecrow to frighten the birds who are gathering now, who are beating their wings, and who, like the drive, keep on coming."[56] Even if we reject the extremes of Edelman's argument, the imagined future Child forces us to confront our assumptions about the kind of legacy we'd like to leave and how we talk about it now.

The Human Afterlife

With these criticisms in mind, how can we salvage a commitment to the future? Philosopher Samuel Scheffler claims that we must look to the human future to make meaning in our lives. Scheffler invites us to imagine a doomsday scenario: he writes, "Suppose you knew that, although you yourself would live a normal life span, the earth would be completely destroyed thirty days after your death in a collision with a giant asteroid. How would this knowledge affect your attitudes during the remainder of your life?"[57]

Few among us would be unmoved. We would lament the deaths of loved ones. And we would mourn the disappearance of the "institutions, practices, activities, and ways of life" that we care about.[58] Without a belief that humanity will live beyond us, Scheffler says, our emotional investment in our everyday activities would weaken. Our desire to bear and raise children would diminish. Our attachment to projects—our interest in teaching or writing—would dry up. The only activities that we might pursue with the same relish would relate to our direct comfort and pleasure.[59]

Yet, in the course of our lives, we pursue all of these activities despite knowing that we are in fact mortal and that we won't live to see all of their consequences. We function quite well despite the knowledge that everyone alive today will very soon be dead.

In other words, Scheffler tells us, the existence of a human afterlife—knowing that human generations will live after us—"matters more to us than our own continued existence."[60] In fact, "the coming into existence of people we do not know and love matters more to us than our own survival and the survival of people we do know and love."[61] And this existence of a human afterlife is more fundamentally important to the meaning-making of our lives than any one particular project or activity we might undertake. Scheffler continues:

> Humanity itself as an ongoing, historical project provides the implicit frame of reference for most of our judgments about what matters. Remove that frame of reference, and our sense of importance—however individualistic it may be in its overt content—is destabilized and begins to erode. We need humanity to have a future if many of our own individual purposes are to matter to us now. Indeed . . . we need humanity to have a future for the very idea that things *matter* to retain a secure place in our conceptual repertoire.[62]

If we believe Scheffler, then we will want to embrace the future of humanity. How do we care about the future in a way that avoids the banality, the kitsch, and the latent violence of "reproductive futurism"? Childless lives suggest three ways to connect with the future without placing such a heavy burden on reproductive acts.

First, connections can occur through our own mentoring of young people. Recall the tailor Louise Le Mace, who cultivated a relationship with her apprentices, the next generation of tailors. As she guided her apprentices to select the fabric and measure the client, she continued a cycle of generativity did not need to include her own biological children. She modeled a certain kind of productive generativity, one engaged in nurturing future generations. Contrary to what we might assume, research into adult generativity development shows no difference between women with children and those without.[63]

This kind of connection is a theme for many childless individuals. Violette Farge, the former nun, reflected, "Living, isn't it among other things the transmission of life?" She fondly recalled a teacher she encountered as a girl: "Not having yourself given birth in the flesh, I think I can write that the generations of women that you have formed have become in their turn, in their own ways, pedagogues, mothers who have given life to the values that 'Mademoiselle' had taught them."[64] Farge planned to continue swimming until age one hundred and writing until the end: "These texts . . . it's my heritage. The link between us."[65]

In a similar vein, Mary Capper found that her calling as a Quaker minister helped her to indirectly nurture the next generation. In a letter written in Birmingham in 1824, she advised a young mother, whom Capper had known since childhood "in the simplicity of a school-girl," in raising her own child. "Parental duties, &c., make a Christian's life serious and important," she wrote, with that telling "&c." that includes, tacitly, her own transferred parenting and the seriousness of purpose it gave to Capper herself.[66]

Second, we might look beyond the individuals and institutions that we ourselves can influence. We might instead consider the ideas and questions we want to keep on the table, even if we can't control how they will be explored or what future generations might make of them.

After a lifetime of searching, Parisian activist-seamstress Suzanne Voilquin did not claim to have a solution to women's lower social status. In fact, she wrote in the 1866, "Of all the women existing in our time none have been able to study our sex enough to understand its needs. . . . All that women can do right now is experiment, in view of the future, at their own risk and peril."[67] But women who take this path "hover *just the same* over the abyss!"[68] The Saint-Simonian circle had discovered free love, but the rest of the world continued to punish and ostracize women for sexual deviation, and Voilquin had learned to mistrust men's motives when they declared women free to love. Her own husband had given her syphilis, which likely caused her sterility, and later left her for another woman in order to have children. Despite Voilquin's years as a newspaper editor and a midwife, she did not feel that she had the tools to help other women understand and improve their own situations.

With so much doubt regarding her own direct impact on the problems she cared deeply about, Voilquin found comfort in anticipating the distant future, in staying up late with her companions dreaming about what it might be like. Could she have imagined Beatrice Webb, Violette Farge, or the women of the twenty-fourth century? In Egypt, she felt a sense of awe from standing before the pyramids of Giza. "It was hard to breathe," she writes, "contemplating the mysteries that these pyramids contain. . . . And how many generations will come after us to visit them again before they've said their final word!"[69]

And so, Scheffler's scenario can help childless individuals to cope with their own mortality and the fact that they are not leaving behind biological descendants. The underpinning for meaning is not our own children, but rather the continuation of humanity and of the questions we care about. It's not just that future generations depend on us to provide a healthy planet; it is that we depend on them to give our lives meaning. And so our obligations to them are not burdens but opportunities to deepen our commitments to the future and thereby to make ourselves whole.[70] At the same time, if Scheffler is correct, then I owe a debt of gratitude to those who bear children, for without them I could not anticipate the flourishing of future generations. It's the ultimate story of which I am part that is not of my own choosing, the pinnacle of transcendent interpersonal connectedness. We might call this the reproduction of wonder.

Indeed, we can turn Scheffler's scenario around. Our existence, too, interplays with the generations that preceded us. Their lives had more meaning because of us, because of who they vaguely imagined us to be. We are, in the words of filmmaker Ava DuVernay, our ancestors' wildest dream.[71] And they left for us the human legacy of an inhabited world with a richness of institutions, values, and debates.[72] The fact that humans require a long period of development spurs adults to greater personal maturity and leads them to ask important questions, develop ethical systems, and found greater institutions.[73] "It is not thanks to children that our species has survived," writes Robert Pogue Harrison. "It is thanks to their parents, teachers, leaders, and sages."[74] We require a love of the world and an appreciation of the foresight and sacrifices of previous generations to build and improve and rebuild the society and institutions and to examine and transmit the values that we hold dear. We're trying to jump on a vast and complex train that's been blowing by for centuries. We didn't invent the train ourselves— we didn't even invent the wheel.

But we might tinker with the gears. Indeed, we need to foster child-like genius—wonder, creativity, openness to novelty, and desire to articulate new problems and seek novel responses, with courage and fearlessness about the unknown—because we are in constant need of new ways to tell the story.[75] With or without children, we can look at the world with amazement and process it with our adult brains, with maturity and agency, with emotional depth, with humor and reference, with the ability to place experience in a critical context and create connections to vast treasures of historical memory. If we are attentive, perhaps we can both transmit and transform the legacies of the past, renew them, and make them real and right for our generation while we hand them down to others who will re-make them yet again.[76]

New Narratives

A third possibility for finding a connection to the future is to reframe our narratives about the past. How do childless lives help us to rethink human history and our place within it? And how can childless live fit into the stories we tell about our common past?

Traditional Western historical narratives have tended to marginalize or exclude childlessness. One well-worn grand narrative of human history posits that humanity has emerged from nature, conquered nature, and progressed to a better state. This narrative gained particular currency in the nineteenth century as historians built off of Hegel's notion of progress through conflict, that a clash of ideas leads to something better. Humans struggled to overcome nature, to transcend nature, and to enter into hier-archical political society. Purveyors of such narratives may not have been thinking all that carefully about the day-to-day reality of raising children or the gendered power dynamics at work in households and in the law—they have tended to focus instead on Great Men, on leaders—but they never-theless permeate many assumptions about our daily lives: that our incomes should rise, that we should pass our knowledge and wealth to our children, that our children's lives should be better than our own. Childlessness is typ-ically excluded from these histories, but this narrative may help explain why it is that, when the childless are noticed, they are seen as hyperfocused on the progress of their careers and on other markers of success.

A variant on the framework of progress is the metaphor of birth: the birth of the modern, the origins of capitalism, the Founding Fathers. These narratives see childlessness, metaphorically speaking, as a dead end and meaningless to our lives today. And literal childless, too, is a dead end, if we take the metaphor of birth seriously as a way to explain who we are and where we are headed. Childlessness, in this view, indicates a refusal to take part in creating the culture, technology or social forms that will make our collective future.

Another long-standing grand narrative is the story of the Fall, which is manifested in the Christian tradition as the notion of the fall of humans into sin, with human redemption possible only through Christ at the end of time. Our sinfulness leads us to sex and therefore to reproduction. Because of our abiding sinfulness, we are all expected to reproduce—with the exception of those who have vowed chastity and commended their bodies to God. Childlessness is only proper when it is the manifestation of spiritual commitment. A secular variant on this narrative is the dystopia. For some, childlessness plays into a dystopian narrative, not so much a "fall" from grace as tragic flaw written into Western society or the symptom of the West gone awry.

These narratives of progress, of birth, or, alternatively, of the fall distort the place of childlessness in human history. In fact, the childless provide insights—not anomalies—for the understanding of flourishing in and of themselves and for the cultures in which they live. They also, by their very existence, alter traditional narratives of what the future might hold; they challenge the inevitability of the reproductive future.[77] What narratives might better suit this reality?

Over the years, historians have developed techniques for more clearly understanding and analyzing people who do not possess power—the poor and oppressed—not just the Great Men. They look for contingency, for diaspora, for resistance, for hegemony and subalternity as ways to explain the complexity of the modern world.[78] One major shift in the historiography of the last several decades has been the excavation of agency among marginalized groups—women, peasants, minoritized populations, those with disabilities—and the story of power and the surprising ways that people can exercise it or navigate it, if only in a limited fashion.[79] The notion of choice resides at the heart of this desire to notice, examine, celebrate, and foster the agency of others.

This historical work makes possible attentiveness to childless lives. Should we now set up the voluntarily childless as another unsung group whose more-or-less agency has now been uncovered? Certainly, as I have described this project in conversation, countless childless colleagues, friends and acquaintances have supported it as a validation of their lives, and I hope that this project will do them justice. Part of this project has been to better calibrate the scales of agency and structure in how we assess the pathways to childlessness, to acknowledge a greater possibility for choice among childless women of the past—that they were not just victims of circumstance—while simultaneously recognizing the forces of culture and structure that have limited the latitude of those women.

Yet the excavation of agency—the validation of the childless—is not the only goal of this study. This book has also sought to unearth the deep and necessary connections between the childless and the childful within the quest for human flourishing. One metaphor that may prove useful as we look to the future, then, is that of the co-evolutionary spiral, in which two or more entities grow and change in tandem with each other. Here, there is no place of origin; instead, in the words of Andrew Shryock and Daniel Lord Smail, we find "two [or more] genealogies entwined and feeding off each other."[80] Childless individuals do not exist in a specific space or neighborhood, not in a diaspora, but as part of a whole, dispersed within and among families, friends, and communities of childful people. Childless and childful are, metaphorically speaking, engaged in a co-evolutionary spiral, defining themselves off of each other, performing the work that allows the other to thrive and, in the best of circumstances, openly supporting each other.

One more metaphor may be illuminating. The fractal is a metaphor that shows how the same events are manifested in a variety of scales, from small groups where everyone knows each other to complex organizations with tens of millions. Even as we have grown into these large groups and looked with amazement at the leaps humans have made at certain moments—the development of cooked food, of agriculture, of industrial power—"we have never stopped living in groups reminiscent of the families, clans, and tribes described by political anthropologists."[81] At each scale, we negotiate hierarchy and power, energy and waste, social nicety, and getting things done. The fractal allows us to imagine each of these successive leaps as momentous, even if they are dwarfed by later leaps.[82] The fractal reminds us to look for the many registers in which childlessness operates: in a household, a town, a country, a world. And it urges us to remember that the historical arc of childlessness is far vaster than our own lifetimes, far greater than the few centuries and locations included in this book. Childlessness is, rather, a part of the human condition stretching back into the deep past and forward into the incomprehensible future.

A few years after my mother and I had that difficult and unfinished conversation about childlessness, we sat down to go through her mother's belongings: a few boxes of papers and mementos. We grouped them into stacks of items to keep, some to share with cousins, and a few to send to the local history museum. The very act of sifting and sorting, of making neat piles, is so very us, so very much how our family operates. These items were not only the final ones from my grandmother's life, but also the last tangible items from her own parents, who had been Russian immigrants at the turn of the last century; I had never seen this clear a picture of my great-grandfather, who, as a boy in Austria–Hungary witnessed the deaths of his parents and siblings in an epidemic ("four coffins" was all he recalled). We examined my great-grandmother's citizenship papers, my great-grandfather's factory ID picture and glasses, my grandfather's union pins. We recalled their particular story of kinship, migration, and finding new ways of belonging, a specific instance of a story repeated on small and large scales throughout human history.

Sometime later, back at the kitchen table, I asked my mother about the conversation we'd had in which we talked past each other about childlessness. "I didn't say anything because I didn't want to be judgmental," she said. We laughed.

If we were to look at only tangible artifacts, it would be as though my family came into being around the year 1907 and then disappeared again when the last of us siblings pass sometime in the twenty-first century. In the end, we might accept that there are three stages: to live, to be dead but remembered, and then not to be remembered at all. At some point, sooner or later, our node in the web will wink off, leaving a faint glow that will then fade away. Yet my mother and I, childful and childless, forever linked, will remain part of a human story that extends across the millennia.

On July 14, 2015, a spacecraft the size of a piano flew just 7,750 miles from the surface of Pluto. Despite its recent downgrade from planet to dwarf planet, Pluto retains its hold on the imagination. So cold, so distant, a tiny rock some three billion miles away, almost thirty-two times further from our sun than we are. Humans did not discover it until 1930, when my grandmother was already eleven years old. Its orbit takes 248 of our earth years; it last reached its present location in Anne Silhes's youth. Yet it circles the same sun that we feel on our skin and taste in our fruit. When it's cold on Pluto, it snows. We're distant kin.

To this orb we sent New Horizons, a probe that operates on less power than the light bulbs in my grandmother's lamps, to study its temperature, atmosphere, and geology.[83] After its Pluto encounter, New Horizons explored another object in the Kuiper Belt three or four years distant, and now continues to hurtle into space indefinitely. Voyager 1, which launched from earth in August 1977, just days after I was born, is doing just that. After having visited Jupiter, Saturn, Uranus, and Neptune, it has continued on toward the outer reaches of our solar system. It will eventually pass out of the Sun's magnetic field and into the vast reaches between the stars. In about 40,000 years, Voyager 1 will reach a star known on earth as AC + 79 3888, in the constellation of Camelopardalis (Figure 10.2).[84] For this to matter to humans, we will need an unbroken chain of human reproduction extending forward for 1,600 generations.

Two years after New Horizons passed Pluto, on September 15, 2017, NASA's Cassini spacecraft ended its twenty-year journey around Saturn. After over a decade of sending its images of the ringed planet and its moons back to earth, its fuel running low, scientists turned Cassini toward Saturn for its final task: disintegrate in the atmosphere so that no trace of Cassini and no hitchhiking microbes could disturb the planet and its moons.[85]

Figure 10.2 Hall, Sidney, Etcher. *Camelopardalis, Tarandus and Custos Messium / Sidy. Hall, sculpt.*, 1825. Photograph. https://www.loc.gov/item/2002695395/. Library of Congress, Prints & Photographs Division, LC-USZC4-10051.

Legacy is not just what we leave behind; it's also what we don't leave. New Horizons and Voyager 1 will continue into the cosmic future, but will hurtle out of the range of communication. Cassini has left no trace of itself, but leaves a legacy of photographic knowledge that will inform our understanding of Saturn for decades to come.

Childful and child free, both fill me with wonder and awe.

Notes

Introduction

1. Pearl A. Dykstra, "Childless Old Age," in *International Handbook of Population Aging*, ed. P. Uhlenberg. (Berlin: Springer, 2009), 674, Table 30.1.
2. Christopher Clausen, "Childfree in Toyland," *American Scholar* 71, no. 1 (Winter 2002): 119.
3. Leonore Davidoff et al., *The Family Story: Blood, Contract and Intimacy 1830–1960* (London: Longman, 1999), 73.
4. Jean-Baptiste Michel et al., "Quantitative Analysis of Culture Using Millions of Digitized Books," *Science* 331, no. 6014 (2011): 176–182.
5. Historical Abstracts, May 21, 2018. Search terms: "children," "mother," and "childless."
6. For example, Julia McQuillan et al., "Does the Reason Matter? Variations in Childlessness Concerns Among U.S. Women," *Journal of Marriage and Family* 74 (October 2012): 1176.
7. Sheryl Sandberg, *Lean In: Women, Work, and the Will to Lead* (New York: Knopf, 2013).
8. See, among others, Patricia Hill Collins, *Black Feminist Thought: Knowledge, Consciousness, and the Politics of Empowerment* (Boston: Unwin Hyman, 1990), 119–123, on othermothers; Matthew Connelly, *Fatal Misconception: The Struggle to Control World Population* (Cambridge, MA: The Belknap Press of Harvard University Press, 2008); Katharine Dow, *Making a Good Life: An Ethnography of Nature, Ethics, and Reproduction* (Princeton, NJ: Princeton University Press, 2016); Elaine Tyler May, *Barren in the Promised Land: Childless Americans and the Pursuit of Happiness* (New York: Basic Books, 1995); Deirdre Cooper Owens, *Medical Bondage: Race, Gender, and the Origins of American Gynecology* (Athens, GA: University of Georgia Press, 2017); Naomi Pfeffer, *The Stork and the Syringe: A Political History of Reproductive Medicine* (Cambridge, MA: Blackwell, 1993); Dorothy Roberts, *Killing the Black Body: Race, Reproduction, and the Meaning of Liberty* (New York: Pantheon Books, 1997); Wanda Ronner and Margaret Marsh, *The Empty Cradle: Infertility in America from Colonial Times to the Present* (Baltimore: Johns Hopkins University Press, 1999); Margaret Marsh and Wanda Ronner, *The Fertility Doctor: John Rock and the Reproductive Revolution* (Baltimore: Johns Hopkins University Press, 2008); Daphna Oren-Magidor and Catherine Rider, "Introduction: Infertility in Medieval and Early Modern Medicine," *Social History of Medicine* 29, no. 2 (May 2016): 211–223; Daphna Oren-Magidor, "From Anne to Hannah: Religious Views of Infertility in Post-Reformation England," *Journal of Women's History* 27, no. 3 (Fall 2015): 86–108; Jennifer Evans, "Female Barrenness, Bodily Access and Aromatic Treatments in Seventeenth-Century England," *Historical Research* 87, no. 237 (August 2014):

423–443; Gisela Bock, "Racism and Sexism in Nazi Germany: Motherhood, Compulsory Sterilization, and the State," *Signs: Journal of Women in Culture and Society* 8, no. 3 (March 1983): 400–421; Molly Ladd-Taylor, "Eugenics, Sterilisation and Modern Marriage in the USA: The Strange Career of Paul Popenoe," *Gender and History* 13, no. 2 (August 2001): 298–327; Philip Nord, *France's New Deal: From the Thirties to the Postwar Era* (Princeton, NJ: Princeton University Press, 2010); Timothy B. Smith, *Creating the Welfare State in France, 1880–1940* (Montreal: McGill-Queen's University Press, 2003); Paul Dutton, *Origins of the French Welfare State: The Struggle for Social Reform in France 1914–1947* (New York: Cambridge University Press, 2002).

9. Suzanne Voilquin, *Souvenirs d'une fille du peuple, ou La saint-simonienne en Égypte*, intro. Lydia Elhadad (Paris: François Maspero, 1978), 108.

10. Davidoff et al., *Family Story*, 74, 77; Barbara Duden, *The Woman Beneath the Skin: A Doctor's Patients in Eighteenth-Century Germany*, trans. Thomas Dunlap (Cambridge, MA: Harvard University Press, 1991), 8.

11. For instance, Julie De Groot, Isabelle Devos, and Ariadne Schmidt, eds. *Single Life and the City, 1200–1900* (Houndmills, UK: Palgrave Macmillan, 2015); Kristin Park, "Stigma Management among the Voluntarily Childless," *Sociological Perspectives* 45, no. 1 (Spring 2002): 21–45; Kristin Park, "Choosing Childlessness: Weber's Typology of Action and Motives of the Voluntarily Childless," *Sociological Inquiry* 75, no. 3 (August 2005): 372–402; Kyung-Hee Lee and Anisa M. Zvonkovic, "Journeys to Remain Childless: A Grounded Theory Examination of Decision-Making Processes among Voluntarily Childless Couples," *Journal of Social and Personal Relationships* 31, no. 4 (2014): 535–553.

12. All names from Association pour l'autobiographie (APA) or names of individuals from my own life are pseudonyms.

13. APA 1833, Joséphine Bruyère (pseudonym), "Seize lustres au fil de la plume," 323.

14. APA 1833, Bruyère, 339.

15. APA 1833, Bruyère, 356–358.

16. Sherryl Jeffries and Candace Konnert, "Regret and Psychological Well-Being among Voluntarily and Involuntarily Childless Women and Mothers," *International Journal of Aging and Human Development* 54, no. 2 (2002): 91.

17. Gladys Martinez, Kimberly Daniels, and Anjani Chandra, "Fertility of Men and Women Aged 15–44 Years in the United States: National Survey of Family Growth, 2006–2010," *National Health Statistics Reports* 51 (April 2012): 1–28.

18. J. Abma et al. "Fertility, Family Planning, and Women's Health: New Data from the 1995 National Survey of Family Growth," *Vital Health Statistics* 23, no. 19 (1997): 4.

19. Park, "Stigma Management," 27.

20. Jeffries and Konnert, "Regret," 92.

21. Quoted in Jeffries and Konnert, "Regret," 100.

22. Jeffries and Konnert, "Regret," 102.

23. Jean E. Veevers, *Childless by Choice* (Toronto: Butterworths, 1980), 159, Table 3.

24. Quoted in Dykstra, "Childless Old Age," 679–680.

25. Kyung-Hee Lee and Anisa M. Zvonkovic, "Journeys to Remain Childless: A Grounded Theory Examination of Decision-Making Processes among Voluntarily Childless Couples," *Journal of Social and Personal Relationships* 31, no. 4 (2014): 535–553.

26. Michael Cobb, *Single: Arguments for the Uncoupled* (New York: New York University Press, 2012), 8.

27. Michael J. Sandel, *Justice: What's the Right Thing To Do* (New York: Farrar, Straus and Giroux, 2009), 261.

28. According to the National Center for Education Statistics, in 2014–2015, 452,118 women earned master's degrees and 93,626 earned doctor's degrees, a total of 545,744. In 2008, twenty-four percent of women ages forty to forty-four with advanced degrees were childless. That was a decline from thirty-one percent in 1994. Still, even if we assume that only twenty percent will be childless, that means that 109,148 women with these advanced degrees will be childless at the age of forty-five. If we assume that only fifteen percent of these women will remain childless, the number is 81,862. https://nces.ed.gov/programs/digest/d16/tables/dt16_318.30.asp?current=yes; Gretchen Livingstone and D'Vera Cohn, "Childlessness Up among All Women; Down among Women with Advanced Degrees." Pew Research Center, June 25, 2010. http://www.pewsocialtrends.org/2010/06/25/childlessness-up-among-all-women-down-among-women-with-advanced-degrees/.

29. Amartya Sen, *The Idea of Justice* (Cambridge, MA: The Belknap Press of Harvard University Press, 2009), x.

Chapter 1

1. Jody Day, "50 Ways Not To Be A Mother . . ." Gateway Women (blog). Accessed June 8, 2018. https://gateway-women.com/50-ways-not-to-be-a-mother-with-apologies-to-paul-simon/.

2. A bracing discussion of the less-than-total patriarchy in Margaret R. Hunt, "English Lesbians," *Singlewomen in the European Past, 1250–1800*, ed. Judith M. Bennett and Amy M. Froide (Philadelphia: University of Pennsylvania Press, 1999), 272–273.

3. In 1920, only 2 percent never married in Japan, and only 1 percent in India ten years later; Mary S. Hartman, *The Household and the Making of History: A Subversive View of the Western Past* (New York: Cambridge University Press, 2004), 21.

4. John Hajnal, "European Marriage Patterns in Perspective," in *Population in History: Essays in Historical Demography*, ed. D. V. Glass and D. E. C. Eversley (London: Edward Arnold, 1965), 101–143; Stephanie Coontz, *Marriage, A History: How Love Conquered Marriage* (New York: Penguin, 2005), 124–132. Late marriage for women has been documented in Roman Egypt and twentieth-century Tibet; Jack Goody, *The Development of Family and Marriage in Europe* (New York: Cambridge University Press, 1983), 8–9.

5. Coontz, *Marriage*, 126.

6. Jewish and Muslim populations in Europe continued the pattern of early marriage and high rates of motherhood; Maryanne Kowaleski, "Singlewomen in Medieval and Early Modern Europe: The Demographic Perspective," in Bennett and Froide, *Singlewomen*, 62.

7. Kowaleski, "Demographic Perspective," 53; Hartman, *Household*, 21; Coontz, *Marriage*, 127. This number varied by country and place.

8. Ariadne Schmidt, Isabelle Devos, and Bruno Blondé, "Introduction: Single and the City: Men and Women Alone in North-Western European Towns since the Late Middle Ages," in *Single Life and the City, 1200–1900*, ed. Julie De Groot, Isabelle Devos, and Ariadne Schmidt (Houndmills, UK: Palgrave Macmillan, 2015), 5.

9. Ruth Mazo Karras, "Sex and the Singlewoman," in Kowaleski, *Singlewomen*, 140; Hunt, "English Lesbians," 278.

10. Schmidt et al., "Introduction," *Single Life*, 11.

11. Hartman, *Household*, 20, 58n71, 60–62. Illegitimacy rates hovered between 1.2 and 4 percent of children in England, where parish records from 1538 to 1754 preserved the details, and at only 1.2 percent in France of the 1740s.

12. Michael Anderson, "Highly Restricted Fertility: Very Small Families in the British Fertility Decline," *Population Studies* 52, no. 2 (July 1998): 179; 24 percent of women who married from ages thirty-five to thirty-nine were infertile in England in the period 1580 to 1837. Philip Kreager, "Where Are the Children?" in *Ageing without Children: European and Asian Perspectives*, ed. Philip Kreager and Elisabeth Schröder-Butterfill (New York: Berghan Books, 2004), 13.

13. Donald T. Rowland, "Historical Trends in Childlessness," *Journal of Family Issues* 28, no. 10 (October 2007): 1328.

14. Robert V. Wells, "The Population of England's Colonies in America: Old English or New Americans?" *Population Studies* 46 (1992): 95. Enslaved women averaged six to eight children; Wells, "England's Colonies," 91; Elaine Tyler May, *Barren in the Promised Land: Childless Americans and the Pursuit of Happiness* (New York: Basic Books, 1995), 27.

15. Leslie Tuttle, *Conceiving the Old Regime: Pronatalism and the Politics of Reproduction in Early Modern France* (New York: Oxford University Press, 2010), 9.

16. Tuttle, *Conceiving*, 11.

17. Hartman, *Household*, 270.

18. Caton's story is recounted in Olwen H. Hufton, "Women, Work and Marriage in Eighteenth-Century France," in *Marriage and Society: Studies in the Social History of Marriage*, ed. by R. B. Outhwaite (New York: St. Martin's, 1981), 186–194.

19. Antonia Fraser, *Marie Antoinette: The Journey* (New York: Anchor Books, 2001), 149.

20. Quoted in Amy M. Froide, *Never Married: Singlewomen in Early Modern England* (New York: Oxford University Press, 2005), 184.

21. Vivien Brodsky Elliott, "Single Women in the London Marriage Market: Age, Status and Mobility, 1598–1619," in Outhwaite, *Marriage and Society*, 90.

22. Merry E. Wiesner, "Having Her Own Smoke: Employment and Independence for Singlewomen in Germany, 1400–1750," in Bennett and Froide, *Singlewomen*, 204–205.

23. Wiesner, "Employment and Independence," 207.

24. Judith M. Bennett and Amy M. Froide, "A Singular Past," in Bennett and Froide, *Singlewomen*, 14.

25. Wiesner, "Employment and Independence," 197–198.

26. James B. Collins, "Women and the Birth of Modern Consumer Capitalism," in *Women and Work in Eighteenth-Century France*, ed. Daryl M. Hafter and Nina Kushner (Baton Rouge: Louisiana State University Press, 2015), 169.

27. Hunt, "English Lesbians," 280.

28. Froide, *Never Married*, 111–112.

29. Carlos Eire, *Reformations: The Early Modern World, 1450–1650* (New Haven, CT: Yale University Press, 2016), 662.

30. Kowaleski, "Demographic Perspective," 55, 60; Hunt, "English Lesbians," 278.

31. Kathleen Wellman, *Queens and Mistresses of Renaissance France* (New Haven, CT: Yale University Press, 2013), 79.

32. Bridget Hill, *Women Alone: Spinsters in England 1660–1850* (New Haven, CT: Yale University Press, 2001), 10.

33. Margaret H. Darrow, *Revolution in the House: Family, Class, and Inheritance in Southern France, 1775–1825* (Princeton, NJ: Princeton University Press, 1989), 129n129.

34. Darrow, *Revolution in the House*, 97–98.

35. Quoted in Froide, *Never Married*, 200–201.

36. Misery of dependency: Hill, *Women Alone*, 68–70.

37. Quoted in Froide, *Never Married*, 76.

38. Froide, *Never Married*, 75–77.

39. Christine Adams, "A Choice Not to Wed? Unmarried Women in Eighteenth-Century France," *Journal of Social History* 29, no. 4 (Summer 1996): 884.

40. Quoted in Adams, "Choice Not to Wed?" 887.

41. Froide, *Never Married*, 156.

42. Froide, *Never Married*, 159–160.

43. "† orb, adj." OED Online. Oxford University Press. March 2017. Accessed June 7, 2017. http://www.oed.com/view/Entry/132223?rskey=9SDOwk&result=3.

44. Quoted in Froide, *Never Married*, 157.

45. Quoted in Hill, *Women Alone*, 145.

46. Hill, *Women Alone*, 19.

47. Monica Chojnacka, "Singlewomen in Early Modern Venice: Communities and Opportunities," in Bennett and Froide, *Singlewomen*, 217.

48. Froide, *Never Married*, 160–161.

49. Froide, *Never Married*, 161.

50. Froide, *Never Married*, 164.

51. Hunt, "English Lesbians," 278.

52. Susan S. Lanser, "Singular Politics: The Rise of the British Nation and the Production of the Old Maid," in Bennett and Froide, *Singlewomen*, 299.

53. Quoted in Lanser, "Singular Politics," 300.

54. Quoted in Lanser, "Singular Politics," 301.

55. Froide, *Never Married*, 159.

56. Lanser, "Singular Politics," 304.

57. Wells, "England's Colonies," 90; Lanser, "Singular Politics," 316.

58. Adam Smith, *An Inquiry into the Nature and Causes of the Wealth of Nations* (New York: Modern Library, 1994), 90 (I.8.37).

59. Nicole Eustace, *1812: War and the Passions of Patriotism* (Philadelphia: University of Pennsylvania Press, 2012), 13.

60. Quoted in Eustace, *1812,* 11.

61. Eustace, *1812,* 12.

62. Dorothy Roberts, *Killing the Black Body: Race, Reproduction, and the Meaning of Liberty* (New York: Pantheon Books, 1997), 26.

63. Kristiaan P. G. Aercke, "Anna Bijns: Germanic Sappho," in *Women Writers of the Renaissance and Reformation,* ed. Katharina M. Wilson (Athens: University of Georgia Press, 1987), 365–397.

64. Quoted in Froide, *Never Married,* 214–215.

65. Froide, *Never Married,* 165–166.

66. Quoted in Froide, *Never Married,* 211.

67. Froide, *Never Married,* 182.

68. Froide, *Never Married,* 216.

Chapter 2

1. S. Philip Morgan, "Late Nineteenth- and Early Twentieth-Century Childlessness," *American Journal of Sociology* 97, no. 3 (November 1991): 785.

2. Morgan, "Late Nineteenth," 782; Pearl A. Dykstra, "Childless Old Age," in *International Handbook of Population Aging,* ed. P. Uhlenberg (Berlin: Springer, 2009), 673–674, Table 30.1; Donald T. Rowland, "Historical Trends in Childlessness," *Journal of Family Issues* 28, no. 10 (October 2007): 1318.

3. Norman MacKenzie and Jeanne MacKenzie, eds., *The Diaries of Beatrice Webb,* abridged by Lynn Knight, preface by Hermione Lee (Boston: Northeastern University Press, 2001), 150 (December 1, 1890).

4. Webb, *Diaries,* 156 (June 20, 1891).

5. Webb, *Diaries,* 183 (July 25, 1894).

6. *The Times,* April 15, 1857, quoted in Michael Anderson, "Highly Restricted Fertility: Very Small Families in the British Fertility Decline," *Population Studies* 52, no. 2 (July 1998):195.

7. Anderson, "Small Families," 178–180.

8. Morgan, "Late Nineteenth," 803.

9. Morgan, "Late Nineteenth," 785.

10. Jean-Claude Chenais, *The Demographic Transition: Stages, Patterns, and Economic Implications. A Longitudinal Study of Sixty-Seven Countries Covering the Period 1720–1984,* trans. Elizabeth and Philip Kreager (New York: Oxford University Press, 1992), 145, 322–324.

11. Chenais, *Demographic Transition,* 322–324.

12. Chenais, *Demographic Transition,* 145. These figures refer to the period total fertility.

13. May, *Barren*, 44.

14. Leonore Davidoff et al., *The Family Story: Blood, Contract and Intimacy 1830–1960* (London: Longman, 1999), 130.

15. Dustin J. Penn, "The Evolutionary Roots of Our Environmental Problems: Toward a Darwinian Ecology," *The Quarterly Review of Biology* 78, no. 3 (September 2003): 280–281.

16. Jan Van Bavel, "Subreplacement Fertility in the West before the Baby Boom: Past and Current Perspectives," *Population Studies* 64, no. 1 (2010): 11.

17. David G. Troyansky, *Old Age in the Old Regime: Image and Experience in Eighteenth-Century France* (Ithaca, NY: Cornell University Press, 1989), 16.

18. Anderson, "Small Families," 178.

19. Dykstra, "Childless Old Age," 680.

20. Bridget Hill, *Women Alone: Spinsters in England 1660–1850* (New Haven, CT: Yale University Press, 2001), 2.

21. Elaine Tyler May, *Barren in the Promised Land: Childless Americans and the Pursuit of Happiness* (New York: Basic Books, 1995), 51.

22. May, *Barren*, 49.

23. Quoted in May, *Barren*, 50.

24. Janet Farrell Brodie, *Contraception and Abortion in Nineteenth-Century America* (Ithaca, NY: Cornell University Press, 1994), 9–37.

25. Brodie, *Contraception*, 1.

26. Brodie, *Contraception*, 9–37.

27. Chenais, *Demographic Transition*, 111; Elinor Accampo, *Blessed Motherhood, Bitter Fruit: Nelly Roussel and the Politics of Female Pain in Third Republic France* (Baltimore: Johns Hopkins University Press, 2006), 3.

28. Brodie, *Contraception*, 293.

29. Brodie, *Contraception*; Rowland, "Historical Trends," 1327; Alain Corbin, *Time, Desire and Horror: Towards a History of the Senses*. trans. Jean Birrell (Cambridge, UK: Polity, 1995), 96; Stephanie Coontz, *Marriage, A History: How Love Conquered Marriage* (New York: Penguin, 2005), 193; Accampo, *Blessed Motherhood*, 4.

30. Anderson, "Small Families," 193.

31. May, *Barren*, 91.

32. Morgan, "Late Nineteenth," 799; Coontz, *Marriage*, 171, 193; Accampo, *Blessed Motherhood*, 45; Angus McLaren, *Birth Control in Nineteenth-Century England* (New York: Holmes & Meier, 1978), 231–253.

33. Matthew Connelly, *Fatal Misconception: The Struggle to Control World Population* (Cambridge, MA: The Belknap Press of Harvard University Press, 2008), 18–19.

34. Quoted in McLaren, *Birth Control*, 157.

35. Offen, "Depopulation," 659.

36. McLaren, *Birth Control in England*, 157, 186; Accampo, *Blessed Motherhood*, 4.

37. Sidney Webb, quoted in McLaren, *Birth Control in England*, 188.

38. Dorothy Roberts, *Killing the Black Body: Race, Reproduction, and the Meaning of Liberty* (New York: Pantheon Books, 1997), 56–103.

39. Quoted in Karen Offen, "Depopulation, Nationalism and Feminism in Fin-de-Siècle France," *American Historical Review* 89, no. 3 (June, 1984): 658.

40. Offen, "Depopulation," 661.
41. Quoted in Accampo, *Blessed Motherhood*, 54.
42. Accampo, *Blessed Motherhood*, 69.
43. Christopher H. Johnson and David Warren Sabean, "Introduction: From Siblingship to Siblinghood, Kinship and the Shaping of European Society (1300–1900)," in *Sibling Relations and the Transformation of European Kinship, 1300–1900*, ed. Christopher H. Johnson and David Warren Sabean (New York: Berghahn Books, 2011), 23.
44. Morgan, "Late Nineteenth," 795.
45. Van Bavel, "Subreplacement Fertility," 6.
46. Quoted in May, *Barren*, 82.
47. Quoted in Arthur W. Calhoun, *A Social History of the American Family from Colonial Times to the Present*. Vol. 3, *Since the Civil War* (Cleveland, OH: Arthur H. Clark, 1919), 249–250.
48. Rowland, "Historical Trends," 1322.
49. Anderson, "Small Families," 190.
50. Jan Van Bavel and Jan Kok, "Pioneers of the Modern Lifestyle?: Childless Couples in the Early-Twentieth-Century Netherlands," *Social Science History* 34, no. 1 (Spring 2010): 63–67.
51. Data refer to marriages of duration of at least fifteen years, as of 1911, and in which the wives had been between the ages of twenty-two and twenty-six at the time of marriage; Anderson, "Small Families," 183.
52. Morgan, "Late Nineteenth," 800; Anderson, "Small Families," 193.
53. May, *Barren*, 81.
54. Morgan, "Late Nineteenth," 801.
55. Anderson, "Small Families," 195.
56. Calhoun, *American Family*, 241.
57. Quoted in Brodie, *Contraception*, 293.
58. Paul Dutton, *Origins of the French Welfare State: The Struggle for Social Reform in France 1914–1947* (New York: Cambridge University Press, 2002), 9–10.
59. Offen, "Depopulation," 658.
60. Philip Nord, *France's New Deal: From the Thirties to the Postwar Era* (Princeton, NJ: Princeton University Press, 2010), 52; Timothy B. Smith, *Creating the Welfare State in France, 1880–1940* (Montreal: McGill-Queen's University Press, 2003), 90.
61. Offen, "Depopulation," 670.
62. Dutton, *Welfare State*, 8; Rachel G. Fuchs, *Poor and Pregnant in Paris: Strategies for Survival in the Nineteenth Century* (New Brunswick, NJ: Rutgers University Press, 1992), 61, 66.
63. Margaret Cook Andersen, "Creating French Settlements Overseas: Pronatalism and Colonial Medicine in Madagascar," *French Historical Studies* 33, no. 3 (Summer 2010): 421.
64. Andersen, "Pronatalism,"422.
65. Andersen, "Pronatalism," 419, 423–425.
66. Morgan, "Late Nineteenth," 782; Dykstra, "Childless Old Age," 673–674, Table 30.1; Rowland, "Historical Trends," 1318.

67. Anderson, "Small Families," 178.

68. P. K. Whelpton and Clyde V. Kiser, "The Comparative Influence on Fertility of Contraception and Impairments of Fecundity," *Social and Psychological Factors Affecting Fertility*, vol. 2, ed. P. K. Whelpton and Clyde V. Kiser (New York: Milbank Memorial Fund Quarterly, 1950 [1948]), 341; See also Edward Pohlman, "Childlessness, Intentional and Unintentional: Psychological and Social Aspects," *Journal of Nervous and Mental Disorders* 151, no. 1 (1970): 12.

69. Jürgen Dorbritz, "Germany: Family Diversity with Low Actual and Desired Fertility," *Demographic Research* 19 (July 2008): 566; Dykstra, "Childless Old Age," 678, Van Bavel, "Subreplacement Fertility"; Paul Weindling, *Health, Race, and German Politics between National Unification and Nazism, 1870–1945* (Cambridge, UK: Cambridge University Press, 1989), 189.

70. Rowland, "Historical Trends," 1322.

71. Dorbritz, "Germany," 569.

72. Van Bavel, "Subreplacement Fertility," 5.

73. Mary S. Hartman, *The Household and the Making of History: A Subversive View of the Western Past* (New York: Cambridge University Press, 2004), 21; Dykstra, "Childless Old Age," 675, Figure 30.1; Katherine Holden, *The Shadow of Marriage: Singleness in England, 1914–60* (Manchester, UK: Manchester University Press, 2007), 11; Dykstra, "Childless Old Age," 674; Dorbritz, "Germany," 569.

74. Elisabeth Badinter, *The Conflict: How Modern Motherhood Undermines the Status of Women*, trans. Adriana Hunter (New York: Metropolitan Books, 2011), 141.

75. Davidoff et al., *Family Story*, 225.

76. Van Bavel, "Subreplacement Fertility," 3.

77. Van Bavel, "Subreplacement Fertility," 11.

78. Van Bavel, "Subreplacement Fertility," 4.

79. May, *Barren*, 63.

80. Frederick S. Crum, "The Decadence of the Native American Stock. A Statistical Study of Genealogical Records," *Publications of the American Statistical Association* 14, no. 107 (September 1914): 221.

81. Calhoun, *American Family*, 240.

82. Calhoun, *American Family*, 241.

83. Calhoun, *American Family*, 242.

84. Jenna Healey, "Rejecting Reproduction: The National Organization for Non-Parents and Childfree Activism in 1970s America," *Journal of Women's History* 28, no. 1 (2016): 139.

85. Quoted in Dykstra, "Childless Old Age," 680.

86. Johnson and Sabean, "From Siblingship to Siblinghood," 1.

87. Holden, *Shadow of Marriage*, 11.

88. Quoted in May, *Barren*, 87.

89. Quoted in May, *Barren*, 87.

90. May, *Barren*, 87.

91. Van Bavel, "Subreplacement Fertility," 5.

92. Van Bavel, "Subreplacement Fertility," 2.

93. Anderson, "Small Families," 196.

Chapter 3

1. Luc Masson, "Avez-vous eu des enfants? Si oui, combien?" Insee dossier, *France, portrait social—édition 2013*, 95); Rebecca Pulju, *Women and Mass Consumer Society in Postwar France* (New York: Cambridge University Press, 2011); Donald T. Rowland, "Historical Trends in Childlessness," *Journal of Family Issues* 28, no. 10 (October 2007): 1327.

2. Elaine Tyler May, *Barren in the Promised Land: Childless Americans and the Pursuit of Happiness* (New York: Basic Books, 1995), 129.

3. S. Philip Morgan, "Late Nineteenth- and Early Twentieth-Century Childlessness," *American Journal of Sociology* 97, no. 3 (November 1991): 801.

4. Quoted in Paul Dutton, *Origins of the French Welfare State: The Struggle for Social Reform in France 1914–1947* (New York: Cambridge University Press, 2002), 212.

5. Richard C. Keller, *Fatal Isolation: The Devastating Paris Heat Wave of 2003* (Chicago: University of Chicago Press, 2015), 123; Timothy B. Smith, *Creating the Welfare State in France, 1880–1940* (Montreal: McGill-Queen's University Press, 2003), 113.

6. Philip Nord, *France's New Deal: From the Thirties to the Postwar Era* (Princeton, NJ: Princeton University Press, 2010), 3.

7. Jürgen Dorbritz, "Germany: Family Diversity with Low Actual and Desired Fertility," *Demographic Research* 19 (July 2008): 561; Laurent Toulemon, Ariane Pailhé, and Clémentine Rossier, "France: High and Stable Fertility," *Demographic Research* 19 (July 2008), art. 16, 507–508 (the more sophisticated measure of parity and duration total fertility rate reached 3.0 for France in 1960).

8. May, *Barren,* 133.

9. According to Toulemon, the baby boom ended in France between 1966 and 1975; Toulemon, "France," 509. Lesthaeghe writes, "From the second half of the 1960s onward, fertility started falling from its 'baby boom' high"; Ron Lesthaeghe, "The Unfolding Story of the Second Demographic Transition," *Population and Development Review* 36, no. 2 (June 2010): 212); Rowland, "Historical Trends," 1325.

10. Laurent Toulemon, "How Many Children and How Many Siblings in France in the Last Century?" *Population & Sociétés* 374 (December 2001): 1.

11. May, *Barren,* 128. Ten percent is for the cohorts of women born between 1915 and 1930. The numbers for France and Germany are for the cohort born in 1935.

12. 3.2 children per family in the 1950s; May, *Barren,* 133.

13. Toulemon, "How Many Children," 2.

14. Sarah Fishman, *From Vichy to the Sexual Revolution: Gender and Family Life in Postwar France* (New York: Oxford University Press, 2017), xxiv.

15. Quoted in Fishman, *From Vichy,* 50.

16. P. K. Whelpton, "Cohort Analysis of Fertility," *American Sociological Review* 14, no. 6 (December 1949): 742.

17. Fishman, *From Vichy,* 64, 175–176.

Chapter 4

1. A 1974 Gallup Poll of a representative sample of Americans (McLaughlin, 1975, 37), cited by Jean E. Veevers, *Childless by Choice* (Toronto: Butterworths, 1980), 168.

2. Ann Landers, *Wake Up and Smell the Coffee! Advice, Wisdom, and Uncommon Good Sense* (New York: Villard, 1996), 107.

3. Landers, *Wake Up!* 107.

4. Landers, *Wake Up!* 108.

5. Landers, *Wake Up!* 108.

6. Dagmar Herzog, "Between Coitus and Commodification: Young West German Women and the Impact of the Pill," in *Between Marx and Coca-Cola: Youth Cultures in Changing European Societies, 1960–1980*, ed. Axel Schildt and Detlef Siegfried (New York: Berghahn Books, 2006), 261–286; Eva-Maria Silies, *Liebe, Lust und Last: Die Pille als weibliche Generationserfahrung in der Bundesrepublik, 1960–1980* (Göttingen, Germany: Wallstein Verlag, 2010).

7. All the numbers in this paragraph are for cohorts born in the early 1960s. Laurent Toulemon, Ariane Pailhé, and Clémentine Rossier, "France: High and Stable Fertility," *Demographic Research* 19 (July 2008), art. 19, 516; Pearl A. Dykstra, "Childless Old Age," in *International Handbook of Population Aging*, ed. P. Uhlenberg (Berlin: Springer, 2009), 673–674, Table 30.1. Livingstone and Cohn found that childlessness for women aged forty to forty-four in the United States was higher, up to 18 percent; Gretchen Livingstone and D'Vera Cohn, "Childlessness Up among All Women; Down among Women with Advanced Degrees," Pew Research Center, June 25, 2010, https://www.pewsocialtrends.org/2010/06/25/childlessness-up-among-all-women-down-among-women-with-advanced-degrees/.

8. Toulemon, "France," 528.

9. Fertility rates: Central Intelligence Agency, "Country Comparison: Total Fertility Rates," in *World Fact Book*. Accessed June 19, 2015. https://www.cia.gov/library/publications/the-world-factbook/rankorder/2127rank.html/; childlessness rates for European women born in 1965: Jürgen Dorbritz and Kerstin Ruckdeschel, "Kinderlosigkeit in Deutschland—Ein europäischer Sonderweg?" in *Ein Leben ohne Kinder: Kinderlosigkeit in Deutschland,* ed. Dirk Konietzka and Michaela Kreyenfeld (Wiesbaden, Germany: Verlag für Sozialwissenschaften, 2007), 64, Figure 9.

10. Jürgen Dorbritz, "Germany: Family Diversity with Low Actual and Desired Fertility," *Demographic Research* 19 (July 1, 2008): 563.

11. Dorbritz, "Germany," 583.

12. Dorbritz, "Germany," 566.

13. Dorbritz, "Germany," 580.

14. A. H. Maslow, "A Theory of Human Motivation," *Psychological Review* 50, no. 4 (July 1943): 382.

15. Maslow, "A Theory of Human Motivation," 383.

16. Maslow, "A Theory of Human Motivation," 383.

17. Sarah Fishman, *From Vichy to the Sexual Revolution: Gender and Family Life in Postwar France* (New York: Oxford University Press, 2017), 142.

18. Fishman, *From Vichy*, xxv.

19. Dirk J. van de Kaa, "Is the Second Demographic Transition a Useful Research Concept: Questions and Answers," *Vienna Yearbook of Population Research 2* (2004): 8.

20. van de Kaa, "Questions and Answers," 8. Ron Lesthaeghe concurs in "The Unfolding Story of the Second Demographic Transition," *Population and Development Review* 36, no. 2 (June 2010): 217.

21. Edward Pohlman, "Childlessness, Intentional and Unintentional: Psychological and Social Aspects," *Journal of Nervous and Mental Disorders* 151, no. 1 (1970): 12.

22. Pohlman, "Childlessness," 11–12.

23. Quoted in Jenna Healey, "Rejecting Reproduction: The National Organization for Non-Parents and Childfree Activism in 1970s America," *Journal of Women's History* 28, no. 1 (2016): 138.

24. Herzog, "Between Coitus and Commodification," 275.

25. Mary S. Hartman, *The Household and the Making of History: A Subversive View of the Western Past* (New York: Cambridge University Press, 2004), 272.

26. Elizabeth Anderson, "What Is the Point of Equality?" *Ethics* 109, no. 2 (January 1999): 316.

27. Henry Greenbaum, "Marriage, Family, and Parenthood," *American Journal of Psychiatry* 130, no. 11 (November 1973): 1264.

28. Lesthaeghe, "Unfolding Story," 233–234.

29. Elisabeth Badinter, *The Conflict: How Modern Motherhood Undermines the Status of Women*, trans. Adriana Hunter (New York: Metropolitan Books, 2011), 2.

30. Gary S. Becker, *The Economic Approach to Human Behavior* (Chicago: University of Chicago Press, 1976), 5.

31. Becker, *Economic Approach*, 174.

32. Becker, *Economic Approach*, 14.

33. Michael J. Sandel, *What Money Can't Buy: The Moral Limits of Markets* (New York: Farrar, Straus and Giroux, 2012), 51.

34. Ursula Henz, "Gender Roles and Values of Children: Childless Couples in East and West Germany," *Demographic Research* 19 (August 22, 2008): art. 39, 1454n2.

35. Henz, "Childless Couples," 1455.

36. Badinter, *The Conflict*, 128; see also Henz, "Childless Couples," 1456.

37. Badinter, *The Conflict*, 136–137.

38. Henz, "Childless Couples," 1456.

39. Dorbritz, "Germany," 563.

40. Katharine Dow, *Making a Good Life: An Ethnography of Nature, Ethics, and Reproduction* (Princeton, NJ: Princeton University Press, 2016), 16.

41. Becker, *Economic Approach*, 178.

42. Henz, "Childless Couples," 1454.

43. Herzog, "Between Coitus and Commodification," 262.

44. Herzog, "Between Coitus and Commodification," 262.

45. Herzog, "Between Coitus and Commodification," 263, 266–267.

46. Herzog, "Between Coitus and Commodification," 265.

47. Herzog, "Between Coitus and Commodification," 269.

48. Herzog, "Between Coitus and Commodification," 281.

49. Linda Gordon, *Woman's Body, Woman's Right: A Social History of Birth Control in America* (New York: Grossman, 1976), 405–406.

50. Gordon, *Woman's Body, Woman's Right,* 405.

51. Gordon, *Woman's Body, Woman's Right,* 405.

52. Fishman, *From Vichy,* 162.

53. Dow, *Making a Good Life,* 66.

54. Rolf A. Peterson, "Attitudes toward the Childless Spouse," *Sex Roles* 9, no. 3 (1983): 321.

55. Lawrence G. Calhoun and James W. Selby, "Voluntary Childlessness, Involuntary Childlessness, and Having Children: A Study of Social Perceptions," *Family Relations* 29 (April 1980): 181–183.

56. Arinae Kemkes, "Is Perceived Childlessness a Cue for Stereotyping? Evolutionary Aspects of a Social Phenomenon," *Biodemography & Social Biology* 54, no. 1 (Spring 2008): 33; Pohlman, "Childlessness"; Denise F. Polit, "Stereotypes Relating to Family-Size Status," *Journal of Marriage and Family* 40, no. 1 (February 1978): 105–114; Calhoun and Selby, "Voluntary Childlessness"; Victor J. Callan, "Perceptions of Parenthood and Childlessness: A Comparison of Mothers and Voluntarily Childless Wives," *Population and Environment* 6, no. 3 (1983): 179–189; Victor J. Callan, "Perceptions of Parents, the Voluntarily and Involuntarily Childless: A Multidimensional Scaling Analysis," *Journal of Marriage and the Family* 47, no. 4 (1985): 1045–1050.

57. Tanya Koropeckyj-Cox, Victor Romano, and Amanda Moras, "Through the Lenses of Gender, Race, and Class: Students' Perceptions of Childless/Childfree Individuals and Couples," *Sex Roles* 56 (2007): 416; Joanna Ross and James P. Kahan, "Children by Choice or by Chance: The Perceived Effects of Parity," *Sex Roles* 9, no. 1 (1983): 69–77.

58. Veevers, *Childless by Choice,* 4, Table 1.

59. Veevers, *Childless by Choice,* 6. Note that Veevers herself did not believe this.

60. Greenbaum, "Marriage, Family, and Parenthood," 1263.

61. cited in Doyle, "Childfree Australian Women," 398.

62. Kemkes, "Stereotyping," 34.

63. S. L. N. Rao, "A Comparative Study of Childlessness and Never-Pregnant Status," *Journal of Marriage and the Family* 36, no. 1 (1974). 151, US Census Bureau, "Table MS-2: Estimated Median age at First Marriage, by Sex: 1890 to Present," September 15, 2004, https://www.census.gov/population/socdemo/hh-fam/tabMS-2.pdf, based on Jason Fields, "America's Families and Living Arrangements: 2003" in *Annual Social and Economic Supplement: 2003 Current Population Survey,* US Census Bureau Current Population Reports, Series P20–553, November 2004, https://www.census.gov/prod/2004pubs/p20-553.pdf.

64. Veevers, *Childless by Choice,* 123.

65. Quoted in Veevers, *Childless by Choice,* 46.

66. Veevers, *Childless by Choice*, 48.
67. Veevers, *Childless by Choice*, 49.
68. Veevers, *Childless by Choice*, 82.
69. Veevers, *Childless by Choice*, 81.
70. Veevers, *Childless by Choice*, 75–76.
71. Elaine Tyler May, *Barren in the Promised Land: Childless Americans and the Pursuit of Happiness* (New York: Basic Books, 1995), 182.
72. Veevers, *Childless by Choice*, 153.
73. Healey, "Rejecting Reproduction," 132.
74. Quoted in Healey, "Rejecting Reproduction," 138.
75. Healey, "Rejecting Reproduction," 142.
76. Quoted in Healey, "Rejecting Reproduction," 140.
77. Quoted in Healey, "Rejecting Reproduction," 141.
78. Healey, "Rejecting Reproduction," 142–143.
79. Healey, "Rejecting Reproduction," 143.
80. Healey, "Rejecting Reproduction," 143, 144.
81. Healey, "Rejecting Reproduction," 145.
82. Its growth slowed, and by 1978 included about 1,600 members. Most child-free people could not be persuaded to remain militant for long; once they were reassured that remaining childless is not deviant, they had little incentive to remain in the organization. NOAP closed its doors in 1982; Veevers, *Childless by Choice*, 153–154.
83. Quoted in Veevers, *Childless by Choice*, 163n3.
84. Suzanne Noordhuizen, Paul de Graaf, and Inge Sieben, "The Public Acceptance of Voluntary Childlessness in the Netherlands: From 20 to 90 percent in 30 years," *Social Indicators Research* 99 (October 2010): 169.
85. Noordhuizen, "Netherlands," 174.
86. Livingston and Cohn, "Childlessness Up."
87. Veevers, *Childless by Choice*, 174.
88. Jonathan Vespa, "Marrying Older, But Sooner?" US Census (blog), February 10, 2014. http://blogs.census.gov/2014/02/10/marrying-older-but-sooner/.
89. Katja Köppen, Magali Mazuy, and Laurent Toulemon, "Kinderlosigkeit in Frankreich," in Konietzka and Kreyenfeld, *Ein Leben ohne Kinder*, 95; see also Toulemon, "France," 519; Luc Masson, "Avez-vous eu des enfants? Si oui, combien?" Insee dossier. *France, portrait social—édition 2013*, 102.
90. Dorbritz, "Germany," 570; see also Heike Wirth, "Kinderlosigkeit von hoch qualifizierten Frauen und Männern in Paarkontext—Eine Folge von Bildungshomogamie?" in Konietzka and Kreyenfeld, *Ein Leben ohne Kinder*, 193.
91. Köppen et al., "Frankreich," 96.
92. Jan Eckhard and Thomas Klein, "Die Motivation zur Elternschaft. Unterschiede zwischen Männern und Frauen," in Konietzka and Kreyenfeld, *Ein Leben ohne Kinder*, 292.
93. Köppen et al., "Frankreich," 99.
94. Doyle, "Childfree Australian Women," 399.
95. Chancey, "Voluntary Childlessness," 29.

96. Masson, "Avez-vous eu des enfants?"
97. Toulemon, "France," 540.
98. Toulemon, "France," 538.
99. Toulemon, "France," 538.
100. Toulemon, "France," 539–540.
101. Toulemon, "France," 506.
102. Toulemon, "France," 505.
103. Henz, "Childless Couples," 1485.
104. Hartman, *Household*, 193.
105. Quoted in Doyle, "Childfree Australian Women," 398.
106. Nicholas Eberstadt, "The Global Flight from the Family," *The Wall Street Journal*, February 21–22, 2015, p. A11.
107. Katherine Holden, *The Shadow of Marriage: Singleness in England, 1914-60* (Manchester, UK: Manchester University Press, 2007), 219.
108. A Roper poll cited in May, *Barren*, 189.
109. Pew Research Center survey, reported in Livingston and Cohn, "Childlessness Up."
110. General Social Survey, reported in Livingston and Cohn, "Childlessness Up."
111. A Pew Research Center poll, cited by Livingston and Cohn, "Childlessness Up."
112. Leslie Ashburn-Nardo, "Parenthood as a Moral Imperative? Moral Outrage and the Stigmatization of Voluntarily Childfree Women and Men," *Sex Roles* no. 76 (2017): 398.

Chapter 5

1. This kind of conversation is not limited to the childless. My friends with one child are told over and over again that one is not enough.
2. For example, Jamie Berube, "You Shouldn't Need a Reason for Not Having Kids," February 10, 2014. http://thoughtcatalog.com/jamie-berube/2014/02/you-shouldnt-need-a-reason-for-not-having-kids/; Ashley Grof, "The Childfree Woman," *Huffington Post*, March 1, 2016. http://www.huffingtonpost.com/ashley-grof/the-childfree-woman_b_9349128.html.
3. Lauren Berlant and Lee Edelman, *Sex, or the Unbearable* (Durham, NC: Duke University Press, 2014), 5.
4. Association pour l'autobiographie 3387, Violette Farge (pseudonym), "L'habit ne fait pas la femme," 18.
5. Jean E. Veevers, *Childless by Choice* (Toronto: Butterworths, 1980), 82.
6. Sarah Blaffer Hrdy, "The Past, Present, and Future of the Human Family" (paper presented at the Tanner Lectures on Human Values, University of Utah, February 27–28, 2001), 90.
7. For examples of stigma management see Kristin Park, "Stigma Management among the Voluntarily Childless," *Sociological Perspectives* 45, no. 1 (Spring 2002): 31.

8. Nina Kushner and Daryl M. Hafter, "Introduction," in *Women and Work in Eighteenth-Century France*, ed. Daryl M. Hafter and Nina Kushner (Baton Rouge: Louisiana State University Press, 2015), 8.

9. Kushner and Hafter, "Introduction," 7.

10. Quoted in Amy M. Froide, *Never Married: Singlewomen in Early Modern England* (New York: Oxford University Press, 2005), 214.

11. Susan S. Lanser, "Singular Politics: The Rise of the British Nation and the Production of the Old Maid," in *Singlewomen in the European Past, 1250–1800*, ed. Judith M. Bennett and Amy M. Froide (Philadelphia: University of Pennsylvania Press, 1999), 299.

12. Mary Astell, *A Serious Proposal to the Ladies*, ed. Patricia Springborg (Peterborough, ON: Broadview, 2002), 51.

13. Astell, *Serious Proposal*, 52.

14. Astell, *Serious Proposal*, 55–56.

15. Astell, *Serious Proposal*, 56.

16. Astell, *Serious Proposal*, 69–70.

17. Astell, *Serious Proposal*, 80.

18. Astell, *Serious Proposal*, 76.

19. Froide, *Never Married*, 172.

20. Froide, *Never Married*, 171.

21. Astell, *Serious Proposal*, 89.

22. Froide, *Never Married*, 173; Bridget Hill, *Women Alone: Spinsters in England 1660–1850* (New Haven, CT: Yale University Press, 2001), 133.

23. Christine Adams, "A Choice Not to Wed? Unmarried Women in Eighteenth-Century France," *The Journal of Social History* 29, no. 4 (Summer 1996): 884, 889.

24. Quoted in Adams, "Choice Not to Wed?" 888.

25. Adams, "Choice Not to Wed?" 887.

26. Beatrice Webb, *The Diaries of Beatrice Webb*, ed. Norman MacKenzie and Jeanne MacKenzie, eds. Abridged by Lynn Knight, preface by Hermione Lee (Boston: Northeastern University Press, 2001), 248. (April 24, 1901). The Webbs had co-authored three books by this point.

27. Webb, *Diaries*, 187 (October 9, 1894).

28. Webb, *Diaries*, 248–249 (April 24, 1901).

29. Webb, *Diaries*, 187 (October 9, 1894).

30. Voilquin, letter to Prosper Enfantin, January 29, 1838, quoted in Claire Goldberg Moses and Leslie Wahl Rabine, *Feminism, Socialism, and French Romanticism* (Bloomington: Indiana University Press, 1993), 275.

31. Voilquin, letter to Prosper Enfantin, January 29, 1838, quoted in Moses and Rabine, *Feminism*, 275.

32. Michael J. Sandel, *Justice: What's the Right Thing to Do?* (New York: Farrar, Straus and Giroux, 2010), 225.

33. Michael Bess, *Our Grandchildren Redesigned: Life in the Bioengineered Society of the Near Future* (Boston: Beacon, 2015), 78–82.

34. Sherryl Jeffries and Candace Konnert, "Regret and Psychological Well-Being among Voluntarily and Involuntarily Childless Women and Mothers," *International Journal of Aging and Human Development* 54, no. 2 (2002): 103–104.

35. Bess, *Our Grandchildren Redesigned,* 81.

36. See Christopher Peterson and Martin E. P. Seligman, *Character Strengths and Virtues: A Handbook and Classification* (New York: Oxford University Press, 2004); Martin E. P. Seligman, *Learned Optimism: How to Change Your Mind and Your Life* (New York: Vintage Books, 2006); Jonathan Haidt, *The Happiness Hypothesis: Finding Modern Truth in Ancient Wisdom* (New York: Basic Books, 2006); Amartya Sen, *The Idea of Justice* (Cambridge, MA: The Belknap Press of Harvard University Press, 2009); Martha C. Nussbaum, *Creating Capabilities: The Human Development Approach* (Cambridge, MA: The Belknap Press of Harvard University Press, 2011).

37. Nussbaum, *Creating Capabilities,* 15; Peterson and Seligman, *Characters Strengths and Virtues,* 31.

38. Nussbaum, *Creating Capabilities,* 33–34.

39. Nussbaum, *Creating Capabilities,* 24.

40. Haidt, *Happiness Hypothesis,* 164.

41. A. H. Maslow, "A Theory of Human Motivation," *Psychological Review* 50, no. 4 (July 1943): 370–396.

42. Nussbaum, *Creating Capabilities,* 18.

43. Nussbaum, *Creating Capabilities,* 33.

Chapter 6

1. Definition from Lecci, Okun, and Karoly (1994), cited in Sherryl Jeffries and Candace Konnert, "Regret and Psychological Well-Being among Voluntarily and Involuntarily Childless Women and Mothers," *International Journal of Aging and Human Development* 54, no. 2 (2002): 91.

2. Natalie Joseph-Williams, Adrian Edwards, and Glyn Elwyn, "The Importance and Complexity of Regret in the Measurement of 'Good' Decisions: A Systematic Review and a Content Analysis of Existing Assessment Instruments," *Health Expectations* 14 (2010): 61.

3. Joseph-Williams, "Regret," 61–62.

4. Joseph-Williams, "Regret," 61; Baine B. Alexander et al., "A Path Not Taken: A Cultural Analysis of Regrets and Childlessness in the Lives of Older Women," *The Gerontologist* 32, no. 5 (1992): 619.

5. Orna Donath, "Regretting Motherhood: A Sociopolitical Analysis," *Signs: Journal of Women in Culture and Society* 40, no. 2 (2015): 346.

6. Donath, "Regretting Motherhood," 346.

7. Donath cites Carolyn M. Morell, *Unwomanly Conduct: The Challenges of Intentional Childlessness* (London: Routledge, 1994), and Alexander et al., 1992.

8. Quoted in Jean-Claude Chenais, *The Demographic Transition: Stages, Patterns, and Economic Implications. A Longitudinal Study of Sixty-Seven Countries Covering the Period 1720–1984,* trans. Elizabeth and Philip Kreager (New York: Oxford University Press, 1992), 344.

9. L.A. Paul, "What You Can't Expect When You're Expecting," *Res Philosophica* 92, no. 2 (April 2015): 8–9.

10. Quoted in Donath, "Regretting Motherhood," 349.

11. Quoted in Amy M. Froide, *Never Married: Singlewomen in Early Modern England* (New York: Oxford University Press, 2005), 201.

12. S. Katherine Nelson et al., "In Defense of Parenthood: Children Are Associated with More Joy than Misery," *Psychology Science* 20, no.10 (2012): 5.

13. Maike Luhmann et al., "Subjective Well-Being and Adaptation to Life Events: A Meta-Analysis," *Journal of Personality and Social Psychology* 102, no. 3 (2012): 605.

14. Sarah Gibney et al., "Lifetime Childlessness, Depressive Mood and Quality of Life among Older Europeans," *Social Indices Research*, (November 21, 2015): 2.

15. Luhmann et al., "Subjective Well-Being," 610.

16. Kei M. Nomaguchi and Melissa A. Milkie, "Costs and Rewards of Children: The Effects of Becoming a Parent on Adults' Lives," *Journal of Marriage and Family* 65 (May 2003): 363.

17. Thirty-one hours a week versus twenty-two hours for nonmothers. Nomaguchi and Milkie, "Costs and Rewards," 364–365.

18. Jeffrey Dew, "Has the Marital Time Cost of Parenting Changed over Time," *Social Forces* 88, no. 2 (December 2009): 519–542; Eli J. Finkel et al., "The Suffocation Model: Why Marriage in America Is Becoming an All-or-Nothing Institution," *Current Directions in Psychological Science* 24, no. 3 (2015): 239.

19. Ranae J. Evenson and Robin W. Simon, "Clarifying the Relationship between Parenthood and Depression," *Journal of Health and Social Behavior* 46 (December 2005): 349; Robin Simon, "Life's Greatest Joy? The Negative Emotional Effects of Children on Adults," *Contexts* 7 (2008): 42.

20. Evenson and Simon, "Parenthood and Depression," 354.

21. Thomas Hansen, "Parenthood and Happiness: A Review of Folk Theories Versus Empirical Evidence," *Social Indicators Research* 108, no. 1 (August 2012): 44; Nelson et. al, "Defense of Parenthood," 2.

22. Ingrid Arnet Connidis and Julie Ann McMullin, "To Have or Have Not: Parent Status and the Subjective Well-being of Older Men and Women," *The Gerontologist* 33, no. 5 (1993): 630–636.

23. Jeffries, "Regret," 102.

24. Hansen, "Folk Theories," 36–38.

25. Hansen, "Folk Theories," 41.

26. Hansen, "Folk Theories," 46–50.

27. Gibney, "Older Europeans," 15.

28. Evenson and Simon, "Parenthood and Depression," 349.

29. Nelson et. al, "Defense of Parenthood," 2.

30. Tanya Koropeckyj-Cox, Amy Mehraban Pienta, and Tyson H. Brown, "Women of the 1950s and the 'Normative' Life Course: The Implications of Childlessness, Fertility Timing, and Marital Status for Psychological Well-Being in Late Midlife," *Journal of Aging and Human Development* 64, no. 4 (2007): 320.

31. Regina M. Bures, Tanya Koropeckyj-Cox, Michael Loree, "Childlessness, Parenthood, and Depressive Symptoms Among Middle-Aged and Older Adults," *Journal of Family Issues* 30, no. 5 (May 2009): 670–687; Matthijs Kalmijn, "The Ambiguous Link between Marriage and Health: A Dynamic Reanalysis of Loss and Gain Effects," *Social Forces* 95, no. 4 (June 2017): 1, 607–11, 636; Bella DePaulo, "Get Married, Get Healthy? Maybe Not," *The New York Times*, May 25, 2017, https://www.nytimes.com/2017/05/25/opinion/marriage-health-study.html?ref=opinion.

32. Gibney, "Older Europeans," 9.

33. Pearl A. Dystra and Michael Wagner, "Pathways to Childlessness and Late-Life Outcomes," *Journal of Family Issues* 28, no. 11 (November 2007): 1487–1517.

34. Thomas Hansen, Britt Slagsvold, and Torbjørn Moum, "Childlessness and Psychological Well-Being in Midlife and Old Age: An Examination of Parental Status Effects Across a Range of Outcomes," *Social Indicators Research* 94, no. 2 (November 2009): 343–362.

35. Karsten Hank and Michael Wagner, "Parenthood, Marital Status, and Well-Being in Later Life: Evidence from SHARE," *Social Indicators Research* 114, no. 2 (November 2013): 639–653.

36. Gibney, "Older Europeans," 12.

37. Tim Huijts, Gerbert Kraaykamp, and S. V. Subramanian, "Childlessness and Psychological Well-Being in Context: A Multilevel Study on 24 European Countries," *European Sociological Review* 29, no. 1 (2013): 32.

38. Timothy D. Wilson and Daniel T. Gilbert, "Affective Forecasting: Knowing What to Want," *Current Directions in Psychological Science* 14, no. 3 (2005): 131.

39. Jordi Quoidbach and Elizabeth W. Dunn, "Personality Neglect: The Unforeseen Impact of Personality Dispositions on Emotional Life," *Psychological Sciences* 21, no. 12 (2010): 1784.

40. Sonja Lyubomirsky, "Hedonic Adaptation to Positive and Negative Experiences," in *The Oxford Handbook of Stress, Health, and Coping*, ed. Susan Folkman (New York: Oxford University Press, 2011), 201.

41. Lyubomirsky, "Hedonic Adaptation," 214–217.

42. Quoted in Maria Catherine Bishop, *A Memoir of Mrs. Augustus Craven (Pauline de la Ferronnays) with Extracts from Her Diaries and Correspondence*, 3d. ed. (London: Richard Bentley, 1896), 103.

43. Quoted in Bishop, *Craven*, 105.

44. Gail DeLyser, "At Midlife, Intentionally Childfree Women and Their Experiences of Regret," *Journal of Clinical Social Work* 40 (2012): 70.

45. Jeffries, "Regret," 103.

46. Quoted in Alexander, "Cultural Analysis of Regret," 620.

47. Quoted in Alexander, "Cultural Analysis of Regret," 621.

48. Quoted in Alexander, "Cultural Analysis of Regret," 621.

49. Ellen B. Gold, "The Timing of the Age at Which Natural Menopause Occurs," *Obstetrics and Gynecology Clinics of North America* 38, no. 3 (September 2011): 425–440, http://www.ncbi.nlm.nih.gov/pmc/articles/PMC3285482/.

50. Alexander, "Cultural Analysis of Regret," 622.

51. Alexander, "Cultural Analysis of Regret," 622.

52. Alexander, "Cultural Analysis of Regret," 624.

53. Jeffries, "Regret," 102.

54. Wilson and Gilbert, "Affective Forecasting," 131.

55. Wilson and Gilbert, "Affective Forecasting," 133.

56. Joanne Doyle, Julie Ann Pooley and Lauren Breen, "A Phenomenological Exploration of the Childfree Choice in a Sample of Australian Women," *Journal of Health Psychology* 18, no. 3 (2012): 404.

57. DeLyser, "Regret at Midlife," 68–69.

58. DeLyser, "Regret at Midlife," 69.

59. Quoted in Jeffries, "Regret," 101.

60. Donath, "Regretting Motherhood," 347.

61. Quoted in Donath, "Regretting Motherhood," 356.

62. Quoted in Donath, "Regretting Motherhood," 359.

63. Quoted in Donath, "Regretting Motherhood," 355.

64. Jean-Baptiste Moheau, "Jean-Baptiste Moheau on the Moral Causes of Diminished Fertility," trans. Etienne van de Walle, *Population and Development Review* 26, no. 4 (December 2000): 824.

65. Quoted in Alexander, "Cultural Analysis of Regret," 625.

66. J. Michael Walton, "Versions or Perversions: Last Call for the Playwrights?" *Arion: A Journal of Humanities and the Classics* 23, no. 1 (Spring–Summer 2015): 163–164.

67. Froide, *Never Married*, 204.

68. Quoted in Froide, *Never Married*, 205.

69. Froide, *Never Married*, 205.

70. Quoted in Froide, *Never Married*, 206.

71. Leo Tolstoy, *War and Peace*, trans. Richard Peveat and Larissa Volokhonsky (New York: Vintage, 2008), 419–420.

72. Tolstoy, *War and Peace*, 423.

73. Darrin M. McMahon, *Happiness: A History* (New York: Atlantic Monthly Press, 2006), 12.

74. Robert Pogue Harrison, *Juvenescence: A History of Our Age* (Chicago: University of Chicago Press, 2014), 7.

Chapter 7

1. EpicFamilyDecals, "No Kids . . . Just Money Family Car Sticker." Accessed March 4, 2017. https://www.etsy.com/listing/84248620/no-kidsjust-money-family-car-sticker.

2. US Department of Agriculture, "Parents Projected to Spend $245,340 to Raise a Child Born in 2013, According to USDA Report," August 18, 2014, https://www.usda.gov/media/press-releases/2014/08/18/parents-projected-spend-245340-raise-child-born-2013-according-usda.

3. Michelle J. Budig and Melissa J. Hodges, "Differences in Disadvantage: Variation in the Motherhood Penalty across White Women's Earning Distribution," *American Sociological Review* 75, no. 5 (2010): 705–728.

4. Corinne Maier, *No Kids: 40 Good Reasons Not to Have Children*, trans. Patrick Watson (Toronto: McClelland & Stewart, 2009), 51.

5. Jan de Vries, *The Industrious Revolution: Consumer Behavior and the Household Economy, 1650 to the Present* (New York: Cambridge University Press, 2008), 33.

6. de Vries, *Industrious Revolution*, 12–13, 270.

7. Michael J. Sandel, *What Money Can't Buy: The Moral Limits of Markets* (New York: Farrar, Straus and Giroux, 2013), 88–89.

8. Sandel, *Money*, 47–51.

9. David Warren Sabean, *Property, Production, and Family in Neckarhausen, 1700–1870* (New York: Cambridge University Press, 1990), 100–101; Leonore Davidoff et al., *The Family Story: Blood, Contract and Intimacy 1830–1960* (London: Longman, 1999), 34.

10. Wendell Berry, *The Unsettling of America: Culture and Agriculture*, rev. ed. (Berkeley, CA: Counterpoint, 1996), 132.

11. Mary Capper, *A Memoir of Mary Capper: Late of Birmingham, England, a Minister of the Society of Friends* (Philadelphia: William H. Pile's Sons, 1888), 65; Amy M. Froide, *Never Married: Singlewomen in Early Modern England* (New York: Oxford University Press, 2005), 187.

12. Froide, "Marital Status," 239–241.

13. Froide, "Marital Status," 242. See also Bridget Hill, *Women Alone: Spinsters in England 1660–1850* (New Haven, CT: Yale University Press, 2001), 38.

14. Association pour l'autobiographie [APA] 3141, Anne Panneton (pseudonym), "Lettres," January 5, 1937, 8.

15. APA 3141, Panneton, [early 1939], 12.

16. APA 3141, Panneton, January 3 [1936], 7.

17. Louise Otto, "Klein–rein–und allein," *Neue Bahnen: Organ des Allegemeinen Deutschen Frauenvereins* 14, no. 3 (1881): 18–20. Reproduced in Eleanor S. Riemer and Jon C. Fout, ed. *European Women: A Documentary History, 1789–1945* (New York: Schocken Books, 1980), 139.

18. APA 3141, Panneton, July 18, 1935, 5.

19. APA 3141, Panneton, [early 1939], 12.

20. APA 3141, Panneton, September 12, 1939, 14.

21. APA 3141, Panneton, October 10, 1939, 15.

22. APA 3141, Panneton, June 4, 1940, 17.

23. APA 3141, Panneton, June 20, 1941, 18.

24. APA 3141, Panneton, June 20, 1941, 18.

25. APA 3141, Panneton, September 21, 1941, 19.

26. APA 3141, Panneton, October 20, 1944, 23.

27. Natalia Sarkisian and Naomi Gerstel, "Does Singlehood Isolate or Integrate? Examining the Link between Marital Status and Ties to Kin, Friends, and Neighbors," *Journal of Social and Personal Relationships* 33, no. 3 (2016): 361–384; Christopher R. Long et al., "Solitude Experiences: Varieties, Settings, and Individual Differences,"

Personality and Social Psychology Bulletin 29, no. 5 (May 2003): 578–683. See also Bella DePaulo, *Singled Out: How Singles Are Stereotyped, Stigmatized, and Ignored, and Still Live Happily Ever After* (New York: St. Martin's, 2006) and Eric Klinenberg, *Going Solo: The Extraordinary Rise and Surprising Appeal of Living Alone* (New York: Penguin Books, 2013).

28. Suzanne Voilquin, *Souvenirs d'une fille du peuple, ou La saint-simonienne en Egypte*, introduction by Lydia Elhadad (Paris: François Maspero, 1978), 124.

29. Voilquin, *Souvenirs*, 59.

30. Voilquin, *Souvenirs*, 137–138.

31. Voilquin, *Souvenirs*, 136.

32. Voilquin, *Souvenirs*, 136–137.

33. Voilquin, *Souvenirs*, 108.

34. Voilquin, *Souvenirs*, 88, 205, 223, 263.

35. Voilquin, *Souvenirs*, 249.

36. de Vries, *Industrious Revolution*, 25.

37. Katherine Holden, *The Shadow of Marriage: Singleness in England, 1914–60* (Manchester, UK: Manchester University Press, 2007), 218.

38. Davidoff et al., *Family Story*, 114.

39. Mary S. Hartman, *The Household and the Making of History: A Subversive View of the Western Past* (New York: Cambridge University Press, 2004), 66.

40. Hartman, *Household*, 238.

41. Hartman, *Household*, 211. See also Lawrence Stone, "Past Achievements and Future Trends," in "The New History: The 1980s and Beyond (I)," ed. Robert I. Rotberg and Theodore K. Rabb, special issue, *The Journal of Interdisciplinary History* 12, no. 1 (Summer 1981): 82.

42. Quoted in Hartman, *Household*, 23–24.

43. Christine Adams, "A Choice Not to Wed? Unmarried Women in Eighteenth-Century France," *The Journal of Social History* 29, no. 4 (Summer 1996): 885–886.

44. Adams, "A Choice Not to Wed?" 885.

45. Davidoff et al., *Family Story*, 20–21.

46. Kelly Lambert, *Lifting Depression: A Neuroscientist's Hands-On Approach to Activating Your Brain's Healing Power* (New York: Basic Books, 2008).

47. Berry, *Unsettling*, 20.

48. Berry, *Unsettling*, 19.

49. Berry, *Unsettling*, 21.

50. Berry, *Unsettling*, 24.

51. Albert Borgmann, "Focal Things and Practices," in *Readings in the Philosophy of Technology*, 2nd ed., ed. David M. Kaplan (Lanham, MD: Rowman & Littlefield, 2009), 70.

52. Sarkisian and Gerstel, "Does Singlehood Isolate or Integrate?"

53. Voilquin, *Souvenirs*, 220.

54. Borgmann, "Focal Things," 57.

55. Felipe Fernández-Armesto with Daniel Lord Smail, "Food," in *Deep History: The Architecture of Past and Present*, ed. Andrew Shryock and Daniel Lord Smail (Berkeley: University of California Press, 2011), 137.

56. Fernández-Armesto, "Food," 143–144.

57. Borgmann, "Focal Things," 65.

58. Borgmann, "Focal Things," 73.

59. Capper, *Memoir,* 328.

60. Davidoff et al., *Family Story,* 35.

61. Andrew Shryock and Daniel Lord Smail, "Body," in Shryock and Smail, *Deep History,* 63–64.

Chapter 8

1. Wilkie Collins, *The Woman in White,* ed., introduction and notes by Matthew Sweet (New York: Penguin, 2003), 46.

2. Suzanne Voilquin, *Souvenirs d'une fille du peuple, ou La saint-simonienne en Egypte,* introduction by Lydia Elhadad (Paris: François Maspero, 1978), 69.

3. Sykes and Matza (1957), quoted in Kristin Park, "Stigma Management among the Voluntarily Childless," *Sociological Perspectives* 45, no. 1 (Spring 2002): 34.

4. David Benatar, *Better Never to Have Been: The Harm of Coming into Existence* (Oxford: Oxford University Press, 2006), 92.

5. Seana Valentine Shiffrin, "Wrongful Life, Procreative Responsibility, and the Significance of Harm," *Legal Theory* 5 (1999): 139.

6. Quoted in Elisabeth Badinter, *The Conflict: How Modern Motherhood Undermines the Status of Women,* trans. Adriana Hunter (New York: Metropolitan Books, 2011), 125.

7. Montesquieu, "Letter Forty," *Persian Letters,* trans. John Davidson (London: Gibbings, 1899), 123, quoted in Benatar, *Better Never,* 212.

8. Gustave Flaubert, "Letter to Louise Colet, 11 December 1852," in *The Letters of Gustave Flaubert 1830-1857,* trans. Francis Steegmuller (London: Faber & Faber, 1979), 174; quoted in Benatar, *Better Never,* 93.

9. Shiffrin, "Wrongful Life," 137.

10. Shiffrin, "Wrongful Life," 137. Shiffrin distinguishes, rightly, between actions that prevent harm and those that add benefit. Procreation adds benefit, namely, the benefit of life, but in doing so, it intrinsically imposes burdens; hence, it is morally hazardous. Imposing burden while preventing harm, however, is more morally defensible.

11. Benatar, *Better Never,* 14.

12. Benatar, *Better Never,* 35.

13. Benatar, *Better Never,* 35.

14. Benatar, *Better Never,* 76–77.

15. Arthur Schopenahuer, "On the Suffering of the World," in *Essays and Aphorisms,* trans. and introduction by R. J. Hollingdale (New York: Penguin, 1970), 47–48.

16. Benatar, *Better Never,* 211.

17. Benatar, *Better Never,* 64–69.

18. Benatar, *Better Never,* 2.

19. Benatar, *Better Never,* 211.

20. Benatar, *Better Never,* 92.

21. Thomas Piketty, *Capital in the Twenty-First Century,* trans. Arthur Goldhammer (Cambridge, MA, Harvard University Press, 2014), 73, 101, Figure 2.5. This is a rough estimates based on the notion that in the year 0 the world population could not have been miniscule. For example, if population growth from 0 to 1700 had been 0.8 percent, and given that we estimate that in 1700 the world's population was about 600 million, that would mean that there were fewer than 10,000 people on earth in the year 0. But our best information suggests that, in fact, there were about 200 million people on earth in the year 0, with 50 million in the Roman Empire alone, so there is no doubt that annual population growth was less than 0.2 percent, and almost certainly less than 0.1 percent.

22. William F. Kenkel, *The Family in Perspective,* 2d ed. (New York: Appleton-Century-Crofts, 1966), 81.

23. Leslie Tuttle, *Conceiving the Old Regime: Pronatalism and the Politics of Reproduction in Early Modern France* (New York: Oxford University Press, 2010), 7.

24. Tuttle, *Conceiving,* 43.

25. Tuttle, *Conceiving,* 11.

26. Piketty, *Capital,* 79, Table 2.3, "Demographic Growth Since the Industrial Revolution (average annual growth rate); 75, Figure 2.1, "The Growth of World Population, 1700–2012."

27. Adam Smith, *An Inquiry into the Nature and Causes of the Wealth of Nations* (New York: The Modern Library, 1994), 91 (I.8.38).

28. Smith, *Wealth of Nations,* 93 (I.8.42).

29. Robert J. Mayhew, *Malthus: The Life and Legacies of an Untimely Prophet* (Cambridge, MA: Harvard University Press, 2014), 128–129.

30. William H. Schneider, *Quality and Quantity: The Quest for Biological Regeneration in Twentieth-Century France* (New York: Cambridge University Press, 1990), 15.

31. Paul Weindling, *Health, Race, and German Politics between National Unification and Nazism, 1870–1945* (New York: Cambridge University Press, 1989), 242.

32. Robert Cantillon's *Essai sur la Nature du Commerce en Général* A Londres: Chez Fletcher Gyles, 1755 (published posthumously) also discusses population limitations.

33. Thomas R. Malthus, *An Essay on the Principle of Population,* ed. and introduction by Donald Winch (New York: Cambridge University Press, 1992), 272.

34. Malthus, *Essay,* 271.

35. Malthus, *Essay,* 273.

36. Malthus, *Essay,* 242.

37. Malthus, *Essay,* 274.

38. Malthus, *Essay,* 40.

39. Malthus, *Essay,* 241.

40. Mayhew, *Malthus,* 99.

41. Nicole Eustace, *1812: War and the Passions of Patriotism* (Philadelphia: University of Pennsylvania Press, 2012), 11, 16, 18.

42. Mayhew, *Malthus,* 88, 97.

43. Malthus, *Essay,* 248–249.

44. Malthus, *Essay,* 266.

45. Malthus, *Essay,* 242.

46. Mayhew, *Malthus,* 141.

47. Quoted in Mayhew, *Malthus,* 142.

48. For example, P.-J. Proudhon, *Système des Contradictions Economiques, ou Philosophie de la Misère,* vol. 2 (Paris: Guillaumin, 1846), 447.

49. A new MOTHER, Unita [possibly Désirée Veret], "A Woman's Voice," *Tribune des femmes* 2 (Paris: Tribune des femmes, 1834): 153–155, a letter from London dated January 10, 1834 and quoted in Claire Goldberg Moses and Leslie Wahl Rabine, *Feminism, Socialism, and French Romanticism* (Bloomington: Indiana University Press, 1993), 322.

50. A new MOTHER, Unita, "A Woman's Voice," 322.

51. Piketty, *Capital,* 99.

52. Piketty, *Capital,* 99.

53. Michael J. Sandel, *What Money Can't Buy: The Moral Limits of Markets,* reprint ed. (New York: Farrar, Straus and Giroux, 2013), 70–71.

54. Elaine Tyler May, *Barren in the Promised Land: Childless Americans and the Pursuit of Happiness* (New York: Basic Books, 1995), 200–201.

55. Jean E. Veevers, *Childless by Choice* (Toronto: Butterworths, 1980), 177.

56. Jenna Healey, "Rejecting Reproduction: The National Organization for Non-Parents and Childfree Activism in 1970s America," *Journal of Women's History* 28, no. 1 (2016): 131.

57. Matthew Connelly, *Fatal Misconception: The Struggle to Control World Population* (Cambridge, MA: The Belknap Press of Harvard University Press, 2008), 222; Dorothy Roberts, *Killing the Black Body: Race, Reproduction, and the Meaning of Liberty* (New York: Pantheon Books, 1997), 89–98.

58. Connelly, *Fatal Misconception,* 117.

59. Connelly, *Fatal Misconception,* 160–161.

60. Amartya Sen, *Development as Freedom* (New York: Knopf, 2000), 218.

61. Piketty, *Capital,* 79, Table 2.3, "Demographic Growth Since the Industrial Revolution (average annual growth rate); 75, Figure 2.1, "The Growth of World Population, 1700–2012."

62. Quoted in Park, "Stigma Management," 38.

63. Paul A. Murtaugh and Michael G. Schlax, "Reproduction and the Carbon Legacies of Individuals," *Global Environmental Change* 19 (2009), 14.

64. Murtaugh and Schlax, "Carbon Legacies," 18, Table 3.

65. Ostrander, "How Do You Decide to Have a Baby When Climate Change is Remaking Life on Earth," *The Nation,* April 11–18, 2016, http://www.thenation.com/article/how-do-you-decide-to-have-a-baby-when-climate-change-is-remaking-life-on-earth/.

66. Quoted in Ostrander, "How Do You Decide."

67. Sandel, *Money,* 86.

68. Jan Van Bavel, "Subreplacement Fertility in the West before the Baby Boom: Past and Current Perspectives," *Population Studies* 64, no. 1 (2010): 11.

69. Piketty, *Capital*, 79.
70. Utopian Charles Fourier, in his manic wisdom, saw this back in 1808, when the global population had just eclipsed one billion: When the population reached three billion, he wrote, "there will be regularly on the globe thirty-seven million poets equal to Homer, thirty-seven million geometers equal to Newton, thirty-seven million playwrights equal to Molière, and so on for every imaginable talent. (These are approximate estimates.)" [Charles Fourier], *Théorie des quatres mouvements et des destinées générales: Prospectus et annonce de la découverte* (Leipzig [actually Lyon: Pelzin], 1808), 117.

Chapter 9

1. Association pour l'autobiographie [APA] 3000, Marguerite Babineaux (pseudonym), "Journal intime d'une veuve," August 18, 1908, 16–17.
2. APA 3000, Babineaux, August 24, 1908, 18.
3. APA 3000, Babineaux, August 29, 1908, 19–20.
4. APA 3000, Babineaux, August 19, 1908, 18.
5. APA 3000, Babineaux, July 10, 1908, 12.
6. APA 3000, Babineaux, May 25, 1908, 7; May 30, 1908, 10.
7. APA 3000, Babineaux, August 19, 1908, 18; August 27, 1908, 19.
8. APA 3000, Babineaux, August 18, 1908, 16–17.
9. APA 3000, Babineaux, May 30, 1908, 10.
10. APA 3000, Babineaux, August 10, 1908, 16.
11. APA 3000, Babineaux, October 29, 1908, 30.
12. Richard C. Keller, *Fatal Isolation: The Devastating Paris Heat Wave of 2003* (Chicago: University of Chicago Press, 2015), 57–58.
13. This number is based on the excess deaths relative to the average number of deaths.
14. Keller, *Fatal Isolation*, 72.
15. Keller, *Fatal Isolation*, 59.
16. Keller, *Fatal Isolation*, 86.
17. Quoted in Amy M. Froide, *Never Married: Singlewomen in Early Modern England* (New York: Oxford University Press, 2005), 199.
18. Quoted in Froide, *Never Married*, 197.
19. Quoted in Froide, *Never Married*, 198.
20. "A Virgin Life," quoted in Froide, *Never Married*, 199.
21. Bridget Hill, *Women Alone: Spinsters in England 1660–1850* (New Haven, CT: Yale University Press, 2001), 5.
22. Susan S. Lanser, "Singular Politics: The Rise of the British Nation and the Production of the Old Maid," in *Singlewomen in the European Past, 1250–1800*, ed. Judith M. Bennett and Amy M. Froide (Philadelphia: University of Pennsylvania Press, 1999), 312.
23. To derive this number, I divided the 18 percent who were childless at ages forty to forty-four (in 2008) by the 0.23 percent who had a first child at ages forty to forty-four

(in 2012). For the percentage of women who are childless at ages forty to forty-four, see Gretchen Livingstone and D'Vera Cohn, "Childlessness Up among All Women; Down among Women with Advanced Degrees," Pew Research Center, June 25, 2010, https://www.pewsocialtrends.org/2010/06/25/childlessness-up-among-all-women-down-among-women-with-advanced-degrees/. For the percentage of women who had a first child at age forty to forty-four, see Centers for Disease Control and Prevention, "Data Brief 152. First Births to Older Women Continue to Rise," May 2014, data table for Figure 1, "First Birth Rates for Women Aged 35–39 and 40–44: United States, 1970–2012," http://www.cdc.gov/nchs/data/databriefs/db152_table.pdf#1/.

24. Tim Huijts, Gerbert Kraaykamp, and S. V. Subramanian, "Childlessness and Psychological Well-Being in Context: A Multilevel Study on 24 European Countries," *European Sociological Review* 29, no. 1 (2013): 36.

25. Jean Twenge, "Will This Fertility Treatment Make Egg Freezing Obsolete?" *The Daily Beast*, September 15, 2015, http://www.thedailybeast.com/articles/2015/09/15/ovaprime-the-end-of-women-s-biological-clock.html

26. Michael Bess, *Our Grandchildren Redesigned: Life in the Bioengineered Society of the Near Future* (Boston: Beacon, 2015), 163.

27. Froide, *Never Married*, 198–199.

28. Age at menopause for white women in industrialized countries falls between fifty and fifty-two, and about two years earlier for black and Latina women in the United States. Ellen B. Gold, "The Timing of the Age at Which Natural Menopause Occurs," *Obstetrics and Gynecology Clinics of North America* 38, no. 3 (September 2011): 425–440, http://www.ncbi.nlm.nih.gov/pmc/articles/PMC3285482/.

29. David G. Troyansky, *Old Age in the Old Regime: Image and Experience in Eighteenth-Century France* (Ithaca, NY: Cornell University Press, 1989), 18.

30. Troyansky, *Old Age*, 23.

31. Barbara A. Hanawalt, *The Ties That Bound: Peasant Families in Medieval England* (New York: Oxford University Press, 1986), 229.

32. Life expectancy was age eight-one for a female born in 2012; a woman who was sixty-five in 2012 could expect to live to be 85.7; Jennifer M. Ortman, Victoria A. Velkoff, and Howard Hogan, "An Aging Nation: The Older Population in the United States. Population Estimates and Projections," US Census Bureau Current Population Reports, May 2014, http://www.census.gov/prod/2014pubs/p25-1140.pdf.

33. This calculation assumes an infertility rate of only 5 percent. Jack Goody, *Production and Reproduction: A Comparative Study of the Domestic Domain* (New York: Cambridge University Press, 1976), 133–134.

34. Goody, *Production and Reproduction*, 88.

35. Donald T. Rowland, "Historical Trends in Childlessness," *Journal of Family Issues* 28, no. 10 (October 2007): 1316.

36. Cross-national study based on surveys of older adults in the 1990s, so these are individuals born from the high point of childlessness to the high point of the baby-boom parents. Tanya Koropeckyj-Cox and Vaughn R. A. Call, "Characteristics of Older Childless Persons and Parents," *Journal of Family Issues* 28, no. 10 (October 2007): 1399.

37. Quoted in Gail DeLyser, "At Midlife, Intentionally Childfree Women and Their Experiences of Regret," *Journal of Clinical Social Work* 40, (2012): 69.

38. Hanawalt, *Ties That Bound*, 227–228.

39. APA 235, Sandrine Keller (pseudonym) "J'ai jeté mes cent ans dans la Seine," 18.

40. Quoted in Froide, *Never Married*, 2–7.

41. Troyansky, *Old Age*, 108.

42. Keller, *Fatal Isolation*, 123–124.

43. Maria Evandrou and Jane Falkingham, "Demographic Change in Europe: Implications for Future Family Support for Older People," in *Ageing without Children: European and Asian Perspectives*, ed. Philip Kreager and Elisabeth Schröder-Butterfill (New York: Berghan Books, 2004), 176–177.

44. Evandrou and Falkingham, "Demographic Change in Europe," 179.

45. Pearl A. Dykstra, "Childless Old Age," in *International Handbook of Population Aging*, ed. P. Uhlenberg (Berlin: Springer, 2009), 683; Hal Kendig et al., "Health of Aging Parents and Childless Individuals," *Journal of Family Issues* 28, no. 11 (November 2007): 1457–1486.

46. Melissa Graham, "Is Being Childless Detrimental to a Woman's Health and Well-Being across Her Life Course?" *Women's Health Issues* 25, no. 2 (2015): 178–180.

47. Julie Cwikel, Helen Gramotnev, and Christina Lee, "Never-Married Childless Women in Australia: Health and Social Circumstances in Older Age," *Social Science & Medicine* 62 (2006): 1999.

48. A well-known study of the British aristocracy born between 740 and 1876 found that childless women were overrepresented among those who lived to age eighty-one or older—in fact, almost half of those women were childless; Rudi G. J. Westendorp and Thomas B. L. Kirkwood, "Human Longevity at the Cost of Reproductive Success," *Nature* 396 (December 24–31, 1998): 743–746). A later study argued that aristocratic family genealogies may have excluded children who died young or happened to be female, and so the parity of seemingly childless women could not be verified; Gabriele Doblhammer and Jim Oeppen, "Reproduction and Longevity among the British Peerage: The Effect of Frailty and Health Selection," *Proceedings of the Royal Society of London* B 270 (2003): 1541–1547; see discussion in Kendig et al., "Health," 1460.

49. Cwikel et al., "Never Married," 1992.

50. Edward Copeland, "Money," in *The Cambridge Companion to Jane Austen*, ed. Edward Copeland and Juliet McMaster (New York: Cambridge University Press, 1997), 135.

51. Troyansky, *Old Age*, 126.

52. Quoted in Troyansky, *Old Age*, 136.

53. Robert D. Plotnick, "Childlessness and the Economic Well-Being of Older Americans," *The Journals of Gerontology. Series B, Psychological Sciences and Social Sciences* 64B, no. 6 (2009): 767–776. However, never-married childless women do not have higher incomes than married women in general; Koropeckyj-Cox and Call, "Older Childless Persons," 1400.

54. Cwikel et al., "Never Married," 1991.

55. Michael Stegmann and Tatjana Mika, "Kinderlosigkeit, Kindererziehung und Erwerbstätigkeitsmuster von Frauen in der Bundesrepublik und der DDR und ihre

Auswirkungen auf das Alterseinkommen," in *Ein Leben ohne Kinder: Kinderlosigkeit in Deutschland,* ed. Dirk Konietzka and Michaela Kreyenfeld (Wiesbaden, Germany: Verlag für Sozialwissenschaften, 2007), 201–241.

56. Troyansky, *Old Age,* 126.

57. Froide, *Never Married,* 103–104.

58. Michael Anderson, "Highly Restricted Fertility: Very Small Families in the British Fertility Decline," *Population Studies* 52, no. 2 (July 1998):194.

59. Quoted in Merry E. Wiesner, "Having Her Own Smoke: Employment and Independence for Singlewomen in Germany, 1400–1750," in Bennett and Froide, *Singlewomen,* 202–203.

60. Troyansky, *Old Age,* 171.

61. Koropeckyj-Cox and Call, "Older Childless Persons," 1400.

62. Dykstra, "Childless Old Age," 683.

63. Lawrence Stone, "Past Achievements and Future Trends," in "The New History: The 1980s and Beyond (I)," ed. Robert I. Rotberg and Theodore K. Rabb, special issue, *The Journal of Interdisciplinary History* 12, no. 1 (Summer 1981): 62.

64. Margaret H. Darrow, *Revolution in the House: Family, Class, and Inheritance in Southern France, 1775–1825* (Princeton, NJ: Princeton University Press, 1989), 190, 206.

65. Evandrou and Falkingham, "Demographic Change in Europe," 181.

66. Note that if they lived in an early-marriage society, women depended even more on producing a son than on their own activities, savings, and relationships. Mary S. Hartman, *The Household and the Making of History: A Subversive View of the Western Past* (New York: Cambridge University Press, 2004), 65.

67. Ron J. Lesthaeghe, *The Decline of Belgian Fertility, 1800–1970* (Princeton, NJ: Princeton University Press, 1977), 148.

68. Hartman, *Household,* 41.

69. Hanawalt, *Ties That Bound,* 229–234.

70. Hartman, *Household,* 65.

71. Philip Kreager, "Where Are the Children?" in Kreager and Schröder-Butterfill, *Ageing without Children,* 18. For urban, the figures are 54 percent for men and 37 to 46 percent for women.

72. Kreager, "Where Are the Children?" 18.

73. Less than 5 percent of men lived alone and less than 5 percent with other kin. Kreager, "Where Are the Children?" 18.

74. Kreager, "Where Are the Children?" 18.

75. Kreager, "Where Are the Children?" 17–18.

76. [Charles Fourier], *Théorie des quatres mouvements et des destinées générales: Prospectus et annonce de la découverte* (Leipzig [actually Lyon: Pelzin], 1808), 166.

77. Kreager, "Where Are the Children?" 18.

78. Anderson, "Small Families," 194.

79. Quoted in Keller, *Fatal Isolation,* 131.

80. Evandrou and Falkingham, "Demographic Change in Europe," 189–190.

81. Quoted in Froide, *Never Married,* 200.

82. Quoted in Froide, *Never Married,* 203.

83. Quoted in Froide, *Never Married,* 203.

84. Quoted in Froide, *Never Married,* 203.

85. Quoted in Froide, *Never Married,* 212.

86. Froide, *Never Married,* 46.

87. APA 1833, Joséphine Bruyere (pseudonym), "Seize lustres au fil de la plume," 529–530.

88. APA 1833, Bruyere, n.p.

89. APA 1833, Bruyere, n.p.

90. J. Bengel et al., "Long-Term Psychological Consequences of Childlessness: A Review," *Zeitschrift für Klinische Psychologie-Forschung und Praxis* 29, no. 1 (2000): 3–15. See also Kristin Park, "Choosing Childlessness: Weber's Typology of Action and Motives of the Voluntarily Childless," *Sociological Inquiry* 75, no. 3 (August 2005): 375; G. Clare Wenger et al., "Social Embeddedness and Late-Life Parenthood: Community Activity, Close Ties, and Support Networks," *Journal of Family Issues* 28, no. 11 (November 2007): 1419–1456; Dykstra, "Childless Old Age," 682.

91. Joanne Doyle, Julie Ann Pooley, and Lauren Breen, "A Phenomenological Exploration of the Childfree Choice in a Sample of Australian Women," *Journal of Health Psychology* 18, no. 3 (2012): 404; Martin Kohli and Marco Albertini, "Childlessness and Intergenerational Transfers: What Is at Stake?" *Ageing & Society* 29 (2009): 1179.

92. Dykstra, "Childless Old Age," 682.

93. Dykstra, "Childless Old Age," 682; Cwikel et al., "Never Married," 1999.

94. Thomas Hansen, Britt Slagsvold, and Torbjørn Moum, "Childlessness and Psychological Well-Being in Midlife and Old Age: An Examination of Parental Status Effects across a Range of Outcomes," *Social Indicators Research* 94 (2009): 355–356.

95. Hansen, "Old Age," 356.

96. Keller, *Fatal Isolation,* 132.

97. Pat M. Keith, "A Comparison of the Resources of Parents and Childless Men and Women in Very Old Age," *Family Relations* 32 (1983): 408.

98. Ingrid Arnet Connidis and Julie Ann McMullin, "To Have or Have Not: Parent Status and the Subjective Well-Being of Older Men and Women," *The Gerontologist* 33, no. 5 (October 1993): 630–636.

99. Baine B. Alexander et al., "A Path Not Taken: A Cultural Analysis of Regrets and Childlessness in the Lives of Older Women," *The Gerontologist* 32, no. 5 (1992): 622.

100. Quoted in Alexander, "Cultural Analysis of Regret," 622.

101. Dykstra, "Childless Old Age," 683.

102. Norman MacKenzie and Jeanne MacKenzie, eds., *The Diaries of Beatrice Webb,* abridged by Lynn Knight, preface by Hermione Lee (Boston: Northeastern University Press, 2001), 555 (February 11, 1938).

103. Webb, *Diaries,* 459–460 (April 14, 1927).

104. Webb, *Diaries,* 431–432 (July 10, 1924).

105. Quoted in Webb, *Diaries,* 431 (July 10, 1924).

106. Webb, *Diaries,* 545 (April 18, 1937).

107. Webb, *Diaries,* 551 (December 14, 1937).

108. Bess, *Our Grandchildren Redesigned*, 20–21.
109. Niko Kolodny, "Introduction," in *Death and the Afterlife* by Samuel Scheffler, ed. Niko Kolodny (New York: Oxford, 2013), 10.

Chapter 10

1. Margaret H. Darrow, *Revolution in the House: Family, Class, and Inheritance in Southern France, 1775–1825* (Princeton, NJ: Princeton University Press, 1989), 173n8.
2. Darrow, *Revolution in the House*, 173.
3. Darrow, *Revolution in the House*, 102–103.
4. Darrow, *Revolution in the House*, 71–72.
5. Darrow, *Revolution in the House*, 72.
6. Kristin Elizabeth Gager, *Blood Ties and Fictive Ties: Adoption and Family Life in Early Modern France* (Princeton, NJ: Princeton University Press, 1996), 54, 71, 80.
7. Darrow, *Revolution in the House*, 82.
8. Darrow, *Revolution in the House*, 72, 79; Jan de Vries, *The Industrious Revolution: Consumer Behavior and the Household Economy, 1650 to the Present* (New York: Cambridge University Press, 2008), 4n11.
9. Quoted in Darrow, *Revolution in the House*, 84.
10. David G. Troyansky, *Old Age in the Old Regime: Image and Experience in Eighteenth-Century France* (Ithaca, NY: Cornell University Press, 1989), 147.
11. De Vries, *Industrious Revolution*, 144.
12. Darrow, *Revolution in the House*, 185.
13. De Vries, *Industrious Revolution*, 144.
14. Maxine Berg, quoted in De Vries, *Industrious Revolution*, 146.
15. De Vries, *Industrious Revolution*, 145.
16. Michael Cobb, *Single: Arguments for the Uncoupled* (New York: New York University Press, 2012), 81–82.
17. Cobb, *Single*, 81.
18. Holden, *Shadow of Marriage*, 221.
19. Andrew Shryock et al., "Imaginging," in *Deep History: The Architecture of Past and Present*, ed. Andrew Shryock and Daniel Lord Smail (Berkeley: University of California Press, 2011), 42.
20. Thomas R. Trautmann et al., "Deep Kinship," in Shryock and Smail, *Deep History*, 186.
21. Shryock et al., "Imaginging," 44.
22. Shryock et al., "Imaginging," 46.
23. Christopher H. Johnson and David Warren Sabean, "Introduction: From Siblingship to Siblinghood, Kinship and the Shaping of European Society (1300-1900)," in *Sibling Relations and the Transformation of European Kinship, 1300-1900*, ed. Christopher H. Johnson and David Warren Sabean Sabean (New York: Berghahn Books, 2011), 1.
24. Gager, *Blood Ties*, 18–19.
25. Shryock et al., "Imaginging," 34.

26. Leonore Davidoff et al., *The Family Story: Blood, Contract and Intimacy 1830–1960* (London: Longman, 1999), 80.

27. Quoted in Baine B. Alexander et al., "A Path Not Taken: A Cultural Analysis of Regrets and Childlessness in the Lives of Older Women," *The Gerontologist* 32, no. 5 (1992): 623.

28. Quoted in Alexander, "Cultural Analysis of Regret," 623.

29. For example, see Angela Davis, "Reflections on the Black Woman's Role in the Community of Slaves," in "Woman: An Issue," ed. Lee R. Edwards, Mary Heath, and Lisa Baskin, special issue, *The Massachusetts Review* 13, no. 1–2, (Winter–Spring 1972): 81–100; Dorothy Roberts, *Killing the Black Body: Race, Reproduction, and the Meaning of Liberty* (New York: Pantheon Books, 1997), 22–55.

30. Patricia Hill Collins, *Black Feminist Thought: Knowledge, Consciousness, and the Politics of Empowerment* (Boston: Unwin Hyman, 1990), 123–129.

31. Jack Goody, *Production and Reproduction: A Comparative Study of the Domestic Domain* (New York: Cambridge University Press, 1976), 88.

32. Goody, *Production and Reproduction*, 86–95.

33. Shryock et al., "Imaginging," 36.

34. Floyd G. Lounsbury, "The Formal Analysis of Crow- and Omaha-Type Kinship Terminologies," in *Explorations in Cultural Anthropology: Essays in Honor of George Peter Murdock*, ed. Ward H. Goodenough (New York: McGraw-Hill, 1964), 367–379; Trautmann et al., "Deep Kinship," 174–176.

35. Shryock et al., "Imaginging," 39–41; Johnson and Sabean, "Introduction," 1–28.

36. Darrow, *Revolution in the House*, 222.

37. Shryock et al., "Imaginging," 39, 43.

38. Norman MacKenzie and Jeanne MacKenzie, eds., *The Diaries of Beatrice Webb*, abridged by Lynn Knight, preface by Hermione Lee (Boston: Northeastern University Press, 2001), 466 (April 18, 1928).

39. Judith M. Bennett, *A Medieval Life: Cecilia Penifader of Brigstock, c. 1295–1344* (Boston: McGraw-Hill College, 1999), 81.

40. Trautmann et al., "Deep Kinship," 170–171.

41. Trautmann et al., "Deep Kinship," 179.

42. Samuel Scheffler, *Death and the Afterlife*, ed. Niko Kolodny (New York: Oxford, 2013), 61.

43. Scheffler, *Death*, 61.

44. Wendell Berry, *The Unsettling of America: Culture and Agriculture* (Berkeley: Counterpoint, 1996 [1977]), 56.

45. Berry, *Unsettling*, 57.

46. Lao-tzu, *Tao Te Ching*, trans. Stephen Mitchell (New York: HarperPerennial, 1991), Chapter 9.

47. Andrew J. Counter, *The Amorous Restoration: Love, Sex, and Politics in Early Nineteenth-Century France* (New York: Oxford University Press, 2016), 79.

48. Lee Edelman, *No Future: Queer Theory and the Death Drive* (Durham, NC: Duke University Press, 2004), 3–4, 154.

49. Edelman, *No Future*, 13.

50. Counter, *Amorous Restoration*, 78.

51. Counter, *Amorous Restoration*, 78.

52. Counter, *Amorous Restoration*, 110.

53. Counter, *Amorous Restoration*, 104.

54. Edelman, *No Future*, 45.

55. Lauren Berlant locates problematic futurism in sex aimed at reproduction. She promotes the project of sex without optimism, a concept that could mean, among other definitions, "seeing that sex becomes more of a threat when it has to hold up a world that spans both chronological and fantastic futures"; Lauren Berlant and Lee Edelman, *Sex, or the Unbearable* (Durham, NC: Duke University Press, 2014), 20.

56. Edelman, *No Future*, 154.

57. Scheffler, *Death*, 18.

58. Scheffler, *Death*, 21.

59. Scheffler, *Death*, 26.

60. Scheffler, *Death*, 26.

61. Scheffler, *Death*, 45.

62. Scheffler, *Death*, 60.

63. Joanne Doyle, Julie Ann Pooley, and Lauren Breen, "A Phenomenological Exploration of the Childfree Choice in a Sample of Australian Women," *Journal of Health Psychology* 18, no. 3 (2012): 398.

64. Association pour l'autobiographie [APA] 3387, Violette Farge (pseudonym), "L'habit ne fait pas la femme," 5 (the pages renumber).

65. APA 3387, Farge, 1 (the pages renumber).

66. Capper, Mary, *A Memoir of Mary Capper: Late of Birmingham, England, a minister of the Society of Friends* (Philadelphia: William H. Pile's Sons, 1888), 309.

67. Suzanne Voilquin, *Souvenirs d'une fille du peuple, ou La saint-simonienne en Egypte*. Introduction by Lydia Elhadad (Paris: François Maspero, 1978), 189.

68. Voilquin, *Souvenirs*, 189.

69. Voilquin, *Souvenirs*, 257.

70. Scheffler, *Death*, 79.

71. Samantha Tomaszewski, "Ava DuVernay Pays Tribute to Michelle Obama's Slave Ancestor," *Huffington Post*, August 5, 2017, https://www.huffingtonpost.com/entry/ava-duvernay-tribute-michelle-obama-slave-ancestor_us_5985f7a3e4b08b75dcc7462e.

72. Robert Pogue Harrison, *Juvenescence: A History of Our Age* (Chicago: University of Chicago Press, 2014), 41–42.

73. Harrison, *Juvenescence*, 40.

74. Harrison, *Juvenescence*, 40.

75. Harrison, *Juvenescence*, 46.

76. Harrison, *Juvenescence*, 41.

77. Sarah Ensor, "Spinster Ecology: Rachel Carson, Sarah Orne Jewett, and Nonreproductive Futurity," *American Literature* 84, no. 2 (June 2012), 417.

78. Andrew Shryock and Daniel Lord Smail, "Preface," in Shryock and Smail, *Deep History*, xi.

79. Andrew Shryock and Daniel Lord Smail, "Introduction," in Shryock and Smail, *Deep History*, 10.

80. Shryock and Smail, "Introduction," 19.

81. Mary C. Stiner et al., "Scale," in Shryock and Smail, *Deep History*, 247.

82. Stiner et al., "Scale," 246.

83. By "we," I mean the Johns Hopkins University Applied Physics Laboratory and its affiliates, but I claim the achievement for humanity. The Johns Hopkins University Applied Physics Laboratory, "New Horizons." Accessed July 14, 2015. http://pluto.jhuapl.edu/Mission/Spacecraft/Systems-and-Components.php.

84. California Institute of Technology, Jet Propulsion Laboratory, "Interstellar Mission." Accessed July 14, 2015. http://voyager.jpl.nasa.gov/mission/interstellar.html.

85. Kenneth Chang, "Cassini Vanishes into Saturn, Its Mission Celebrated and Mourned," *The New York Times*, September 14, 2017, https://www.nytimes.com/2017/09/14/science/cassini-grand-finale-saturn.html.

Index

Note: Page numbers followed by *f* or *t* denote figures and tables.

For the benefit of digital users, indexed terms that span two pages (e.g., 52–53) may, on occasion, appear on only one of those pages.